The Architectural Association
in the Postwar Years

Patrick Zamarian

LUND
HUMPHRIES

First published in 2020 by Lund Humphries

Lund Humphries
Office 3, Book House
261A City Road
London EC1V 1JX
UK

www.lundhumphries.com

The Architectural Association in the Postwar Years
© Patrick Zamarian, 2020
All rights reserved

ISBN: 978-1-84822-406-3

Cover: Final Jury, Architectural Association, 1962
The models show development schemes for the Waterloo Road area in London, completed by groups of fourth-year students under year master John Winter.

Photo: AA Photolibrary / Courtesy of Julyan Wickham.

Copyedited by Pamela Bertram
Cover design by Stefi Orazi
Proofread by Patrick Cole
Set in Arnhem Pro and Circular Std
Printed in Malaysia

Contents

Acknowledgements

My research into the Architectural Association began in 2013, and it humbles me to think of the number of people who over this period of time have – each in their own way – helped me in my efforts.

I wish to convey my deep-felt gratitude to Mark Swenarton and Barnabas Calder, who supervised the doctoral thesis on which this book is based and have been unfailingly supportive of my work ever since. I am lucky to conduct my teaching and research at the University of Liverpool in close contact with distinguished colleagues. I wish to thank all academic and administrative staff, and in particular the head of our department, Soumyen Bandyopadhyay, his predecessors Andy Brown and Andrew Crompton, and Martin Winchester.

My research took me to a good number of libraries and archives, which as a general rule are always staffed by the most helpful people one can meet. I owe a tremendous debt to my friend Ed Bottoms and his colleagues, who gave me unfettered access to the treasure trove that is the AA Archive. I am also grateful to the archivists and librarians at the Modern Records Centre in Coventry, the Centre for Research Collections at the University of Edinburgh, the National Archive in Kew, Lancaster University, Liverpool John Moores University, the University of Liverpool, Imperial College London, the Royal Institute of British Architects in London, the London Metropolitan Archives, the British Library in London and its Boston Spa outpost, Manchester Central Library, the People's History Museum in Manchester, the Avery Architectural & Fine Arts Library at Columbia University, the Houghton Library at Harvard University, the Stuart Weitzman School of Design at the University of Pennsylvania, and the Institute for the History and Theory of Architecture at ETH Zurich.

I have had the pleasure and privilege to meet many former AA students and staff, some of whom welcomed me in their homes and allowed me to look through their private papers and student work. In particular, I wish to thank Jean and Stephen Macfarlane, Jenny and the late Martyn Haxworth, Alison and the late Bob Maguire, the late Geoff Spyer, Jean and Tim Sturgis, the late Chris Whittaker, and also Peter Ahrends, John Miller, Derek Montefiore, Bill Mullins, the late John Partridge, Michael Pearson, and Tim Tinker. I am equally grateful to those who took the time to talk to me on the phone or on Skype, specifically the late Sir Andrew Derbyshire, Tony Eardley, the late Michael Glickman, Kenneth Grieb, Malcolm Higgs, Diana Lee-Smith, and the late Peter Rich, and to many more who communicated with me in writing, including Dargan Bullivant, the late Gabi Epstein, Bob Garratt, the late Bob Gatje, John Godwin and Jill Hopwood, Allen Greenberg, Hans Heyerdahl Hallen, Elizabeth Hill-Smith, Paffard Keatinge-Clay, Alec Livock, the late Bob Maxwell, Peter Phippen, Marius Reynolds, Stephen Rosenberg, Joseph Rykwert, Elizabeth Scott, Grahame Shane, Charmian Shenton, and David Wild.

Nick Allen and Nicholas Boyarsky both gave me generous access to their respective father's papers. I am equally grateful to John Frazer, John Martin, Simon Pepper, Denise Scott Brown, Tim Sturgis, and Roger Whitehouse, who made privately held drawings and images available to me, and also to Nigel Coates, Sir Jeremy Dixon, Tony Dugdale, Tony Eardley, Eldred Evans, Adrian Gale, Sir Nicholas Grimshaw, Birkin Haward, Edward Jones, John Outram, Eric Parry, Richard and Ruth Rogers, Tim Tinker, Bernard Tschumi, Julyan Wickham, Christopher Woodward, and the Zaha Hadid Foundation, who gave me permission to publish their work.

Mark Swenarton's advice in transforming my thesis into this book was invaluable, and the same applies to Tim Brittain-Catlin, Murray Fraser, Iain Jackson, Simon Pepper, and Alan Powers. Countless others, including Rob Adams, Chris Barker, Alistair Bevington, Judy Carter, Jiat-Hwee Chang, Nick Coombe, Yvonne Glennie, Elain Harwood, Harry Hobin, Ben Johnson, Joshua Mardell, Jim McCann, Stephen Parnell, Chris Rogers, Andrew Saint, and Greg Smith, provided useful information and leads for further investigations.

Last but by no means least, I wish to extend my thanks to Val Rose and Rochelle Roberts at Lund Humphries for their help and patience, and to the members of the 'Architectural History of the British Isles' series board for their valuable input. The University of Liverpool and the Paul Mellon Centre for Studies in British Art both awarded generous grants to cover the illustration and production costs of this book, and I am very grateful to Soumyen Bandyopadhyay and Mark Swenarton for supporting these applications.

Having left my home country many years ago, I have come to treasure family and friendship ties which have remained unaffected by, what used to be, geographical irrelevancies such as the English Channel. My parents, my sister Katja and my godson Remo have always been enthusiastic about everything I do, including this book. Banham brought – and Sophie continues to bring – balance and joy to my life. For all of the above and more I wish to thank my Julie, to whom I dedicate this book.

Introduction

The school's most marked differences from other schools of architecture are its size, its minimal administration and its reliance on myths, both in the proper sense of explanations that relate architecture to the real world, and the degraded sense of beliefs that can be contradicted by facts.

Fred Scott, 1975[1]

The Architectural Association (AA) is a fascinating place. It was founded as an independent school at a time when school-based training in Britain was as yet unknown, and its history is the history of its struggle for survival as an independent school. This in itself makes it a unique institution in the architectural world. Short-lived pedagogical experiments notwithstanding, all other major schools are rooted in a particular educational system (nowadays mainly the German model of technical universities, in previous eras the French Beaux-Arts system). Driven by an unshakeable belief in the superiority of its own approach, the AA has always defined itself *against* the prevailing methods of training. Its roots lie firmly in itself, and like similarly esoteric societies it has developed and nurtured its own impenetrable customs and myths, in both of the senses identified by Fred Scott. Over its long existence the AA has been a constant point of reference in British architectural education, alternately eliciting admiration, envy and scorn – but never indifference.

I was not born in Britain and did not study here. The indigenous infatuation with the AA's idiosyncrasies has thus largely passed me by. Indeed, with its glorified amateurism and its penchant for eccentricity, the AA always seemed to me to be a profoundly English construct and like most such things an acquired taste. Certainly, when I studied architecture at ETH Zurich in the late 1990s, we had little time for the AA and its fanciful paper visions. We saw the AA as an art academy rather than a school of architecture, and as such it figured fairly low in our estimation. Conditioned by a subliminally anti-artistic Zwinglian utilitarianism, our interest in the architectural drawing lay solely in its potentiality as an actual building, and the AA seemed to make no obvious contribution to this. (Of course, history proved us wrong on this point.)

What we could relate to was the AA's hermetic snobbishness and entitlement mentality – common Swiss traits not limited to ETH but particularly prevalent there. However, in our case – or at least in my case as a Zurich native – exaggerated feelings of self-importance derived largely from the fact that ours was far and wide the only school of any standing. Other architectural schools in small European countries find themselves in similarly dominant positions – TU Delft, the University of Porto or the major Scandinavian schools being prime examples – and this may offer some explanation why it is often in such countries that we can find something resembling a coherent national attitude towards modern architecture.

The situation in Britain could not be more different. Today, there are about 50 validated schools of architecture, a dozen of them in London alone. In the postwar period there had been 73 such schools, 20 of which (including the AA) offered a full-time five-year course which was recognised by the Royal Institute of British Architects (RIBA) for exemption from its final examination. The AA was thus far from unique. Yet in spite of this, the school could claim to have produced a quarter of all major competition winners in the postwar period,[2] and while the exact figure may be debatable, the overall success of the school in this respect is not. Beginning with the first significant competition after the war – the Pimlico housing scheme, won by Philip Powell and Hidalgo Moya in 1946 – AA graduates strung together a succession of similar accomplishments in the following years and decades. In 1951, the AA dominated both competitions organised in connection with the Festival of Britain, winning two first and two third prizes.[3] Two years later, John R. Harris won the contest for a new state hospital in Doha, and in 1959, members of three of the four finalist teams for the Churchill College competition currently taught at the AA, while the lead designer of the winning scheme – Bill Mullins for Sheppard Robson – was a recent graduate (as were the two named partners of his firm). In the following year, Nigel Farrington and John Dennys submitted a successful entry for the new civic centre of Corby in collaboration with their erstwhile tutor Enrico de Pierro. In 1961, Paul Koralek won Trinity College in Dublin and founded a practice with his former fellow students Richard Burton and Peter Ahrends, while Eldred Evans took first prize in the Lincoln civic centre competition with a project based on her final thesis (Fig.57). Three years later, Francis Pym won the contest for an extension of the Ulster Museum, and in 1971 Richard Rogers, with Renzo Piano, scored a surprise victory in the international competition for the Centre Pompidou in Paris.

Of course, not all distinguished architects came from the AA. Stirling studied at Liverpool, Gowan at Glasgow and Kingston, and the Smithsons in Newcastle. 'We did not go to the AA – that's why we're good', Alison Smithson reportedly proclaimed,[4] yet for many others the AA was high on the wish list and failure to be admitted a cause for regret.[5] Indeed, the list of AA graduates reads like a who's who of British postwar architecture and includes private practitioners such as Peter Cook, Edward Cullinan, Nicholas Grimshaw, Michael and Patty Hopkins, Robert Maguire, Cedric Price, Quinlan Terry, John Voelcker and Elia Zenghelis, as well as RMJM partners Francis Baden-Powell, Andrew Derbyshire, Hugh Morris, Peter Newnham and Alan Wightman, three-quarters of both HKPA (Howell, Killick and Amis) and DEGW (Duffy, Eley and Worthington), and all original partners of Colquhoun + Miller, Dixon + Jones, Shankland Cox, and Austin-Smith:Lord (Michael Austin-Smith, Inette Austin-Smith, Peter Lord and Geoffrey Salmon). Many lesser known but equally influential architects who attained high positions in the public sector also graduated from the AA, including Neave Brown, George Finch, John Kay, Henry Swain, Patricia Tindale and Gordon Wigglesworth. At a rough estimate the AA produced half of the country's leading postwar architects. In addition, there were those who went on to illustrious careers abroad, among them Ram Karmi, Ada Karmi-Melamede and Thomas Leitersdorf in Israel; Mick Pearce in Zimbabwe; John Godwin and Gillian Hopwood in Nigeria; Geoffrey Bawa in Sri Lanka; Kamil Khan Mumtaz in Pakistan; Frank Musson and Peter Dickinson in Canada; and Donald Appleyard, John Belle, Paffard Keatinge-Clay and Denise Scott Brown in the United States.

The AA was for much of the postwar period the country's largest and – if one accepts the subsequent careers of its graduates as a measure of its success – most eminent school of architecture. How was it possible that an institution, whose value as a training ground for practising architects I dismissed, had managed to produce all these architects whose work I admired? Of course, it did not take me long (and came as no great surprise) to apprehend that the postwar incarnation of the AA school had been an altogether different entity to the one on which I based my prejudices. Rather more surprising was the realisation that nobody had been sufficiently intrigued by the school's tremendous efficacy to investigate the matter in any depth. The AA, it seemed, reflected Goldhagen and Legault's assessment of the postwar period as an 'interregnum between an expiring modernism and a dawning postmodernism', worthy of consideration only in so far as it allowed occasional glimpses of things to come.[6]

There has been tentative research into the period leading up to the Second World War, when the students staged a campaign against the school's Beaux-Arts methods which would, as Elizabeth Darling argues, 'ultimately [. . .] secure modernism's domination over British spatial culture'.[7] Likewise, the so-called 'Electric Decade'[8] from the mid-1960s onward, which reached its apex in the early 1970s, when Alvin Boyarsky reinvented the school as an 'intellectual infrastructure for architectural postmodernism', has attracted considerable interest from historians such as Andrew Higgott, Igor Marjanović and Irene Sunwoo.[9] Bridging these two landmark events in the AA's history, the two decades from the end of the war until the mid-1960s have received only perfunctory treatment and generated little more than anecdotal evidence. In a compellingly neat narrative, the postwar years emerge as a transitional and largely inconsequential phase during which the pioneering spirit of the pre-war insurgents lay dormant until it eventually stimulated Boyarsky and a new generation of staff and students to salvage the moribund AA from imminent closure. Given the unquestionable success of the school in the postwar period, this seemed a blatantly absurd proposition. Six years ago, I therefore decided to leave my home in Spain and move to England to dedicate my doctoral research to the matter. The book you are holding in your hands is the outcome of this research.

Historically, control over education, the setting of competition standards and the establishment of provincial societies formed the tripod on which the RIBA's efforts to spread professionalism rested.[10] In sharp contrast to the state-dominated educational systems in continental Europe, architectural training in Britain was (and remained) tightly linked to, and guided by, the practical demands of the profession. This raises the question as to the basic suitability of architectural education as a subject in its own right and, contingent on this, the potential validity of any study which centres upon the contribution of one particular school, no matter the significance of that school within its broader setting. Andrew Saint, in his selective study of the profession, argues that 'the nature of architectural teaching at any given time proceeds from the state of the profession, rather than the other way round', and he therefore omits any discussion of the subject altogether.[11] Yet the reality of British architectural education in the postwar years paints a more complex picture than Saint suggests. In the mid-1950s, there existed six different routes into the profession as intending architects could learn their trade by becoming articled pupils; taking a correspondence course; studying part-time at a so-called 'facilities school'; taking both RIBA examinations externally while attending a so-called 'listed school'; taking the final examination externally after completing the three-year course at a school exempt from the RIBA's intermediate examination; or studying at a fully recognised school (which in turn could be part of a university, an art school, a technical college or independent like the AA). Moreover, even among the recognised full-time schools there was a marked discrepancy in methodology, ranging from the Beaux-Arts-derived education at the Bartlett to the more vocational training offered by the London polytechnics. It seems that the setting of educational parameters was largely left to the schools, either because the profession had limited control over them or because it lacked the ability to agree a coherent policy.

Arguably, both were the case. The rise of full-time school training in the early 20th century and the corresponding emergence of a sub-profession of architectural teachers, particularly in the universities, made the schools less susceptible to the pressures exerted upon them by the RIBA. More importantly, the diversity of pedagogical approaches in the postwar period reflected the identity crisis of a profession which, faced with an expanded spectrum of tasks and unprecedented government interference, struggled to redefine its role in the nascent welfare state. As public and private practitioners vied for influence within the RIBA, their conflicting priorities frustrated any attempt at arriving at a coherent educational agenda. Significantly, throughout the period leading up to the seminal Oxford Conference of 1958, which finally crystallised the diverging views of its members into a unified and rigorously enforced policy centred upon higher entry standards and a preference for full-time university education, both factions saw educational policy as an instrument with which to mould the future trajectory of the profession. In other words, in the postwar period, architectural education shed any passive role it may have had and turned into an active agent of change. In Crinson and Lubbock's view, it became 'one of the major forces shaping the built environment [. . .], perhaps the most important'.[12]

The interdependence between education and professional practice is of particular interest in our context since the AA school was the only architectural school, certainly in Britain, which was controlled and operated by a professional body. Throughout the postwar period the membership of the association, whose primary purpose was the running of the school, consisted – on the basis of a closely observed formula – of at least 89 per cent architects. The AA council as the governing body was, with few exceptions, composed of practising architects while almost all members of the studio staff served in a part-time capacity and were – in contrast to most other schools at the time – not just encouraged, but explicitly required to engage in architectural practice. In light of this, we should expect the AA to be particularly responsive to the changing demands and preoccupations of the profession.

Likewise, the gradual change from the loosely controlled educational framework of the postwar years to the tightly regulated setup of the early 1960s was bound to have implications for an independent school such as the AA. Without academic oversight by either a government agency or a university senate, the AA had over the course of its history developed a highly adaptive educational system. The composition of the council changed annually, and with the sole exception of the principal all members

of the academic staff were appointed on short-term contracts, which enabled the school to effect changes to policy and curriculum almost instantly. Moreover, many of these changes originated in suggestions from the student body, which enjoyed unparalleled participatory privileges. Unsurprisingly perhaps, AA graduates retained an unusual degree of loyalty to their alma mater, enabling the school to draw upon a virtually unlimited pool of practising architects to recruit to its part-time teaching staff. The sum total of these features had allowed the AA to pioneer a number of experimental pedagogical schemes and underpinned its self-conception as 'the most imaginative and progressive radiating point of architectural ideas in Britain'.[13]

The AA was fiercely alert to external developments which in the postwar period jeopardised its autonomy and the educational benefits it derived from it. It is therefore not without irony that arguably the greatest threat to this autonomy was homemade and arose from the AA's precarious financial position. Unlike the university schools, which received generous funding from the Treasury through the University Grants Committee, and technical colleges such as the London polytechnics, which were under the charge of local education authorities (which were in turn subsidised by the Ministry of Education), the AA school was dependent on students' tuition fees to cover its running costs. Throughout its history the AA struggled to balance its books, and the state-funded expansion of higher technological education in the wake of the 1945 Percy Report inevitably put it at a competitive disadvantage. This is a matter which will concern us throughout the book as, with the systemic shortage of money and the growing regulatory pressure from government agencies curtailing its room for manoeuvre, the advantages of the school's independence, and indeed the very idea of this independence, came into question. The overall picture which emerges of the postwar period is that of the government and the RIBA acting as dual forces pushing for greater conformity and control in architectural education. Broadly speaking, for approximately a decade after the end of the war the advantages of the AA's independence outweighed any potential drawback arising from its scarce finances; yet in the mid-1950s this independence began to look out of touch with the changing political and educational realities and threatened to leave the school marginalised within a tightening national framework of architectural education.

The ultimate responsibility for negotiating these conditions lay with the council, an annually elected body consisting largely, albeit not exclusively, of AA graduates. Some members of the council play a major, and at times determining, role in the events recounted, particularly where they concern negotiations with outside bodies or the arbitration of internal disputes. For instance, President Hugh Casson, newly knighted for his work on the Festival of Britain, emerges as a key figure in the turbulent events of the early 1950s; Casson's successor Peter Shepheard was chiefly responsible for obtaining the government's approval for a partial reinstatement of the students' voting rights in 1956; John Brandon-Jones and Denis Clarke Hall, successive presidents in the late 1950s, were, on opposing sides of the argument, instrumental in the AA's deliberations regarding an integrated college of architecture and building; and in the first half of the following decade, Leo De Syllas and Anthony Cox masterminded a complete repositioning of the school to prepare it for a merger with the Imperial College of Science and Technology. However, more often than not, the annual changeover of the council prevented members from exercising a sustained influence on the direction of the school, and even when they served for an extended period they usually did so with restraint – as was indeed the intention. The council was neither expected nor able to formulate and implement a policy for the school, which was – at least in theory – the principal's domain. Though in practice this setup proved flawed, not least because control over the school's finances gave the council a powerful tool to make its changing viewpoint felt, the degree of authority which rested with the AA principal was considerable, and changes in school policy and outlook usually did correspond with changes in leadership. The basic structure of this book is

therefore chronological and reflects the succession of principals. The chapters themselves, however, are topical, and issues which may take centre stage at a specific moment in the school's history often have their roots in previous years. In such instances, the discussion is not confined to a narrow time frame.

Chapter 1 gives a thumbnail history of the AA until the end of the Second World War. The focus lies in the tumultuous events of the late 1930s, when the students rallied in opposition to a council seemingly intent on suppressing the modernist tendencies which were gaining ground in the school. Chapters 2, 3 and 4 address themselves to the immediate postwar years from 1945 to 1951. Chapter 2 describes how the school, under Gordon Brown (1912–62; principal 1945–9), sought to cope with a sudden increase in student numbers and enhance its international reputation. Brown's successor Robert Furneaux Jordan (1905–78; principal 1949–51), whose term in office is the subject of Chapter 3, found the school in a rare state of affluence, which allowed him to operate within looser financial constraints. Driven by firm political convictions, Jordan implemented a teaching model which aimed at preparing his students for a professional future within the collaborative work environment of an all-embracing public sector. The postwar students themselves, many of them ex-service personnel, instigated an extraordinary range of activities within and beyond the AA. These are discussed in Chapter 4, which spans the same period as the previous two. Chapters 5, 6 and 7 cover the decade-long tenure of Michael Pattrick (1913–80; principal 1951–61), each with a different theme. Chapter 5 continues the discussion of student activism and traces the early years of Pattrick's tenure, during which he became the target of a sustained campaign by the students' committee to remove him from office – an unparalleled course of events in the history of British architectural education, unprecedented even at a school which had had its fair share of controversy in the past. Chapter 6 examines Pattrick's changes to the educational model in the mid-1950s, which saw the foundation of the famous Department of Tropical Architecture as well as the introduction of a modified unit system and the appointment of a distinguished teaching staff around Peter Smithson and John Killick. Chapter 7 explores the school's difficulties in adapting its policy to the changing realities in British architectural education in the second half of the 1950s as the AA came under growing political and financial pressure. Chapter 8 discusses the appointment of William Allen (1914–98; principal 1961–5) and the plan to merge the AA school with Imperial College, both driven by the intention to enhance the professional status of AA graduates and expand their sphere of influence. This technocratic vision manifested itself in a rebalancing between studio teaching and lecture courses, which met with fierce resistance from the staff and student body and left Allen increasingly isolated in the school. Chapter 9 discusses the aftermath of Allen's departure, culminating in the failure of the Imperial College merger scheme and the election of Alvin Boyarsky as chairman in 1971. Complementing a body of existing literature which highlights the novelty of his pedagogical experiments, the chapter seeks to explain Boyarsky's rise to power within the particular institutional context of the AA and tentatively extends the narrative to the more recent past.

1 Prologue: A Brief History of the Architectural Association (1847–1945)

The AA, the RIBA and the Systematisation of Architectural Education

In Victorian Britain, young men (and rarely women) who wished to train as architects did so by attaching themselves to a practising master who, for a period of five or six years and in return for a fee, gave them instruction in drawing, measuring, site work and office organisation.[1] Pupillage provided a fluent passage from training to practice, but it had its drawbacks. Articled pupils did not necessarily share the fate of Martin Chuzzlewit, who, in Charles Dickens's eponymous novel of 1843, endures exploitation at the hands of his hypocritical master. Yet the lack of regulation left the pupillage system open to abuse and the quality of training varied considerably. Pupillage was, moreover, an inherently restrictive teaching method, which at best perpetuated a master's craft, but which gave ambitious students little scope to expand their knowledge and develop their design skills. The Royal Academy offered a limited range of supplementary facilities, including a library, drawing classes and lectures on architectural theory, and from the early 1840s both King's College and University College arranged preparatory courses in architecture for intending pupils. Yet none of these institutions offered design classes, nor did they provide a forum for debate on architectural matters.

The formation of the Architectural Association (AA) was a direct response to this state of affairs.[2] In September 1842, James Wylson, chief assistant in a London practice, formed the 'Association of Architectural Draughtsmen' (AAD), whose members sought to perfect their trade through self-improvement, build up a collection of architectural drawings and keep an employment register. Soon after, an articled pupil named Robert Kerr, using the pseudonym 'R', launched a diatribe against the vices of pupillage in the correspondence columns of the *Builder*. In September 1846, Charles Gray, another pupil, writing over the signature 'An Architectural Student', complained to the same paper about the impossibility of obtaining any substantive instruction in architectural design and suggested that, if the government was unable or unwilling to pit itself against the vested interests of their masters, the pupils themselves might take the initiative and organise their own school. By the end of the year, Kerr had made contact with Gray, and together they persuaded the AAD to join forces by establishing a new architectural society for that purpose.

The AA, whose inaugural meeting took place on 8 October 1847, thus owed its existence to the initiative of youth – Kerr was 23, Gray only 18 – and though the average age of its members soon rose, as many of them retained their membership after completing their training, the AA in principle remained receptive to the ideas of its youngest and most rebellious members. In other ways, too, the early activities of the AA set the tone for its future proceedings. Initially, these were a weekly affair taking place on Friday evenings, alternately in the form of general meetings or design classes. General meetings provided a forum for the uninhibited and often passionate discussion of papers read by members, which contrasted with the more august occasions at the RIBA. The real novelty, however, were the AA's design classes. In the absence of teachers, the learning process was based on mutual criticism: subjects were announced on a printed circular, and students brought their schemes to the following meeting for an informal discussion with their peers. Even when the AA eventually hired professional instructors, the relationship between tutors and students remained collegial and informal, and the same egalitarian spirit was to pervade the AA's pioneering open juries. These invited the active participation of students and observers and thus, despite their nomenclature, differed substantially from the closed and monologic Beaux-Arts juries.

The AA initially flourished and within four years managed to increase its membership from an initial two dozen to 166. Yet the charm of novelty soon wore off: attendance at meetings declined, and by 1854 the AA, which depended on membership dues to cover its costs, was facing insolvency. The RIBA, which had witnessed the rise of its 'adolescent rival'[3] with suspicion, launched a takeover bid and in 1856 proposed 'amalgamation' of the two bodies. It was this threat to its independence which pulled the AA out of its lethargy and revived members' interest in the association. In 1860 they passed a momentous resolution stipulating the annual changeover of officers on its governing body, which not only stimulated the inflow of new members and helped reverse the trend of the previous years, but effectively enshrined the principle of perpetual change and the corresponding absence of any long-term policy in the AA's constitution.

Meanwhile, the AA had set in motion a scheme which was to have a profound impact on the nature of British architectural education itself. This scheme aimed at the creation of an examination system as

the basis for a qualifying diploma for architects – an idea first advanced by James Knowles in an AA prize essay of 1853 and endorsed by AA President Alfred Bailey in a paper two years later. RIBA President William Pite, who attended Bailey's talk, adopted and promoted the scheme, and in 1863 the RIBA staged its first voluntary examination. In anticipation of this, the AA had, in the year before, launched a 'voluntary examination class', thus 'crystallizing', as Summerson put it, 'for the first time, the concept of organized study tested by examination as the foundation of the architect's training'.[4] The voluntary examination class, the original design class and a 'junior class', started in 1869, were the three pillars of the AA's educational system at the time, with additional classes added if and when required.

Despite the AA's advocacy, the RIBA's examinations remained of marginal interest until, in 1882, they were made a mandatory requirement to attain associateship. Five years later, the RIBA divided its examination system into three distinct stages – preliminary, intermediate and final – and the AA responded by aligning its syllabus to this new tripartite structure and remodelling its own educational setup. The evening course now lasted four years, all classes were supervised by experienced tutors (so-called 'visitors'), and from the early 1890s the school engaged paid experts to deliver its extended lecture programme. At the same time, Leonard Stokes, the AA's president from 1889 to 1892, instigated a substantial revision of its administrative apparatus. After the slump in the mid-1850s the membership had increased rapidly, and by 1890 it stood at 1,129. In the following year the AA appointed a secretary as its first paid official to take charge of the day-to-day running of the association and to oversee its vastly expanded activities, which included the publication of a monthly journal, custodianship of a fast-growing library collection and an annual summer excursion in Britain or abroad.

Although by the turn of the century the AA and the RIBA were pursuing their educational objectives in concert, the relationship between the two bodies remained ambivalent. In part this was due to a fundamental difference in class, or rather status – the RIBA was controlled by its 'Fellows', members in private practice (and thus usually in charge of one or more pupils), whereas the AA was effectively a pressure group of their underlings. The more important reason for the latent tensions between the AA and the RIBA was that of jurisdiction. The AA never questioned the RIBA's prerogative as examining and degree-awarding body, but it saw itself – with some justification – as the initiator of the examination system on which the RIBA based this prerogative and thus, effectively, of British architectural education itself. The AA inferred from this a sense of entitlement in educational matters: it expected to be consulted on major decisions and never felt entirely bound by the standards set by the RIBA's Board of Architectural Education (BAE), established in 1904. Inevitably, the existence of two organisations, both with a tenable claim to setting the agenda in architectural education, would give cause for conflict for decades to come.

The Rise of the Beaux-Arts System

By the early 1890s, the AA had evolved from a 'happy-go-lucky club for self-improvement'[5] into a professionally organised educational establishment with paid lecturers and instructors. Changing attitudes in style and pedagogy accompanied this development as the AA, which had upheld a fiercely neutral stance throughout the mid-19th-century 'battle of styles', entered a distinct Arts and Crafts phase, setting up a 'School of Design and Handicraft' and arranging workshop demonstrations for its students at William Lethaby's Central School (Fig.1). In 1901 the AA established complementary day classes, intended to replace articled pupillage and therefore purposely put under the direction of practising architects. As anticipated, the full-time day school gradually superseded the evening school (and eventually, in 1917, eradicated it altogether). At the same time, Arts and Crafts ideals lost traction as the AA's main competitor – Charles Reilly's Liverpool School – remodelled its curriculum along Beaux-Arts lines. In 1912, the AA followed suit

by appointing as its new principal Robert Atkinson, then an unknown young architect, who steered the school resolutely towards a neo-classical approach.[6]

The outbreak of the First World War in July 1914 put any further development on hold as within the space of a few months only 20 students (out of more than 200) were left in the school. Cut off from its main source of income, the AA devised a number of measures to generate additional revenue – in 1917 it finally admitted women to the school (if not yet to membership of the association); it launched an appeal for money (and received a generous donation from the RIBA); and it sold the lease for its headquarters on Tufton Street and took up a more favourable one on its present premises, a Georgian terrace in Bedford Square, which for the first time allowed it to provide club amenities for its non-student members.

When the war ended in November 1918, the student population at once returned to its pre-war size. Institutionally, this marked the moment when the AA set itself up in the form in which it would operate for the next 50 years, and in some part beyond that. In March 1920, the AA was incorporated, and the articles of association for the first time made provisions for women to join the association. The governance of the AA was entrusted to a council composed of ten ordinary members elected annually by the membership plus eight officers, who were returned unopposed, and organised into different committees transacting specific aspects of its business. By far the largest and most important of these was the school committee, which was usually chaired by the AA president and advised the principal on broader educational policy, the actual running of the school being left entirely to his own devices. Meanwhile, the various student societies were reconstituted as sections of the 'students' club', which comprised the entire student body and was managed by the students' committee. Staff and students were represented on various committees, though significantly never on the school committee. In addition, the council could draw on the expertise of an advisory committee consisting of its past-presidents and other eminent members of the profession, which existed since 1885 but, like

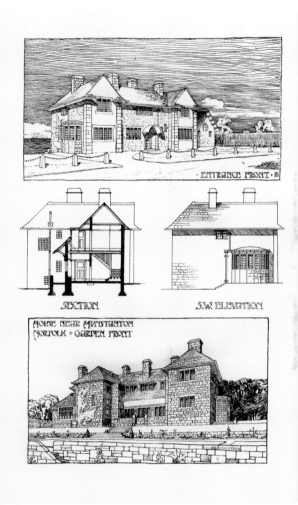

1   House near Hunstanton, Norfolk (Edwin Gunn, Advanced Class of Design, 1901/02)

Around the turn of the century, the AA entered its Arts and Crafts phase. Studio programmes asked for houses and small public buildings on rural or suburban sites. The designs were asymmetric in plan and characterised by the use of traditional building methods and local materials.

2　Roman Composition (Judith Ledeboer, second year, 1927/28)

Compositions of classical elements in the Beaux-Arts manner were a regular feature of the curriculum throughout the 1920s. They were gradually phased out in the following decade although Trajan lettering and the drawing of the orders experienced a brief revival after the war.

the students' committee, had neither legal nor statutory standing.

Pedagogically, the school continued to follow Liverpool's example in embracing a 'half-understood Beaux-Arts style'[7] derived from French and American models – a succession of drawing exercises and increasingly complex design schemes in the classical manner, culminating in a 'grand' thesis at the end of the curriculum (Fig.2). In 1920, the AA instituted a five-year course, to which the RIBA granted exemption from its final examination, along with Liverpool the first in the country to be so recognised. Later that year, Robert Atkinson, whose practice specialised in the then-fashionable American-style movie palaces, retired to the less demanding position of 'director of education'. The council appointed as his successor Howard Robertson, who had briefly trained at the AA before completing his course at the École des Beaux-Arts in Paris just prior to the outbreak of war. Highly decorated for his service in the army, Robertson returned to London in 1919 to set up in private practice with John Murray Easton and run a Beaux-Arts-type 'atelier' at the AA school. As expected, Robertson continued Atkinson's educational policy, aligning the AA's course with the RIBA's examination syllabus and abandoning its evening classes, the last vestiges of the pupillage system.

The Question of Modernism: *Focus* and the Unit System

The rise of modernism in the early 1920s did not go unnoticed at the AA. Indeed, it was chiefly through a series of travel reports in the *Architect and Building News* written by Robertson and AA secretary Frank Yerbury, that in the second half of the 1920s a broader British public woke up to the new phenomenon on the continent.[8] According to Summerson, the influence of modernism 'spread furiously',[9] though perhaps not quite as furiously as he seemed to remember. In 1962, Robert Furneaux Jordan, who – unlike Summerson – had studied at the AA at the time, told a general meeting of the association:

Let us not in our loyalty to the Architectural Association imagine that it was always in the van of modern architecture. I was a student in the AA in the late 'twenties; I was here when *Vers Une Architecture* and the *Ville Radieuse* were being published. [. . .] Our attention was not drawn to them. In fact let us be honest; I think that many of my generation were not even aware of the Bauhaus until it was shut.[10]

Be that as it may, in the early 1930s modernist ideas began to infuse the training at the AA. Howard Robertson, whose own work defied easy categorisation and ranged from the self-conscious eclecticism of the British Pavilion for the Paris Exhibition of 1925 to the structurally striking Art Deco style of the Royal Horticultural Hall, was equally broad-minded in his pedagogical work and allowed for a variety of formal expressions as long as they arose logically from the problem in hand. The future members of Berthold Lubetkin's ground-breaking modernist practice Tecton were among the first who produced drawings that were manifestly inspired by contemporary work on the continent. Lindsay Drake, for instance, abandoned Beaux-Arts-style ink wash rendering in favour of Bauhaus-type axonometric dyeline drawings for his final-year thesis in 1932 (Fig.3). Others soon followed their lead, and by the mid-1930s a significant proportion of student work showed signs of a distinctively modernist vocabulary (Figs 4–9; Plate 1). More importantly, the spirit of social idealism and scientific enquiry which had inspired the creation of this vocabulary infected a growing number of students and staff, challenging the ideological certainties of the 'establishment' as represented by the AA council. This generational conflict soon escalated, not least because it coincided with a constitutional crisis which seriously and permanently damaged relations between students and school authorities.

Following the AA's incorporation in 1920, the students' club had retained its social function, but the sole responsibility for educational policy was henceforth delegated to the council. Significantly, this did not alter the status of students within the

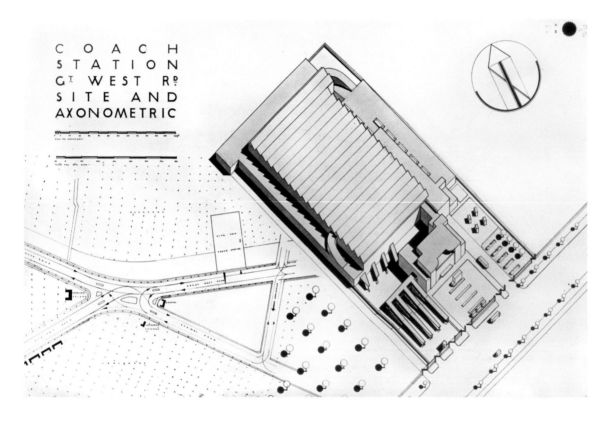

3 Motor Coach Station (Lindsay Drake, thesis, 1931/32)

Asymmetric composition, dyeline drawing, axonometric view – the hallmarks of a functionalist plan layout. Val Harding, a fellow student and future partner in Tecton, had visited Germany in 1930 and carried the technique into the AA.

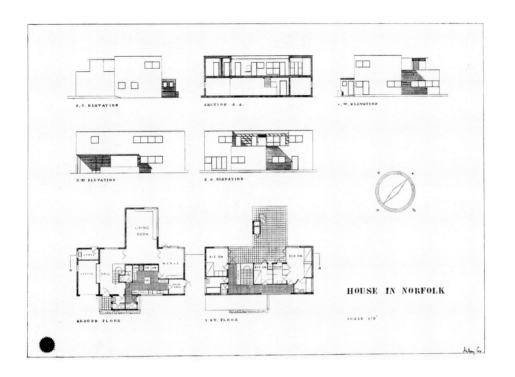

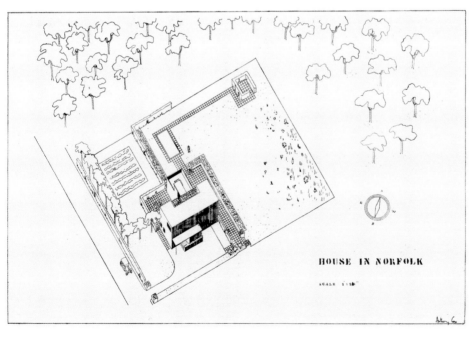

Cox's suburban family home was the first unapologetically modernist design at the school. Living spaces were arranged on an open plan; there was no projecting roof; and the absence of fireplaces suggests that the building was to incorporate central heating. The layout shows affinities with contemporary work on the continent, but at the AA, and in British architecture more generally, it was without precedent – a remarkable achievement by a student who had only just finished his first-year course.

4   House in Norfolk (Anthony Cox, second year, 1934/35)

*This proposal for the replanning of a congested working-class
neighbourhood in central London reflects the growing interest in
planning issues following the passing of the Housing Act of 1930
and the subsequent slum clearance drive of the British government.
The plan is for 1,425 flats, distributed into five-storey slabs and
fifteen-storey Y-shaped towers. The latter were a novel feature
in British architecture at the time and show the influence of Le
Corbusier, who was then developing the 'chicken claw' variation of
his Cartesian skyscraper as an alternative to the cruciform towers
of the Ville Radieuse. The thesis group included Gordon Brown,
a future principal of the school. Richard Sheppard, who drew the
axonometry, later formed a successful partnership with another AA
graduate, Geoffrey Robson.*

5   Rehousing in St Pancras (Gordon Brown, Reginald A. Kirby, Bernard Le Mare, Richard Sheppard, thesis, 1934/35)

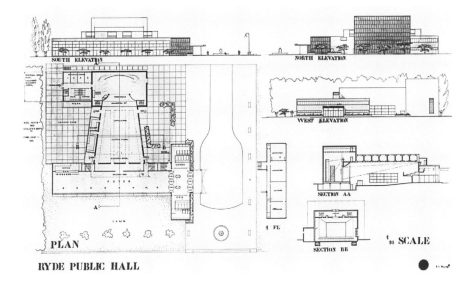

6   Ryde Public Hall (Richard Llewelyn Davies, Unit 11, fourth year, 1936/37)

In the second half of the 1930s, modernist designs became the norm rather than the exception at the AA. There was a tendency to let the plan inform the shape and appearance of the building by arranging different functions in separate but closely interlocked volumes. Llewelyn Davies's idea of resolving a number of symmetrical elements in a loose and asymmetrical layout is typical of its time and reflects the mindset of a generation which as yet lacked the strength of its modernist convictions.

7   Elementary School (Leonard Manasseh, Unit 7, third year, 1936/37)

Manasseh submitted the winning scheme in a competition between students from Bristol, Liverpool and the AA organised by the News Chronicle *in December 1937. The chief assessor was Denis Clarke Hall, who had won the professional competition in March 1937, less than a year after graduating from the AA.*

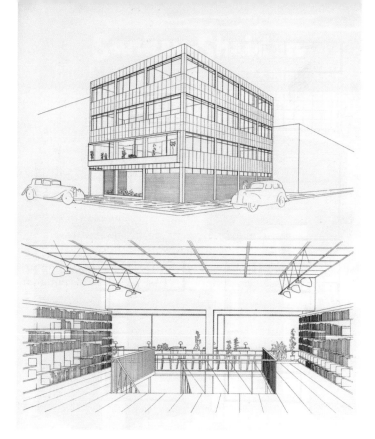

8 Administrative Offices and Main Branch of a Lending Library (Bruce Martin, Unit 9, third year, 1938/39)

The brief asked for a library to set the standard for all subsequent branches in compliance with London building regulations. Martin based his project on a structural grid of 405 cm × 405 cm, which is clearly expressed both inside and outside and allowed for the prefabrication of all major elements. There is an unusually direct link between Martin's student work and his future practice as an architect. His ideas on 'modular coordination', which he developed as a key figure in the Hertfordshire schools programme, are prefigured in several of his student schemes.

9 Dock Offices (Geoffrey Robson, Unit 9, third year, 1937/38)

Sketch designs featured prominently in the AA's curriculum as the ability to think and draw quickly was seen as an essential part of an architect's armoury. Geoffrey Robson's project for dock offices is rife with period features – note, for instance, the Calder mobile hanging from the neighbouring building and the anti-Fascist graffiti underneath it. The stencil lettering and the use of initialised project titles followed by a project number (in this case taken from his unit) were both borrowed from Le Corbusier's Oeuvre complète.

association as they remained equal members, entitled to vote and, indeed, stand for council.[11] Although this never actually occurred, it did potentially undermine the authority of the school executive, which in May 1933 prevailed upon the council to create a non-voting class of membership for students.[12] Having cleared all legal hurdles, on 26 February 1935, the council sought to get the necessary alterations of the bylaws approved by a general meeting of members, yet the students spotted the item on the agenda and attended in force to oppose (and defeat) it. Though outnumbered by a ratio of seven to one, the students had managed to turn the vote in their favour, and the council was determined not to allow this to happen again. At another general meeting a few months later, shrewdly scheduled during the summer vacation, when most students were absent, a majority of members supported the council's motion to introduce a postal ballot instead of a vote by show of hands, which permanently weakened the students' influence.[13]

The events of 1935 opened a gulf between the council and an increasingly distrustful student body. Unwilling to indiscriminately accept the council's educational policy, the students' committee began to shift its priorities from social to pedagogical issues – 'away from the world of nail-brushes and soap in the lavatories and into the world of conscious expression on the way they were being taught'.[14] This change of emphasis was further stimulated by the introduction, in the spring of 1936, of an entirely new teaching system at the school. Three years prior, Robertson had followed Atkinson's example and retired from the principalship to take up the less time-consuming post of director, appointing E. A. A. Rowse as his assistant director. Rowse, who held professional qualifications in architecture, town planning and structural engineering, soon displayed remarkable organisational acumen as he single-handedly devised the scheme for a new postgraduate department at the AA. Drawing on sociology, economics and a range of other disciplines, the pioneering School of Planning and Research for National Development (SPRND), inaugurated in January 1935, was the first to consider planning as a subject in its own right rather than merely an

extension of architectural studies in scope and scale. It proved an instant success, and when Robertson resigned at the end of the year the council promoted Rowse to principal and appointed Harry Goodhart-Rendel to the senior, but largely ceremonial, role of director. A former president of the AA and current Slade Professor of Fine Art at Oxford, Goodhart-Rendel was a self-taught architect of the Francophile persuasion, and his appointment was an obvious attempt to preserve the school's Beaux-Arts traditions against Rowse's modernism.[15]

On 14 January 1936, at his first school committee meeting as principal, Rowse presented his proposal for a fundamental reorganisation of the school.[16] Rowse considered the division of the school into five large year groups fundamentally flawed in that it prevented a free adjustment of the curriculum to meet the changing demands of the profession, discouraged close contact between staff and students (as well as among the students themselves), deterred staff from recommending relegation due to its relatively severe implications, and led to over- or underused studios depending on the size of the year group. To address these issues, Rowse devised a new system – the so-called 'unit system' – which was based on a division of the school into 15 term-based units, each under the charge of a different master. In other words, the cycle of studio tuition would be trimestrial rather than annual as each term a new group of students would enter Unit 1 and begin their 15-step progression through the school. This would allow the principal to relegate weak students by a single term rather than an entire year; talented students could be allowed to progress more rapidly through the course; and candidates could be admitted three times a year, which was likely to increase the school's revenue.

The school committee passed Rowse's report on to the council with a 'strong recommendation that it be adopted', and on 22 January 1936, the council resolved 'that the scheme be proceeded with immediately, in an experimental form'.[17] The students, too, approved of the new system and put forward a number of suggestions to improve it, including the extension of group work arrangements, the abolition of marks (or the introduction of a simplified system of 'Mention, Pass, Fail') and the participation of students in the writing of programmes.[18] In light of the students' interest in the parameters of their training, the staff began to meet with them on a regular basis to discuss the curriculum and, in January 1937, invited them to compile their ideas in the form of a report.

The work of the students' sub-committee set up to this end coincided with a controversial speech on architectural education given by Goodhart-Rendel in February 1937.[19] In his first address to the school after one year in office, the director rejected the pedagogical changes which were taking place and defended Beaux-Arts exercises, such as the drawing of the orders, not because he considered them to have any practical applicability to the contemporary architect, but because their abolition had left a normative void in the curriculum. Yet

to the authors of the 'Report of Students' Sub-committee on the School System', issued in May 1937 and better known as the 'Yellow Book', these changes did not go nearly far enough as they called for higher entry standards to facilitate a more advanced lecture course, criticised the compartmentalisation of subjects and, inspired by their history lecturer Robert Furneaux Jordan, demanded a complete remodelling of the history course as a 'history of social movements' rather than a 'history of architecture', and with particular emphasis on the immediate past.[20]

The students envisaged the Yellow Book as 'the first tentative step to clarify the basis on which a modern school should rest',[21] but their intention to follow it up with a second report advancing definite proposals to improve the curriculum was soon confounded by events in the school. In February 1938,

10

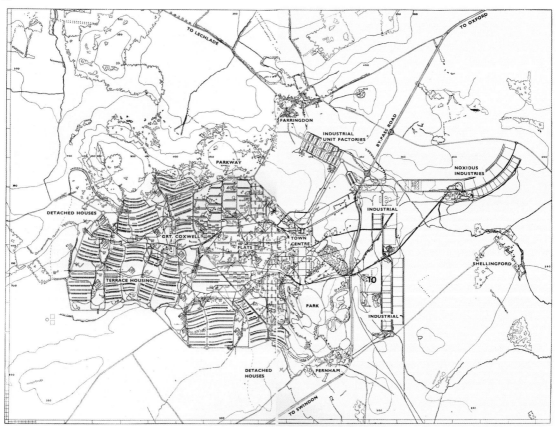

In the previous year, the same students had prepared a hypothetical scheme for a new town of 50,000 people as their pre-thesis subject. For their thesis, they adapted this scheme to a specific site near Faringdon in Oxfordshire. Drawing on extensive research ranging from soil conditions to methods of prefabrication, the group proposed a town consisting of five neighbourhood units located around a town centre and separated by a green belt from the surrounding industrial areas. The combination of detached houses, terrace housing and twelve-storey flats showed the influence of both Gropius's Törten Estate in Dessau and Tecton's recently completed Highpoint in London.

11

Town Plan (Arnulf Brandt, Elizabeth Chesterton, Peter Cocke, Ralph Crowe, Richard Llewelyn Davies, David Duncan, David Gladstone, John C. de C. Henderson, J. Hinchcliff, Anthony Pott, Peter Saxl, Frederick Lamond Sturrock, Peter Thornton, John Wheeler, Unit 15, thesis, 1937/38)

Goodhart-Rendel addressed a general meeting of the AA on 'The Training of an Architect'.[22] To the students' consternation, Goodhart-Rendel remained steadfast in his appreciation of the virtues of Beaux-Arts training and left no doubt about his desire to reverse the educational trends of the past couple of years. The director's bone of contention was not the unit system, as the students subsequently claimed, but the growing tendency for students to collaborate in groups on unnecessarily complex design programmes and, as a consequence, the prevalence of 'untimely and time-wasting research', much of it without obvious architectural implications.[23] The council concurred with Goodhart-Rendel's view and felt that a new principal was needed to effect the desired change of direction. On 3 May 1938, it relieved Rowse of his duties, and two months later it appointed Fernand Billerey, the former partner of Detmar Blow, as interim principal for the period

until Christmas.[24] Rowse himself remained principal of the planning school, which – having been abandoned by the council for financial reasons – continued to operate as an independent institution.

Rowse's dismissal as a result of the council's desire to 'stamp out as far as possible the political and sociological tendencies in the School'[25] occurred at just the moment when his methods began to bear fruit. The annual exhibition of student work, held two months after Rowse's departure, contained as its *pièce de resistance* the famous 'Town Plan', a cooperative thesis produced by an entire 15-strong unit comprising, among others, Elizabeth Chesterton and Richard Llewelyn Davies.[26] Highly praised in the professional press, the meticulously planned scheme illustrated the potential of Rowse's research-driven group work approach (Figs 10–11). 'I hate being optimistic', wrote Summerson, 'but I cannot help the feeling that a school which can turn out an exhibition

25

as bursting with initiative as this, is a bright spot in contemporary architecture.'[27] Rowse's replacement by a devoted (if eventually surprisingly moderate) French Beaux-Arts classicist spelled doom for the further evolution of these initiatives.

It was in this seemingly desperate situation that two students, Tim Bennett and Leo De Syllas, decided to stem the wave of defeatism and launch a magazine to rally the support of those who shared their desire for a reform of their training. With the financial backing of Maxwell Fry, and with Anthony Cox, a recent graduate of the school, as joint editor and main contributor, *Focus* was chiefly responsible for making the tumultuous events at the AA known to a broader audience and securing their place in the narrative of the modern movement in Britain. The inaugural issue of the magazine in the summer of 1938 featured a censorious letter from Anthony Cox to Goodhart-Rendel in reply to his talk at the AA, and the second one, published half a year later, a brief justification of the students' conduct in their recent altercation with the school authorities.[28] Meanwhile, the council's deliberations were taking an unexpected turn as Goodhart-Rendel, who was working with Billerey on a scheme for the reorganisation of the school in the form of a modified unit system, urged it to either extend the contract of the principal by another year, or appoint another suitable person for the same period of time to get the new system running before a new principal took over.[29] The council rejected Goodhart-Rendel's suggestion of another short-term appointment and advertised the position, despite the fact that there was one candidate – Maxwell Fry – who had the support of students, staff and, indeed, Goodhart-Rendel himself.[30] Dissatisfied with the council's decision, Goodhart-Rendel resigned in August 1938, and his plans were put on hold pending the appointment of a new principal.[31]

The Abolition of the Student Vote

The students appeared to have won their battle against the establishment, and the combined achievement of Yellow Book and *Focus* (two more

issues of which were published) would be a source of inspiration for the succeeding generation of AA students. However, the more immediate outcome of the turbulent years between 1935 and 1938 was the disenfranchisement of the students at the behest of the government's Board of Education. In July 1920, the BOE had approved the AA's application for recognition despite reservations regarding its status and curriculum, and only on the provision that it would become an incorporated body and provide a building research laboratory (the latter because it had applied as a 'technical institution').[32] The AA had since received a vital annual grant from the BOE even though it failed to deliver on its promises regarding the facilities for technical training. In light of this, it can be assumed that when in May 1937 the BOE carried out its first full inspection of the school, it did not do so entirely without bias, particularly as the controversy surrounding the general meeting of the AA in February 1935 had not escaped its attention. In a preparatory meeting for the visit in April 1937, the reporting inspector, Martin Briggs, told the council that the BOE 'was perturbed that students had voting powers on important affairs, and had heard of the attempt to alter this', suggesting that it 'might help the council in this matter'.[33] Accordingly, his report listed the constitution of the governing body as one of 12 points requiring 'immediate and serious consideration'[34] and stressed that 'the present position, which makes it possible for students to control educational policy, remains highly unsatisfactory and calls for action which will put an end to such a system'.[35] The council addressed these concerns in a letter to the BOE in February 1938, stating with respect to the constitution of the governing body that new bylaws introducing postal ballots had been passed which would henceforth prevent students from exerting disproportional influence in elections and referenda. The obvious attempt to gloss over the contentious issue of the student vote proved successful as the BOE advised the council that it 'was very satisfied with the manner in which the AA had met the Board's suggestions, and the matter was now closed'.[36]

It would almost certainly have stayed closed had it not been for a spectacularly ill-timed editorial comment on the recent council elections in the 2 June 1938 issue of the *Architects' Journal*:

> It seems that eight out of ten members nominated by the school [i.e. the students] were successful. Which means, presumably, that only the other two are anti-student-co-operation and all that goes with it. This goes to show what concerted action can do. And if the majority of senior members are too lazy to vote, it's fair enough the students should have their way.[37]

In the following week, the editors retracted their insinuation that the students were able to dominate this (or any other) election, yet the damage was done.[38] On 13 June 1938, the council received a letter from the BOE threatening to withhold its grant unless immediate steps were taken 'to stop the students controlling the affairs of the Association'.[39] Only ten days later, the BOE suspended its grant, and the council felt compelled to initiate the process leading to the abolition of the student vote. The ballot papers were issued in November 1938, and when two months later the results were announced, the required two-thirds majority of members had narrowly voted in favour of the proposed changes to the bylaws, framed to include a probationary, non-voting class of student members.[40] Thus, on 31 January 1939, the association disenfranchised its own founding body – 'perhaps the only backward step in the AA's history', as the *Architectural Review* later reminisced.[41]

Wartime Exile

Goodhart-Rendel's resignation, though greeted with regret, had presented the council with an opportunity to abolish the post of director and thus address the BOE's criticism concerning the 'system of dual control' operating at the AA.[42] The council briefly considered Arthur Kenyon, a representative of the old guard, as possible head of the school, but those who eventually emerged as the frontrunners in the race for principal – Maxwell Fry, R. A. Duncan, Robert Furneaux Jordan and Leslie Martin – were all part of the early wave of British modernists. Deeply polarised, the council was unable to give any of them its unanimous support and instead, in October 1938, agreed a compromise in the person of landscape architect Geoffrey Jellicoe, a former member of the teaching staff and sufficiently detached from either of the warring factions.[43]

Jellicoe, who delivered his inaugural address on 15 February 1939, struck a conciliatory note with his audience.[44] He announced that in compensation for the loss of their voting rights the students would be entitled to choose two members of council as their so-called 'liaison officers', to whom they could appeal directly to make their grievances heard. Informal meetings between staff and students (which the council had disallowed seven months prior) would be reinstated, and the present school system would be continued pending a review of the curriculum, for which he assembled an advisory panel comprising A. F. B. Anderson (representing the council), Robert Furneaux Jordan (representing the staff), Anthony Cox (representing the students) and John Henry Forshaw, at the time chief architect to the Miners' Welfare Association (representing the 'outside world'). An early outcome of these consultations was, in March 1939, the modification of the marking system in favour of written reports and one of three grades (namely, 'mention', 'pass' or 'fail').[45]

These measures calmed the waters, and the outbreak of the Second World War rendered the quarrels of the past few years immaterial. Like other institutions in the capital, the AA bowed to government pressure and evacuated its school to safer quarters when the war broke out. It took refuge in Mount House, a Georgian residence in the leafy suburb of Barnet – 'a setting as lovely as a Gainsborough', as Summerson found.[46] As in the previous war, the sudden drop in numbers and the corresponding fall in revenue caused financial problems. Given that travel was almost impossible and vacations therefore of little value, in May 1940 the school announced the introduction of a four-term year, which raised the school's income by

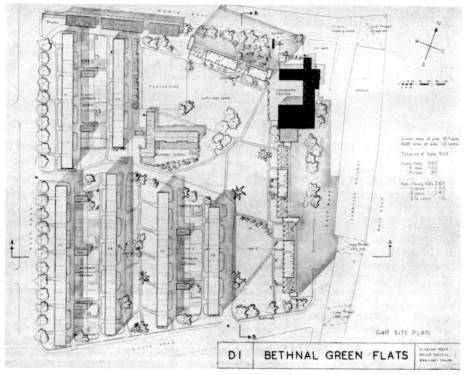

12   Flats at Bethnal Green (Philip Powell, Hidalgo Moya, Margaret Taylor, thesis, 1944/45)

This thesis for a housing estate in Bethnal Green was the first collaboration between Powell and Moya, which continued briefly in Frederick Gibberd's practice and culminated 30 years later in the award of the RIBA Gold Medal. The layout, consisting of parallel rows of slabs on a trapezoid plot severed by a central access corridor, anticipates the basic diagram of their much larger Churchill Gardens Estate, which they would win in an international competition a year after leaving the AA.

a third and allowed students to graduate in four instead of five years (and thus ideally before they were called up). Two months later, Jellicoe relayed the findings of his panel, the most significant of which was its condemnation of the unit system, which it deemed 'unsatisfactory' and 'undesirable' owing to the impracticality of harmonising the term-based cycle of the studio teaching with the annual cycle of the lecture course.[47] Adopting – ironically – the core idea of Goodhart-Rendel and Billerey's scheme for the reorganisation of the school, the panel proposed that in peacetime the system of annual entry should be re-established, with year groups divided into parallel units.[48]

Overburdened with administrative work, Jellicoe left in September 1941. In his resignation letter to Kenyon, now the president of the AA, Jellicoe warned that with growing competition from other institutions – specifically Liverpool, which had largely adopted the 'advanced thought and method' pioneered by the AA but had the additional advantage of being adequately funded, equipped and staffed – the AA school would face 'extinction' unless it managed to reassert its leadership position, a task for which he, Jellicoe, considered himself unfit:

> Our School has one advantage only over all others; it need not compromise. On this depends survival and leadership. My own appointment was a compromise. It gave stability in a time of clashing ideologies. But I must state that my aspirations lie beyond the world of associations and preconceptions, in which my generation and myself are contained. The youth of the country will desire a leader of their own who has already his own established convictions, rather than one like myself, who is engaged in establishing them afresh. [. . .] Certainly now is the moment for this change.[49]

Jelllicoe recommended his friend and fellow teacher Frederick Gibberd as his successor, and the council appointed him in November 1941. Gibberd was the designer of Pullman Court, a pioneering modernist housing scheme in London,

and co-author of a seminal book on modern flats.[50] He was (and remained) the only distinguished architect who was ever put in charge of the AA school, and the only one with a clearly defined design attitude. As anticipated, Gibberd provided the spiritual leadership the students were craving by unapologetically promoting modernism as the guiding philosophy of the school. The RIBA's visiting board, which inspected the AA in October 1942, commended the students' work though it noted that their designs had 'little or no traditional basis' and were 'perhaps too experimental'.[51] The board was also critical of the unit system and recommended that it should be 'reconsidered when normal conditions obtain' – a view with which Gibberd concurred (see p.32).[52]

The small cohort of students which found itself secluded to rural Barnet developed into a tight-knit community, whose social and artistic life centred on Mount House as well as 'Taliesin', a boarding house where, to the council's embarrassment, students of both sexes lived together – 'in heathen disarray', as one of them jestingly recalled.[53] The diminutiveness of the school and the lack of metropolitan peacetime distractions were conducive to the development of a distinguished group of students which included Leonard Manasseh, Geoffrey Robson (Sheppard Robson), Geoffry Powell (Chamberlin, Powell and Bon), Neville Conder (Casson Conder) and Gerhard Kallmann (Kallmann McKinnell & Wood), as well as Philip Powell and Hidalgo Moya, whose competition-winning scheme for Churchill Gardens built on the housing thesis they jointly submitted with a fellow student, Margaret Taylor (Fig.12). According to the visiting board, it was 'evident that the school is vigorous' and the students appeared 'keen [and] genuinely interested in their work'.[54] Gibberd himself was convinced that the success of the school owed a great deal to the close affinity between students, staff and principal:

> The AA is indeed fortunate in having got over its growing pains. After the war it will be at a great advantage over those schools which have yet to face the fact that you cannot teach students something in which they do not believe.[55]

2   After the War (1945–1949)

New Beginnings

If one were to pinpoint the moment at which the war's fortunes began to turn in Britain's favour, the 22 June 1941 would probably be as good a guess as any. On that day, the Third Reich launched a surprise offensive against its Soviet ally, thereby incurring a 2,000-mile front line which was to absorb a fast-growing portion of its troops. This in turn rendered the continuation of the sustained air raids which had plagued the British Isles for almost a year unlikely and allowed the country to apply its thoughts to the aftermath of war. By the autumn of 1943, Italy had surrendered and the allied forces were closing in on Germany. The end of the war within sight, in November 1943 the AA council invited its principal to formulate his ideas for the postwar school. Four months later, Gibberd submitted a report which, in addition to substantive changes to the teaching system, proposed a new office training scheme and a separate building department, both to overcome the artificiality of the architectural course.[1] Though the council approved of his plan, it insisted that in view of the financial position the suggested changes would have to be implemented gradually, and it was not prepared to offer Gibberd the permanent contract he asked for. Unsatisfied with these conditions, the principal resigned on 14 July 1944, and the council shelved his proposal.[2]

Gibberd's departure forced the AA council to find a replacement to tackle the challenges awaiting the

school in the postwar period. With many potential candidates serving in the forces, the response to the job posting was meagre, and the council made abortive approaches to more suitable candidates (notably William Holford, who opted to return to Liverpool instead). For better or worse, the choice was between five shortlisted contenders, two of whom failed to make an impression at the interview, while a third – Colin St Clair Oakes – was stationed in Burma and therefore unable to attend.[3] The decision thus boiled down to the two remaining candidates, Anthony Chitty and Raymond Gordon Brown. The council favoured Chitty, formerly of Tecton and now in partnership with Robert Hening. Chitty's ambitions, however, resided in practice, and he was therefore not prepared to undertake a long-term academic commitment. Brown, on the other hand, consented to devote ten years to the school and give it priority over his private work, which was the main reason behind the council's decision to appoint him on 13 November 1944.[4]

Born in South Africa in 1912, Gordon Brown had studied at Natal before completing his course at the AA in 1935 (Fig.5). Following a short stint with Willem Dudok, he worked as chief assistant for Michael Tapper and for Richardson & Gill and then set up in private practice. When the war broke out, he volunteered for the army, serving in the Essex Regiment and the Commandos before joining the Parachute Regiment.[5] At the time of his application, Brown was just 32, and while it was in the tradition of the AA to appoint a youthful man as the head of its school, there can be little doubt that Brown's limited experience as a practitioner, let alone teacher, would under normal circumstances have disqualified him from being considered for this position.

The controversies of the late 1930s still fresh in the memory, the council sought to avoid putting a man in charge whose approach might polarise the association. Similarly to Jellicoe, Brown was seen as someone who 'was not wedded to any particular school of architecture, [yet] sufficiently progressive [. . .] to appreciate the general trend of architecture'.[6] More important than Brown's non-partisan outlook, however, were the leadership qualities he had demonstrated in the war. The new principal would have to cope with a neglected infrastructure and a drastically inflated student body. At least initially, this would require organisational and improvisational skills rather than pedagogical ones. The council evidently felt that a young paratroop major who had led a successful airborne assault on a heavily defended artillery position in preparation for the D-Day landings was just the right man for the job.[7]

With the question of leadership settled, the council re-focused its efforts on planning the relocation of the school back to London. Throughout the war the association had retained its ground-floor rooms in Bedford Square and organised a series of social events for members stationed in the Home Counties or on leave from the services. The segregation of the school meant that the students were excluded from these activities, and the council was eager to reunite them with the membership sooner rather than later. The onset of flying-bomb attacks on London confounded the plan to move the school after the end of the summer term of 1944; it eventually reopened its doors in Bedford Square on 8 January 1945.

A Numbers Game

The idea to put a military man in charge to get things up and running in London failed as the

War Office denied repeated requests for Brown's release. In his place construction lecturer George Fairweather, a key figure on Gibberd's staff, headed the school in the first half of 1945. It was not until May 1945 that Brown got transferred to England; he finally received his discharge in September, in time for the beginning of the new academic year. The school to which he returned had suffered considerably from enemy action, and the combined shortage of money, material and labour had by the end of the war created a substantial maintenance backlog. The fact that the council in 1946 instigated a three-year plan to bring the premises back into a 'reasonable state of repair' conveys a sense of the scope of damage which still existed and the necessary timeframe anticipated to dispose of it.[8]

To make things worse, there was need for additional studio space as large-scale demobilisation seemed imminent. The government's 'Further Education and Training' (FET) scheme, launched in early 1943, provided grants covering tuition fees and maintenance allowance to military personnel whose post-school education had been interrupted or suspended by the war. FET grants removed the financial obstacle for a large number of ex-servicemen to take up or continue their academic training, and as a consequence Bedford Square quickly filled with students. In July 1944, when there were just over 100 students at the school, the council predicted that this figure was likely to increase to 270 after the war – roughly the number in attendance a decade before. After the return to London, the student population grew gradually to approximately 150 in May 1945, when hostilities in Europe ended, whereupon they more than doubled in the space of a few months. Matters were exacerbated by the fact that Brown, to the council's dismay, exercised his discretion in admitting applicants liberally, accepting both new entrants and ex-service personnel who had not previously been students of the AA. To cope with the rapid influx of students, in early 1946 the council commissioned the erection of a large Nissen hut on a bombed site adjacent to the main studio block, which was complemented by two standard Ministry of Work (MOW) huts shortly after.

While the overall tendency in the late 1940s was steeply upward, there was considerable variance in the intake of students. Given the circumstances, one might expect the AA to have welcomed any temporary relief, but this was not the case. Unlike many universities, whose recurring grants from the University Grants Committee (UGC) had been maintained at pre-war levels despite lower staff expenditures and which had therefore been able to build up substantial reserves during the war,[9] the AA had only managed to keep its school operational by abandoning the summer break in favour of a fourth teaching term and thus increasing its earnings. With fatigue affecting the quality of student work, Gibberd had, in March 1944, single-handedly abolished this scheme, leaving the council no other option than to levy higher charges to avoid a financial deficit.

The costs involved in moving back to Bedford Square aggravated the need for additional revenue, and in January 1946 the school felt compelled to raise its tuition fees once more. This met with strong disapproval from the Ministry of Education (MOE), which – embarrassed by the 'suggestion that public funds were being used to subsidise a school which could only be attended by the children of the comparatively rich' – threatened to withdraw its annual grant unless the school restored its fees to their former level.[10] Assured that this would not affect the AA's status as a recognised school and therefore the awards made to its students under the FET scheme, in March 1946 the council reluctantly decided to dispense with the grant, anticipating that the additional income through student fees would compensate for its loss, which indeed it did.[11] It was a momentous decision as it marked the moment when the AA effectively opted out of the emerging state system of higher education, becoming, for the first time since its incorporation in 1920, a truly independent institution.

As a result, the school was now completely dependent on students' fees and forced to keep their number to the maximum as any temporary drop would instantly put it in financial jeopardy.[12] This explains why the council, despite the lack of space and an already overstrained administration, was hesitant to halt Brown's generously handled intake of students and allowed him to fill unexpected vacancies at once. Since the AA had committed itself to accepting ex-AA students without delay, and with admissions therefore a weekly occurrence, it stands to reason that the numbers were bound to spiral out of control and that, regardless of the creation of any additional studio space, permanent overcrowding had to be accepted as a fact of life. Student numbers eventually peaked at 532 in October 1948 and remained at that level for two years before starting to drop again with the end of the FET scheme in 1951.[13] An enlarged student body necessitated a correspondingly enlarged workforce, and rising costs for accommodation and wages sustained a continuous cycle of fee increases. By 1948, the AA levied student fees of £100 per year, more than twice as much as any other school of architecture in the United Kingdom.

Teaching under Brown: The Stream System

The swelling of the student population not only affected the school's finances but had consequences on its educational setup. In 1944, the AA was still operating under the unit system, which divided the five-year course into 15 terms and combined a termly cycle for studio work with an annual cycle for the lecture course. Gibberd shared Jellicoe's misgivings about a mechanism which led to the absurd situation that some students had to work reversely through the lecture course: 'The complications that ensue must be experienced, they are beyond imagination.'[14] To combine the strengths of the year and unit systems, Gibberd in his plan for the postwar school revived the idea of a parallel unit system, first suggested by Goodhart-Rendel and Billerey and subsequently adopted by Jellicoe, whereby year groups would be divided into units of 15 students run as parallel streams through the year.[15] Although a full implementation of this system presupposed a return to annual entry, Gibberd tested the division of large units into parallel sections in the spring term of 1945, and, encouraged by the results, both he and Fairweather continued the experiment in the following terms. In March 1945, the council effectively sealed the fate of the unit system when it decided to reintroduce annual entry for the coming session (except for those students joining upon their release from the service), and Brown's version of the 'stream system', which envisaged an intake of 60 students to be distributed into three groups and reshuffled after each term according to their respective abilities, was a further variation on a now familiar theme.[16]

The reversion to the year system freed tutors from administrative duties, but staff shortages remained a problem. To guarantee each student a specified period of personal tuition, in January 1946 Brown therefore implemented a more highly organised tutorial system. While the mornings were reserved for informal studio teaching in the conventional way, the afternoons were allocated to tutorial sessions of 20 minutes per student, requiring teachers to work to a precise time plan and making their attendance throughout the day indispensable. Though commonplace in other schools, the new system was a departure from the casual working patterns at the AA and not to everyone's liking. Fairweather, who had just been appointed senior master in appreciation of his work as caretaker principal, resigned at once citing 'fundamental disagreements as to the teaching system now used in the school'.[17]

The new system impaired the working conditions at the AA, which, compared to other institutions of higher education, had not been favourable to begin with. True to its origin as a self-help organisation of students, the AA had taken a long time to start paying competitive wages, and when it finally did, the standard it adhered to was the so-called 'Burnham Scale', that is, the pay grades of primary school teachers. More importantly, the AA could not offer long-term employment: full-time staff were engaged for one academic year, part-time tutors for a term only.

Low wages and lack of job security meant that high staff turnover was inherent at the AA. On the other hand, the school's central London location and its unique link with a professional association gave it unrivalled access to a large pool of practising architects, many of whom had themselves trained at the AA or were otherwise sympathetic to the school. Conscious of the limited resources it had at its disposal, they were often prepared to take on temporary teaching duties for little or, in some cases, no money at all.[18] Moreover, precisely *because* teaching at the AA did not involve a long-term commitment, it was a welcome stopgap for aspiring young architects in the course of setting up in private practice. This was particularly the case in the immediate postwar years, when the licensing of building materials made the resumption of professional work outside public offices all but impossible. Unlike Gibberd, who often had to employ staff regardless of their aptitude as teachers, Brown had the option (if not always the funds) to choose between candidates, not least because the accelerated pace of demobilisation, which otherwise put a strain on the school, did have the benefit that potential tutors, too, became available.

Two general tendencies in Brown's staffing policy are discernible. First, he embraced the time-honoured policy of feeding young professionals, many of them recent AA graduates, back into the school. Some of them, including Jim Cadbury-Brown, Hidalgo Moya and Denys Lasdun, only taught for a short period before their private work gained momentum; others such as Colin Penn and Andrew Carden, however, stayed on well into the next decade. Incidentally, it was also Brown (rather than his successor Robert Furneaux Jordan, as is sometimes claimed), who conceived the idea of engaging the members of the Architects' Co-operative Partnership (ACP), a seven-strong practice consisting of recent graduates of the school, including Anthony Cox and Leo De Syllas, under a collective contract.[19] A second tendency lay in an increasingly cosmopolitan personnel. In January 1942, the council had imposed a ban on the engagement of foreign teaching staff, and although it gradually lifted this policy from 1944 onward, it urged its principal to 'make every effort to employ British staff first'.[20] Accordingly, at the time of Brown's inauguration German architect Walter Segal, who had been appointed the year before, was still the only non-British teacher at the school. Ignoring the council's request, Brown hired a number of foreign tutors, two of whom would have a lasting impact on the school. Canadian Enrico de Pierro was to stay for almost a decade, having previously taught at McGill University under John Bland (who had himself studied under Rowse). Brown's key appointment, however, was Arthur Korn, the mastermind behind the 1942 MARS Plan for London, whom he enticed away from Oxford's School of Arts & Crafts in August 1945 and who was to become a major influence on successive generations of AA students throughout the postwar period. Korn, who had been affiliated with German avant-garde groups in the 1920s, was joined on the AA staff by a number of other émigré architects with links to continental modernism, including Egon Riss, Alexander Kurz and Jaromír Krejcar.

In keeping with his military background, Brown installed a hierarchical chain of command: he rallied a small group of trusted year masters, to whom he delegated much of the running of the school and with whose programmes he did not interfere. Brown chose his adjutants for their teaching skills and suitability within the year masters' collective rather than their architectural predilections. In comparison with the tutors they were therefore a more eclectic and, on the whole, considerably less progressive lot. Two of them were already at the AA when Brown arrived: Eric Jarrett, in charge of the first year, had been on the staff since 1919, and David Goddard had started his appointment under Fairweather. In addition, Brown engaged Colin St Clair Oakes and John Brandon-Jones, two of his competitors for the principalship, as well as Michael Pattrick, who became his second-in-command. Although he reshuffled their assignments occasionally, Brown stuck to this nucleus of year masters and went to great lengths to retain them.[21]

'Draughtsmanship and the Technical Side' – The Postwar Curriculum

Rising numbers and the uncertainties caused by the delayed demobilisation of expected students on the one hand, and the call-up of existing ones on the other, made it exceedingly difficult to institute and maintain a structured curriculum. This was all the more worrying as, notable exceptions notwithstanding, the overall quality of student work had suffered under wartime conditions. When in January 1945 Ralph Tubbs, the secretary of the MARS Group and a member of the AA council, visited the school alongside Fairweather, he delivered a damning indictment of the standard of education offered.[22] Brown's verdict later that year was, if anything, even more scathing. Though sympathetic to the difficulties under which the students had to complete their course, he disapproved of much of their work and considered it in many cases below the high standards required to obtain an AA diploma.[23] To tackle the problem, Brown defined the improvement of 'draughtsmanship and the technical side' as the two cornerstones of his pedagogical concept.[24] Indeed, rather than familiarising his students with particular design strategies, Brown's curriculum aimed at equipping them with sound technical expertise based on which such strategies could be developed and the necessary drawing skills to translate them into architectural schemes.

The students' lack of drawing skills may come as a surprise given that prior to the introduction of universal entrance examinations at the beginning of the 1945/46 session candidates were judged solely on the strength of their portfolios. Yet these comprised mainly free-hand sketches, which were examined for 'evidence of creative ability rather than technical skill'.[25] Echoing Lethaby's approach to 'draughtsmanship', Gibberd wrote:

As drawing to the architect is only a means to an end, the end being an actual building, it does not matter whether the student is naturally gifted at drawing or not. [. . .] The school curriculum has been designed to teach automatically anyone to draw. Automatically, not consciously; in this respect it differs from most other schools where emphasis is attached to drawing as an end in itself.[26]

Yet it appears that, perhaps as a result, many drawings were in fact deficient even as a means to an end. Under Brown, measured drawings and outdoor sketching figured prominently on the timetable, and

Eric Jarrett developed a series of Beaux-Arts-type exercises for his first-year students, ranging from life drawing to Trajan lettering and study of the classical orders. Thus, contrary to the belief that from the late 1930s the AA gradually abandoned its Beaux-Arts traditions, many of them – including a succession of unworldly one-day sketches for Roman villas and Victorian mansions – were in fact revived after the Second World War (Fig.13).

13   Victorian Mansion (Michael Willis, first year, 1946/47)

Day-sketches for whimsical subjects offered some relief at a time of food rationing and material shortages. First-year master Eric Jarrett asked his students to base their design for an eclectic Victorian mansion on an extract from Osbert Sitwell's novel Those Were the Days. *Michael Willis later became a partner with Kenneth Scott Associates and practised widely in Ghana.*

More important than these drawing exercises was the vastly extended lecture syllabus which Brown introduced to strengthen the technical competence of his students. Anticipating the growing demand for lecturers in this field, the AA council had, in December 1944, approached the government's Building Research Station (BRS) with a view to engaging its specialists before other schools could put them under contract.[27] Although William Allen, the future head of its architectural division, did not (as was hoped) join the AA at the time, one of his colleagues, John Eastwick-Field, did, while another, Cecil Handisyde, who had been teaching at the AA since 1935, was now released from studio duties to focus exclusively on his services lectures.

Eastwick-Field took charge of the new practical training site, which involved students erecting life-size structures in timber, brick or concrete and allowed them to gain an understanding of building processes at a time when building restrictions limited such opportunities elsewhere. According to the *AA Journal*, the scheme followed the wartime training methods of the British Army,[28] yet it did in fact have a precursor at the AA itself. In 1938, unit master Douglas Jones had realised two 'live projects' with his students – an idea which was to be at the heart of his pedagogical approach as head of the Birmingham School of Architecture from 1951 onward and had itself been anticipated by Lethaby's School of Building in Brixton.[29] Gibberd picked up the thread in his plan for the postwar school, which was to incorporate a 'school of building', and Fairweather subsequently set it up among the MOW emergency hutments behind the main building. Brown was thus the latest in a line of AA educators who sought to inject the course with Lethabite ideas, and the dominance of technical studies within the curriculum became such that in July 1946 he felt it necessary to appoint a director of technical studies to coordinate the lecture syllabus with the practical training site.

Brown expected the quality of training provided by the AA to be of a considerably higher order than the standard set by the RIBA and took pride in the fact that the course of technical lectures

at the AA was 'the best produced by any school'.[30] At the same time, he was conscious that the extended lecture programme affected the time his students could afford to work on their design tasks, and he therefore reduced these in both scope and number. Alan Colquhoun remembered the teaching as 'unremarkable'[31] – indeed, to some degree it was non-existent, for given the sheer number of students even a weekly tuition time of 20 minutes per student proved impracticable. With year groups regularly exceeding a hundred students, Brown's original idea of splitting an intake of 60 students into three 'streams' soon became obsolete, and from session 1947/48 onward, students were grouped in sections of about ten, loosely supervised by often changing and rarely present staff. This setup suited mature students such as Michael Ventris, Graeme Shankland and Oliver Cox, who organised their education as a largely self-guided process, taking liberties in the interpretation of their tasks and – encouraged by the staff, notably fourth-year master David Goddard – often tackling them collectively (Figs 14–15; Plates 2–3).[32] Ventris, a language prodigy who died young in a car accident, is best known for deciphering the ancient Mycenaean Greek script Linear B; Shankland and Cox, however, were to have successful careers in the public sector and later revived their collaboration by forming an international architecture and planning consultancy which still bears their names today.

International Entanglements: The AA and the CIAM Summer School

Brown was convinced that the school was 'too large to train the best possible architect'.[33] Given the number of distinguished architects who emerged from his course, one may question this assessment, and his superiors at least wholly disagreed with it. Whether it was due to Brown's leadership, his panel of year masters, the revised syllabus or the curricular permissiveness and the type of student to whom it was granted, the excellent outcome was generally

14 Opera House (John Briars, Peter Dickinson, Stephen Gardiner, Michael Nesbitt, fifth year, 1947/48)

This is the earliest example of a group scheme involving students from different years. Large teams of fourth- and fifth-year students worked on layouts for a drama centre in central London and then divided the work on individual buildings – an opera, a theatre and a cinema – between them. Peter Dickinson, the leader of this particular fifth-year group, was perhaps the most uniquely gifted student of his generation and went on to have a short but tremendously successful career as an architect in Toronto.

15 Yacht Club (Patrick Horsbrugh, third year, 1946/47)

Few remained unaffected by the collective spirit which pervaded the AA at the time. Patrick Horsbrugh, later a professor of landscape architecture at Notre Dame, insisted on completing even the most comprehensive schemes completely on his own. He startled his external examiners by presenting no fewer than 20 models for his yacht club; in the following year, he single-handedly designed an entire drama centre and each of its three constituent buildings (see previous figure); and one year later, he took up an entire library space for his thesis project. The extensive use of models – a Lethabite reaction to the Beaux-Arts obsession with drawings – had its roots in the mid-1930s and remained a distinctive and controversial feature in AA student work.

recognised. In March 1947, Anthony Chitty, by then a member of the council, felt that 'the conditions at the school have improved to an extent he had not thought possible so soon after the war',[34] and Howard Robertson, himself a former principal of the school, opined that the 'teaching, in spite of congestion at the entry point, has never been at a higher level'.[35] The architectural press shared these sentiments. Both the *Architect and Building News* and the *Builder* praised the annual school display of 1947,[36] and the *Architects' Journal* was in no doubt that the AA had reasserted its position as 'the unquestionable seat and centre of *avant-gardism* in architecture for the whole country'.[37]

Meanwhile, the country's standing was itself changing as Britain turned from being a latecomer to international modernism to becoming its driving force. Although the MARS Group had met only occasionally in the early 1940s, due to the virtual dissolution of most of its continental counterparts it almost by default emerged as the leading CIAM section after the war. With roughly 100 members it vastly outnumbered any other branch within the organisation and started to take a key role in shaping its agenda, hosting two of its three conferences in the immediate postwar period.[38] The AA was intimately involved in these developments, not least because at the time of the sixth CIAM congress at Bridgwater in the summer of 1947, many MARS members were associated with the school. Three of them – Furneaux Jordan, David Goddard and John Broadbent – had been on the studio staff when Brown took over, and they were soon joined by Korn, Cadbury-Brown, Christopher Nicholson and the seven members of ACP. In addition, senior lecturers Felix Samuely, Richard Sheppard and Sergei George Kadleigh, the director of technical studies, belonged to the MARS Group, as did six of the 18 members of council.

In 1947, the AA celebrated its centenary, and the council intended to organise its festivities concurrently with CIAM 6, allowing visitors from abroad to attend both events and thus boosting the prestige of the occasion. To the same end, the AA invited King George VI to deliver the opening address and waived its usual election procedures

to appoint as its president for the centenary year Howard Robertson, at the time Britain's representative on the UN Board of Design and as such 'in a sense the ambassador of our profession', as councillor Henry Braddock put it.[39] By and large, these plans failed as neither the King nor any other member of the royal family was inclined to attend and the celebration itself had to be deferred to cause less disturbance to the school. In fact, limited resources and austerity measures forced the AA to curtail the event to an extent that Robertson, in fear of embarrassment, suggested that for the time being it be cancelled altogether.[40]

The scaled-back festivities eventually took place shortly before Christmas and, despite travel difficulties caused by currency restrictions, attracted 700 visitors from 11 different countries. More telling for the international renown of the AA, however, was the reaction of some who were unable to attend. To the indignation of the Swiss CIAM group, the AA had invited Hans Hofmann, the comparatively traditionalist Dean of ETH Zurich, but not CIAM Secretary-General Sigfried Giedion or any other of its core members.[41] Effectively barred from teaching positions in their own country, they complained bitterly about the lack of support from what they publicly referred to as 'Europe's most advanced architecture school'.[42] Alarmed by his colleagues, Robertson sent a last-minute invitation, but at this juncture Giedion was either unable or unwilling to attend.[43]

While the centenary was primarily an association affair, whose organisation lay in the hands of the council (which might explain the blunder with Giedion), Brown on his own initiative set schemes in motion which aimed specifically at raising the school's international profile. Most of these took the form of reciprocal visits with foreign schools over the summer vacations. Successful excursions to Denmark, Sweden, Switzerland and Italy provided the groundwork for Brown's major undertaking, which in the late 1940s briefly positioned him, and thereby the AA, at the forefront of the international discourse on architectural education. Drawing on his impressions of schools on the continent,

Brown identified a 'reactionary tendency [. . .] in architectural education in all countries', and in the spring of 1947 he approached Giedion with a proposal for a permanent 'CIAM International School' for postgraduate students in Zurich in order to give 'serious challenge' to this undesirable development.[44] Brown's plan was for a full-time course of one year's duration modelled on the AA school. Led by an independent director under the auspices of a CIAM-appointed council, the aims of the course would be to cultivate 'draughtsmanship' and 'building technique' (complete with a practical training site) as well as 'creative ability and aesthetic appreciation' and, somewhat vaguely, 'logic'.[45] Giedion, who shared Brown's view of the state of architectural education, mistakenly assumed that Brown was acting in conjunction with the MARS Group and suggested that they discuss his ideas in plenum so that, at the forthcoming congress in Bridgwater, 'the problem of educational reform could be brought forth by the members of the English group'.[46] The permanent commission on architectural education, which was inaugurated at the congress, included half a dozen MARS members, two of whom, George Kadleigh and Leo De Syllas, were on the AA teaching staff at the time.[47] However, in the absence of Brown, who had to cancel his appearance, and without the official support of the MARS Group, the item was dropped from the agenda.[48]

Nonetheless, the plan had clearly aroused an interest in Giedion, who – together with Maxwell Fry on behalf of MARS but without Brown himself – initiated informal consultations with Julian Huxley, the Director-General of UNESCO, putting forward Swiss architect Ernst Burckhardt as the prospective principal of the school.[49] Irritated at being sidelined, Brown advised Giedion that he was anxious to proceed with the scheme as quickly as possible and was in a position to organise it, 'whether it is inside or outside CIAM'.[50] Trying to circumvent the MARS Group, who appeared to have appropriated his idea, Brown cunningly suggested that, since the school was to be located in Zurich, the affair should be placed in the hands of the Swiss group, which could co-opt him as a special member to assist Burckhardt

in preparing a draft curriculum.[51] Sceptical about Brown, whom he wrongly blamed for the AA's slight against the Swiss CIAM group ahead of the centenary celebrations, Giedion deferred his reply until January 1948, by which time Brown had managed to persuade the MARS Group to recognise him as their official representative in dealing with the proposed CIAM school.[52] The arrangement, however, was short-lived as within two months of submitting an official MARS proposal for a summer course at the AA, directed by Brown as a test-run for the permanent school, he was once more replaced by Maxwell Fry.[53] In light of currency and travel difficulties, the MARS Group ultimately cancelled the summer course, and Brown, having lost any interest in CIAM, sought to realise his scheme in collaboration with TU Delft instead.[54] Nothing came of it, but organised by Maxwell Fry and Jaqueline Tyrwhitt as a follow-up to the seventh CIAM congress at Bergamo, the CIAM Summer School did eventually take place at the AA in the following year and was to become a regular feature at Venice until the dissolution of CIAM in 1956.

A Tragic Person

When the 1948/49 academic session began, the school's infrastructural problems were under control, its leadership was firmly in place and its national and international reputation was restored. Yet Brown was not content with the state of affairs and, in a paper read to the AA on 24 November 1948, proposed radical changes to its organisational and educational setup.[55] Brown's bone of contention was the persistent lack of realism in student work, which he blamed on the enduring legacy of the school's 'digression' to the Beaux-Arts system in the early decades of the century.[56] The revision of the technical syllabus, specifically the practical training site, had been a first step toward resuscitating the Arts and Crafts-inspired methods employed in the school around the turn of the century and realigning it thus to what Brown considered to be the 'main stream which the policy and development of the AA were [and should again be] following'.[57]

Brown advanced two further schemes aimed at pulling students out of their academic isolation. First, students were to be attached to an architectural practice from their first day at the school and give it a month's unpaid vacation work each year, thus making office training an integral part of the basic course. Second, Brown proposed the integrated training of architects and artists, thereby reflecting the revived interest of the profession in questions of architectural expression, which, inspired by Giedion's influential essay on 'The Need for a New Monumentality' of 1944, emerged as a key topic of the international – and particularly British – postwar discourse. More prosaically, Brown saw the cooperation with art schools as a way to secure his students a foothold in the emerging field of industrial design. In the previous session fourth-year students from the AA and the Royal College of Art (RCA) had collaborated on theatre designs for a drama centre (Fig.14), and Brown intended to forge a permanent liaison with the RCA, which under its new principal Robin Darwin was undergoing an ambitious and generously funded expansion programme. After a first-year foundation course devoted to general education and design basics the two schools were to combine for an extended period of joint training in a new 'country school', reflecting Brown's conviction that an architectural training in entirely urban surroundings lacked balance.[58] Students would then be given the choice between completing their architecture course in the fifth year or embarking upon a two-year course which would earn them an additional degree in either town planning or industrial design.

The principal was, as the *Architects' Journal* noted, 'flying a pretty powerful kite',[59] levelling criticism at the RIBA (for preserving Beaux-Arts traditions through its student prizes), the Ministry of Education (for underfunding students) and above all his own council which, despite appointing a special 'development subcommittee', seemed unable to agree a much-needed policy to safeguard the school's long-term independence in the face of growing government intervention in technical education (see p.57). Nonetheless, the tone and content of Brown's paper suggested that, in his

view, the question was not if but when his proposals would be put in motion. It seems surprising, therefore, that less than a week after delivering his paper Brown established contact with the University of Edinburgh, where a new chair in architecture had been instituted.[60] The council was unaware of this development and caught by surprise when Brown, shortly before the end of the year, informed it of his intention to resign.[61] Urged to reconsider his decision, Brown demanded a long-term contract and the right to 'consult the council from time to time, but not to be bound to adopt any of its suggestions as an order', thus effectively reducing it to an advisory body and assuming complete authority over the school.[62] Attesting to the high regard in which Brown was held, the revised contractual terms he was offered not only met these demands but exceeded them.[63] Brown would assume the responsibilities of the abolished school committee and only be required to report to the council once a year. In addition, his new 15-year contract would offer Brown more favourable financial terms and would – astonishingly – be breakable only on his part. In light of these generous terms, the councillors expected Brown to withdraw his resignation and were clearly taken aback when, on 3 January 1949, he reaffirmed his wish to be released from his contract.[64]

Brown may have reached the conclusion that his idea of synchronising the teaching between different schools, in which he saw the 'nucleus of a University of the Arts', would be easier to put into practice within the departmental structure of an existing university rather than the capricious AA.[65] However, the course of events – particularly the short time gap between his lecture and the initial contact with Edinburgh – suggests that such considerations were not the decisive factor for Brown's sudden departure. The public announcement cited 'personal reasons' for his resignation,[66] and John Brandon-Jones – only slightly less nebulously – recalled that 'things started to get a bit hot for Gordon Brown, and he suddenly [. . .] disappeared from the London scene'.[67] Although there is no direct evidence, one can presume that Brown's problems were of a financial nature. In 1946, he had (inadvertently) misappropriated a grant provided by the Swedish Institute in London for the students' summer excursion, which left the AA liable to reimburse the hosts.[68] James Richards stressed that Brown was 'not dishonest; rather accident-prone where money was concerned' and his subsequent career seems to confirm this verdict.[69]

Brown relinquished his chair at Edinburgh after only 18 months, having accumulated significant debts for which the university stood as guarantor.[70] He accepted an offer from the University of Hong Kong, where he set up a highly successful course modelled on the AA (including a country school on nearby Lantau Island) while virtually monopolising the building programme of the university, for which he designed a number of student hostels, staff flats and laboratories as well as two new colleges and a library. In addition, Brown developed a vast harbour reclamation scheme in Hong Kong and, from October 1951, acted as planner to the government of British North Borneo, entrusted with the development of four new towns. Yet, despite his high salary and a thriving practice, Brown's finances soon got out of hand again, due in part to his flamboyant lifestyle – he owned several cars, a sailboat and a motorised Chinese junk – but mainly because, as one student remembers, 'he was generous to a fault' and regularly covered the school fees of students in financial difficulties.[71] Increasingly frustrated by the RIBA's refusal to award recognition to his school, Brown resigned his position in November 1957, when the university decreed that the faculty would no longer be allowed to engage in private practice.[72] He subsequently lectured in the United States and acted as consulting architect to Miguel Ydígoras Fuentes, the president of Guatemala, before returning to England in 1960 to resume his private practice.[73] On 17 March 1962, the day before his 50th birthday, he shot himself – 'a tragic person whose undoubtedly great potential was never fulfilled'.[74]

3 Architecture as Collaborative Practice (1949–1951)

'Socialist, Scientific and Sophisticated'

The AA had emerged from the war with little more than its reputation intact. Its premises had been in a state of disrepair, and a desperate shortage of money had placed the school at a distinct disadvantage relative to its competitors. Gordon Brown had navigated these conditions with remarkable ease, and his resignation evoked strong sentiments among the council – oscillating between genuine regret about his departure and indignation as to the manner in which it had come to pass. The council thought about holding Brown to his contractual period of notice, but it ultimately felt it injurious to continue under a principal desperate to leave and decided, as a show of confidence in the current staff, to promote the new principal from within their ranks. Brown himself recommended Cecil St Clair Oakes as his successor, but the council appears not to have seriously considered him. Instead, an overwhelming majority favoured Robert Furneaux Jordan, who was appointed by unanimous decision less than a week after Brown had tendered his resignation.

Jordan was a polymath who combined his architectural practice with an interest in historical scholarship and a commitment to teaching. Born in Birmingham in 1905, he studied for three years at the local school of architecture and then transferred to the AA to complete his course. After qualifying in 1928, Jordan practised in his hometown before returning to London six years later. In 1934, he joined the AA as assistant fourth-year master, and from 1936 he lectured in history and design as well. One year later Jordan was promoted to senior design master, but he resigned in March 1939 in reaction to Rowse's dismissal. While at the AA, Jordan had set up in private practice with two fellow staff members, Cecil Charles Handisyde and George Fairweather, and after the war the firm (now without Handisyde) briefly flourished thanks to a number of school and housing commissions. Jordan rejoined the teaching staff as third-year master under Brown but resigned this position after only one term for health reasons. One year later, in February 1947, he returned as senior lecturer and henceforth focused on his academic work, refining and disseminating an idiosyncratic interpretation of history which formed the philosophical foundation of his pedagogical approach as principal.

The rise of modernism with its ahistorical pretensions called into question the sense and purpose of teaching architectural history in its prevalent classical mode, aimed at extracting eternal principles of design and composition from the study of ancient masterpieces. Not surprisingly, in schools which from the mid-1930s aligned themselves with the modernist ethos, the teaching of history – divorced from any immediate practical applicability – suffered what could, as Lionel Budden wrote, 'not unfairly be described as a partial eclipse'.[1] When the Board of Education inspected the AA in 1937, it noted with regret that the subject was unpopular with students, who regarded it 'as an obstacle in the path towards their schemes of social regeneration', and criticised the school, whose 'concession to students' preferences seems to have gone too far'.[2] Nonetheless, even at that time the syllabus included an average of 20 history lectures per year, and there was no intention to reduce this number any further.

At the AA the rejection of history was thus less pronounced than, for instance, at Harvard, which – in the absence of similarly progressive schools in Europe – was increasingly seen as a benchmark. This was arguably due to the publication, in 1936, of Pevsner's seminal *Pioneers of the Modern Movement*, which drew a genealogical line from William Morris to Walter Gropius and the early German modernists and thus legitimated English forays into modern architecture in terms of their historical continuity with a specifically English progenitor.[3] Tellingly, in the early 1940s, AA students were required to pass a paper on the 19th and 20th centuries in addition to the 'classical' subjects stipulated as part of the RIBA's intermediate examination.[4] Moreover, while in the United States the teaching of history lay in the hands of art historians with little interest in architectural history in its own right, at the AA (as well as most other English schools) the subject was traditionally entrusted to architect members of the teaching staff.[5] Despite the growing influence of the more rigorous German art historiography through émigré scholars such as Wittkower, Gombrich and to a lesser degree Pevsner, all of whom lectured regularly at the AA, the general approach towards history teaching therefore remained essentially 'architectural' and thus supposedly more accessible for students.

Robert Furneaux Jordan's synthesis of art and social history fitted neither category. According to Saint, his lectures were 'the first in a British school of architecture to bring social, economic and technological concepts to bear upon the understanding of style'.[6] Indeed, according to Jordan, 'supreme art' could only emerge from a 'complete culture' encompassing society, science and art as three facets of an indivisible whole, for it was this integrity which caused a civilisation's

ascension to greatness but also ultimately its demise[7] – a key tenet of Jordan's Marxist-Hegelian worldview, applicable to any period in history and repeated in memorable phraseology throughout the lecture course.[8] Torn between dichotomous tendencies – industrialism and the rise of the engineer on the one hand; Victorian romanticism, ending with William Morris and the Arts and Crafts movement, on the other – the 19th century emphatically lacked such integrity, its 'fascination and tragedy' being that 'its quintessence was in itself a conflict'.[9]

Jordan believed that modern society was on the verge of resolving this dialectic by once again becoming a complete culture united by a common system of thought and a common technology. It was the task, and indeed the historic mission, of the modern architect to find the expression of his or her age – 'an age which is socialist, scientific and sophisticated' – by acquiring a complete understanding of society and its technical resources.[10] Thus, Jordan not only vindicated the active quest for a contemporary architectural expression in historic terms, he also provided a justification for history teaching itself:

> First, if the relationship of building technique to life is once again to be a great art, then that relationship – in those times when architecture was a great art – must be studied. Second, if that relationship, between 1800 and 1950, was such that architecture ceased to be a great art, then a diagnosis of the disease must be made. It is the recognition of this twofold value of history – what was right with man when architecture was great and what was wrong with man when architecture was not great – that must form the basis of our history teaching.[11]

Changing of the Guard – Jordan's Staffing Policy

The council expected its new principal to carry on and further develop Brown's educational programme, 'continuity being thus assured'.[12]

Indeed, Jordan had spoken in support of Brown's valedictory paper, and a comparative reading of his inaugural address, given two months later, shows the proximity of their ideas.[13] Jordan endorsed Brown's idea of a country school, and he seconded his proposal for a trainee scheme whereby each student would become 'the adopted child of some office [. . .] making a general nuisance of himself every vacation'.[14] Conscious of the council's wishes, Jordan stressed that any novelties he put forward were not 'a diplomatic foreshadowing of something dramatic or immediate in the way of a new curriculum, a new staff or a new house'.[15] Yet, while there were indeed no immediate changes to the 'curriculum' or the 'house', the 'staff' was an altogether different matter.

In June 1949, Jordan announced the abolition of the year master system for the upcoming session and the creation of a tighter, more manageable administration by dividing the school into three administrative units, namely, the 'preliminary school' (first year), the 'intermediate school' (second and third years) and the 'final school' (fourth and fifth years).[16] The directors of these three 'schools', along with the principal, his administrative assistant, and Michael Pattrick as the director of technical studies, formed the new six-strong executive. Jordan portrayed this as a purely organisational measure, which would not affect the educational programme. Yet it had profound implications as it meant, in effect, the disempowerment of the existing year masters with the exception of Pattrick (who was, however, relieved of teaching duties) and Goddard, who was promoted to vice-principal and put in charge of the final school.

Once again bypassed for the position of principal, fifth-year master Oakes had left the AA in April 1949 to become the chief architect for the pharmaceutical manufacturer Boots. In the same month, second-year master John Brandon-Jones – whose view of Arts and Crafts as an ongoing tradition, and of modernism as a misguided deviation from it, proved incompatible with Jordan's resolutely modernist agenda – was forced to resign.[17] Even more controversial was, in January 1950, the departure of

Eric Jarrett, who had been teaching at the school since the end of the First World War and expressed the wish to stay until 1951 to increase his pension. Sparking outrage among senior AA members, Jordan put Jarrett on leave after only one term and hired painter Olive Sullivan from the Manchester School of Art to replace his old-fashioned exercises in draughtsmanship with Bauhaus-derived studies in colour and abstract form (Plate 4).[18] Jordan himself meanwhile drafted the brief for the first-term design project in the autumn of 1949. The famous 'primitive hut' programme required the student to imagine himself [sic] as 'the hero of some Robinson Crusoe type of story',[19] choosing one of three climates and using local resources to erect a simple shelter for himself and his wife ('respectability being the keynote of the AA school', as the *Architect and Building News* quipped).[20] Originally conceived in the late 1930s by George Keck at Moholy-Nagy's 'New Bauhaus' in Chicago, the primitive hut exercise was an object lesson in basic three-dimensional planning and – with its reference to Laugier – thinking in 'first principles'. Under Leonard Manasseh, who took charge of the preliminary school in July 1950, it was to become a signature programme of the AA, from where it spread to other British schools, as well as – through AA graduate Denise Scott Brown – the University of Pennsylvania (Fig.16).[21]

Completing the triumvirate of directors, Kenneth Capon, one of the members of ACP, took charge of the intermediate school, assisted by Fello Atkinson, a recent graduate and partner in James Cubitt's up-and-coming practice. While Brown had surrounded himself with an eclectic group of older and more experienced teachers, Jordan's lead tutors were all younger than himself, and they were – with the exception of Goddard and his second-in-command Henry Elder – all former students of his with little or no teaching experience. Jordan's personnel policy was driven by the desire to attract the vanguard of the profession to the AA – a strategy which proved increasingly difficult to pursue when in the late 1940s the building industry began to recover and employment opportunities for architects improved.

To fill the vacancies, Jordan invited a growing number of foreign architects to the teaching staff. The most notable of these were Argentine Eduardo Catalano, who had studied under Gropius at Harvard and would later hold a chair at MIT, and leading Italian practice BBPR, whose partners Ernesto Rogers and Enrico Peressutti taught successively at the AA and over the years accommodated at least a dozen of its students as trainees at their Milan headquarters. Moreover, Jordan persuaded Alvar Aalto to teach at the AA for four weeks – a coup with great publicity value, especially as it coincided with a visit by Frank Lloyd Wright, who attended the annual award ceremony in July 1950.[22]

The broadened inclusion of foreigners might suggest that Brown's 'internationalism' was seamlessly continued, yet the underlying thinking was altogether different. Prominent visitors such as Aalto and Rogers were invited for their qualities as practising architects rather than teachers. With the exception of Charles Burchard, a young Harvard professor who spent a year at the AA in exchange for Atkinson, their presence, therefore, did not reflect an interest in the workings of foreign schools, let alone an attempt at making an institutional impact on international architectural education itself. Paradoxically then, despite the unprecedented number of international staff, the school itself had a rather more self-referential outlook. Jordan – who, so far as can be ascertained, did not leave the country once during his tenure – certainly lacked Brown's missionary zeal and did not share his international ambitions. Reciprocal visits with foreign schools were discontinued, and when the CIAM Summer School eventually took place in 1949, the AA played no significant part besides providing the infrastructure.

Real Sites, Real Problems, Real Clients

The previous chapter showed how Brown responded to criticism regarding the practical shortcomings of his students by strengthening 'draughtsmanship'

and 'the technical side'. Jordan, too, was aware of the charge that the AA 'had produced some brilliant and several sound architects, but that it was not producing good assistants', and he regarded this 'weakness in the school [. . .] as a serious matter'.[23] The resumption of building production in the late 1940s enabled the new principal to link his course in a more sustained manner to real-life processes than had previously been possible. He therefore gradually abandoned the practical training scheme and encouraged his students to gain work experience on construction sites and in factories instead. School trips to manufacturers featured prominently on the agenda, as did Saturday visits to new buildings such as ACP's rubber factory at Brynmawr, Powell & Moya's housing scheme at Pimlico or the Hertfordshire schools, which were usually led by their respective designers, many of them members of staff.

Much the most popular destination was, of course, the South Bank site of the Festival of Britain, which was proudly, and quite rightly, seen as an AA enterprise. As President Anthony Chitty pointed out, 'of the 26 architects commissioned [. . .] three-quarters [are] members of this association and more than half were trained here [. . .]'.[24] Hugh Casson, the architectural director of the Festival, for instance, was a long-time member (and future president) of the council. Casson had made a name for himself as an active and well-connected advocate for a tempered form of modernism, both through his partnership with the recently deceased AA tutor Christopher Nicholson but particularly through his regular contributions in the architectural press.[25] The choice of designers for the various pavilions on the South Bank reflected his undogmatic take on modern architecture and included several members of the AA teaching staff, specifically Jim Cadbury-Brown, Stefan Buzas, Paul Boissevain and the seven members of ACP. Moreover, AA graduates Leonard Manasseh and Powell & Moya won the two architectural competitions for the Festival, and two current students – A. K. Allen and G. J. Briggs – received a special honourable mention for their proposal for a 'Vertical Feature'. Student drawings at the AA 'positively breathe South Bankism', wrote

16   Primitive Hut (John Bicknell, first year, 1949/50)

'In your first AA design project you are asked to forget the complex activities of modern man, to forget the specialised "cells" of the house, to forget "Architecture" and return to the simple problem of enclosing a space, a shelter for habitation. You must try, like the savage, to be direct, simple, resourceful.' (Extract from the studio programme, Builder, *4 Nov 1949.)*

17 Theatre School (Bill Howell, fourth year, 1948/49)

More than a hundred fourth-year students collaborated with colleagues at the Old Vic on designs for a theatre school building containing a large auditorium as well as classrooms, rehearsal studios and a smaller theatre for experimental work. Though little more than wishful thinking in times of austerity, Robert Furneaux Jordan anticipated that postwar reconstruction and the accompanying socio-cultural changes would fuel the demand for a full-scale modernisation of the theatre stock in the country. The schemes were seen as pointers to a future which would eventually arrive a decade later.

the *Guardian*, 'for it is from the school, fully of its day, [. . .] that a good deal of the South Bank has indirectly come'[26] (Plate 5).

The quest for realism was not limited to extramural activities but permeated the curriculum itself. The basic approach – encapsulated in the formula 'real sites, real problems, real clients' – had been introduced by Robertson in the 1930s and subsequently remained a constant, if at times marginal, feature of the course. Under Brown's aegis, for instance, teams of fourth-year students had developed a cluster of factory and office blocks for Penguin Books, based on a programme provided by the project architect Ralph Tubbs, who, along with the company's founder-director Allen Lane, also served on the final jury (Plate 2). However, unlike Brown, under whom such programmes remained the exception, Jordan considered the 'real sites, real problems, real clients' approach 'one of the AA's best contributions to design teaching'[27] and made it the core of the curriculum, particularly in the senior years. Fourth-year programmes included the replacement of a joinery factory for John Sadd & Sons, which involved students visiting the company's existing plant in Essex to familiarise themselves with its work processes, or a theatre school developed in cooperation with students of the Old Vic, for which its principal, Michel St Denis, acted as make-believe client (Fig.17).

Jordan's lecture syllabus, the studio curriculum with its underlying sense of 'realism' and the various extramural activities were the pillars of a coherent pedagogical strategy which aimed at enabling students to pursue their profession with a grasp of 'the true nature and significance of the contemporary scene'.[28] This 'scene' was characterised by unprecedented building challenges and a shift of patronage from the individual client to collective bodies acting on behalf of the general public, adding, as Robert Matthew put it, the complication of 'finding out not just what the client wants but [. . .] who the client is'.[29] In other words, set within the changed realities of the welfare state, the 'contemporary scene' made the interpretation of the neat formula 'real sites, real problems, real clients' a rather intricate task.

Research and Collaboration – Training for Public Practice

Orchestrated by a coalition government, the country's wartime effort had demonstrated the potential of state interventionism, and the election victory of the Labour Party in 1945 ensured that similar directive powers were now applied to the rebuilding of the country. Effectively turning architecture into a public service, the agencies of the welfare state assumed responsibility for the provision of housing and schools as the twin engine of the reconstruction drive and, through a plethora of building regulations, curtailed private practice to an extent that it 'might', as Summerson wrote, 'with only slight exaggeration, be described as illegal'.[30]

With the spectre of nationalisation looming, the future of private architectural practice was the prevailing concern of the profession in the immediate postwar period, dominating the editorials and correspondence columns of the technical press and prompting the formation of a special RIBA committee under Percy Thomas to report on the matter. Within the AA, these debates were infused by a sense of pragmatism, epitomised by Roderick Enthoven's remark that '[it] is not for us to be concerned whether architecture, like music, is produced by solo instrumentalists or by orchestras, provided it is in fact good'.[31] The rise of the public sector was accepted as a fact of life, and discussions revolved around the question as to how, within its multidisciplinary environment, architects could uphold their traditional role as leaders of the building team and retain creative control over its output.

In April 1948, Anthony Cox read a paper to the AA in which he laid out how, by dividing them into semi-autonomous units and implementing a mechanism of continual research and development, departments could be organised in a way which would avoid the inhibiting effect of a rigid administrative hierarchy and foster the creativity and self-responsibility of its architect members.[32] Jordan, who considered the existing setup of the architectural profession and its education to be 'quite unrelated either to the scope or the scale of modern needs',[33] actively sought the proximity of the London County Council (LCC) and Hertfordshire County Council, whose architect's departments were pioneering the compartmentalised and collaborative work environment Cox called for. Though unable to get official architects directly involved in the teaching of his students, Jordan managed to forge close links with them. The LCC, in particular, became a haven for those who qualified in the late 1940s and early 1950s – partly because of the social aspirations underpinning its expansive building programme, but also because few private practices had job vacancies and even fewer were in a position to satisfy the creative ambitions and salary expectations of AA graduates.

To prepare his students for their work for public authorities, Jordan often modelled studio programmes on their real-life tasks. In 1949, fourth-year students were asked to design a secondary school based on the Hills prefab system used in Hertfordshire, assisted by members of its architect's department, who provided site material, technical details and critical input.[34] A similar programme in the following year conformed to MOE specifications, and Jordan reported with satisfaction that 'the Architects Group at the MOE have virtually written this programme and are maintaining a close interest in it'.[35] Inevitably, much of the student work had the somewhat impersonal look associated with system-built architecture, increasingly overlaid by a Miesian formalism inspired by depictions of recent American architecture in the professional press (Figs 18–21; Plate 6).

Of course, the key novelty advanced by the Hertfordshire architects was not the application of an existing building system but the decision to adapt it to their specific requirements, based on a thorough analysis of the building problem and in close collaboration with the manufacturer.[36] Moreover, they implemented a revolutionary 'rolling programme'[37] whereby user feedback was gathered to inform future stages of the

undertaking. In other words, Hertfordshire suggested a method to approach an unprecedented 'problem' and bridge the gap to the anonymous 'client' by linking up technological and consumer research. Jordan sought to incorporate this notion of research into the curriculum, believing that it was only through enquiry and analysis that the student could hope to acquire an understanding of the 'contemporary scene' in its unprecedented complexity. Consequently, he gave his students far-reaching liberties in the interpretation of the tasks they were set – indeed, subject to satisfactory performance in previous terms, students had the option to disregard these altogether and draft their own briefs, enabling the best of them to write a large proportion of their programmes themselves and thus, to a considerable degree, devise their own course of studies.

Whether working to a given brief or writing their own, students were encouraged to work in groups, not least because the sheer scope of the tasks usually made this a necessity. Unlike Brown, who dismissed the 'big subject' as a Beaux-Arts relic and preferred students to design smaller projects in a more thorough manner instead,[38] Jordan considered any diminution in the scope of programmes to be at odds with the conditions students were likely to encounter upon entering the profession:

> Building programmes generally (e.g. new towns, C.C. schools, health centres or industrial buildings) are likely to be larger rather than smaller – the client a corporate body rather than a single patron – and in such schemes the vision of the artist will be preserved and implemented only if he can co-operate and organise with others.[39]

A fairly regular feature under the unit system, group work had been temporarily abandoned after the war – presumably for organisational rather than pedagogical reasons, for it was Brown who re-introduced it in the spring of 1947, when fourth-year students collaborated on their Penguin schemes.[40] Unlike his predecessors, who limited

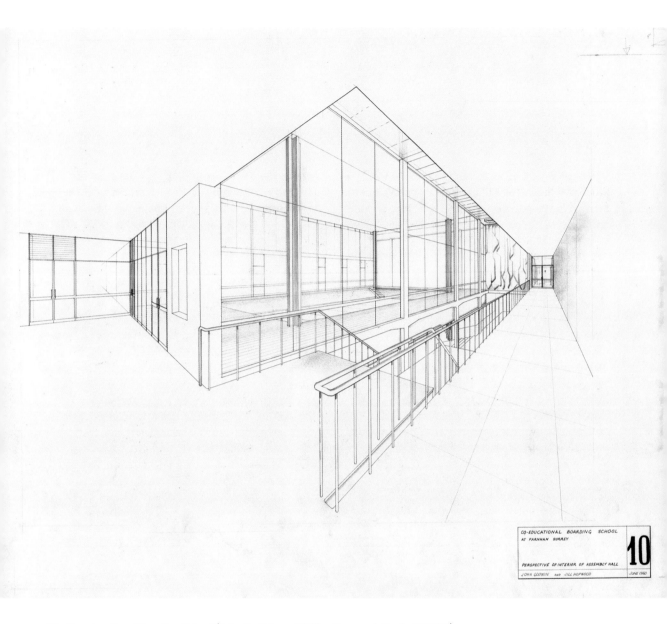

CO-EDUCATIONAL BOARDING SCHOOL
AT FARNHAM SURREY

PERSPECTIVE OF INTERIOR OF ASSEMBLY HALL

10

JOHN GODWIN AND JILL HOPWOOD | JUNE 1950

18   Co-educational Boarding School (John Godwin and Gillian Hopwood, thesis, 1949/50)

Godwin and Hopwood met as first-year students in 1945 and began their life-long collaboration in their senior years at the AA. For their joint thesis, they proposed a three-storey building centred upon a fully enclosed courtyard. When, in 1954, the couple started their own practice in Nigeria, they drew on their thesis scheme to develop a template for a series of multi-storey primary schools, with full-height window walls on both side elevations of the classroom blocks providing cross-air movement for greater comfort, privacy and noise control. The couple were helped with their perspective drawings by Godwin's father, who had graduated from the AA shortly after the First World War.

19   Storey's, Kensington (Robert Maguire and Peter Matthews, third year, 1950/51)

In the early 1950s, curtain walls became a popular feature in student work. This scheme for a store in Kensington was a forerunner of this trend and achieved top marks (in spite of the spelling error on the shop sign). The students tried to avoid the monotony that often comes with large glass frontages by altering the fenestration and incorporating the proto-High Tech feature of a lift in a partially glazed shaft.

group work to the senior years, Jordan extended the idea over the entire curriculum. In fact, the 'primitive hut' was one of only three (out of a total of 25) subjects for which it was explicitly prohibited, and while it was not compulsory for the remainder of programmes, Jordan was unambiguous that it soon would be.[41] He strongly encouraged his students to form themselves into permanent groups early in the course, whether or not they chose to tackle their design projects as teams, and to elect a chairperson who would represent them in fixed weekly meetings with the respective year staff.[42] Group working was thus more than simply an ad hoc design method; it gave students formal status within the administrative machinery of the school. Jordan hoped that these student groups would form the nuclei of more highly organised working partnerships which would persist throughout, and possibly beyond, the duration of the course:

> The AA should produce a 'school' of architects – in the sense in which one speaks historically of a 'school' of painters – but this, in the conflicts of contemporary life, can only be done when there is a conscious effort to form a corporate will.[43]

Two group theses epitomise the high ambitions of Jordan's school, both selected by the MARS Group as its official contributions to the CIAM congresses of, respectively, 1951 and 1953. 'Pin Green, Stevenage', was submitted in 1950 by a group comprising John Killick, Hugh Morris, Stephen Macfarlane, Bill Howell and his future wife Jill Sarson (Figs 22–23). Taking the existing master plan of Stevenage New Town as a starting point, the group developed one of the proposed six neighbourhood units by combining single-storey houses with a number of high-rises. In doing so, the students arrived at densities which proved incompatible with the original plan, inducing them to reconceive the town as a whole. Upon graduation, Howell and Killick joined the housing section of the LCC and used their thesis as the basis for their Alton West Estate in Roehampton; they retained a close connection with the AA and

effectively supervised three thesis groups which concurrently developed schemes for the same site.[44]

The second of the seminal group theses of the period was 'Zone', completed in 1952 as the result of a two-year collaboration between Pat Crooke, Andrew Derbyshire and John Voelcker (Figs 24–25). Unlike the Stevenage project, which did not question the underlying thinking of the New Town programme, 'Zone' was an explicit and prescient critique of prevailing urban theory. The students devised a self-sufficient and hierarchically structured 'micro-region' for 72,000 residents, consisting of a high-density city core surrounded and supported by an interdependent network of farming communities – 'a staggering piece of student work which is still referred to with respect and awe', as Gowan reminisced more than a quarter of a century later.[45]

Shades of Left – The AA in the Crossfire of Political Controversy

Jordan's emphasis on collaborative methods was a way to meet the needs of a society whose progression toward socialism he considered a historical inevitability. Among the first wave of British modernists, to which Jordan belonged, such views were by no means exceptional. Although the British generally lacked the fervour of their continental counterparts, in the 1930s the political connotation was pronounced enough for 'Modernismus' to present an easy target for chauvinist polemic. Shared wartime experiences of air raids and rationing momentarily reconciled antagonisms of class and politics, and the landslide victory of the Labour Party in 1945 indicated that hitherto distinctively leftist causes had acquired broad appeal across the political spectrum. Jordan's assumption of office thus coincided with a brief period in which his radical political views were commonly deemed acceptable.

Yet the political climate was changing. The Czech coup and the division of Germany in 1948 cemented the Cold War, while Britain's active role in setting up the North Atlantic Treaty Organization (NATO) in 1949 and its participation in the Korean War in the following year crushed the widespread (if entirely illusory) hope of many on the left that a socialist Britain might establish itself as a third, non-aligned power on the world stage. Domestically, in 1948, the government initiated a purge of the civil service, and the Labour Party disallowed any form of affiliation between its members and communists, who in turn hardened their stance towards an administration they had initially welcomed. Fuelled by fierce anti-communist rhetoric from both the government and large sections of the press, the schism between the political mainstream and the Communist Party (CP) widened, leaving its supporters marginalised and deeply suspect.

With architecture a part of the state machinery and thus an inherently political subject, it was inevitable that it got caught up in these controversies, and the AA proved particularly vulnerable to politically motivated defamation. The student rebellion of the 1930s had in some corners been seen as the result of concerted agitation by a small group of communist students, and left-wing undercurrents were traditionally strong in the school. Of the many political student societies which emerged within the AA after the war, the Communist Society (ComSoc) was by far the most active. With estimates ranging between eight and 25 members, the ComSoc was, as one of them remembered, 'absolutely a tiny cluster of people'.[46] Nonetheless, in the politically charged climate of the late 1940s they were conspicuous enough to arouse the interest of the secret service, who questioned a disgusted Gabriel Epstein about his communist students[47] – partly because they were disproportionately represented on the students' committee, but mostly because they overlapped with a prominent group of AA students who edited the student magazine *PLAN* and used it as a platform for the dissemination of their (anarchist-pacifist rather than communist) ideas.

While the students' political activities had been a feature at the AA since the war, under Jordan the school itself became a forum for political debate. Rules prohibiting students from using school premises for political meetings or providing them to outside bodies applied equally to the association itself, and when in April 1948 the MARS Group asked for permission to use AA facilities for the CIAM Summer School, the council – against legal advice – consented only because it was assumed that 'half of the course would be English and probably AA members'.[48] One year later, no such pretext seemed necessary to loan a lecture hall to the Association of Building Technicians (ABT), the communist-led trade union of salaried architects and technicians, and the Society for Cultural Relations between the British Commonwealth and the USSR (SCR) for a jointly organised talk by Marxist scientist J. D. Bernal on his recent visit to the Soviet Union. In March 1950, the AA itself hosted a discussion of the Architecture and Planning Group of the SCR, which suggests that it, too, was composed predominantly of AA members and that the council, somewhat naively, did not consider the SCR to be a political organisation.[49]

Governed by a council which seemed oblivious to the political sensitivities of the wider populace and showed no signs of attempting to contain the fomenting activities of its students, the AA made itself an easy target for those intent on pursuing an anti-communist witch-hunt. On 19 July 1950, Jordan informed the council that he had asked for the immediate resignation of his vice-principal, David Goddard, deploring his poor work ethics and 'excessive rudeness' to both students and staff, many of whom had asked not to have to work under him anymore.[50] Goddard rejected Jordan's accusations, expressing the view 'that the Principal is on the edge of a breakdown [and] that the whole business had been engineered by the communists, of which [*sic*] party the Principal had been a member (and probably still is)'.[51] Goddard refused to tender his resignation and only changed his mind when the AA's solicitor threatened to terminate his contract for serious neglect of duty and misconduct. With Jarrett's similarly contentious departure still fresh in the memory, the council became increasingly concerned about Jordan's direction of the school though it refrained from investigating Goddard's allegation as to a

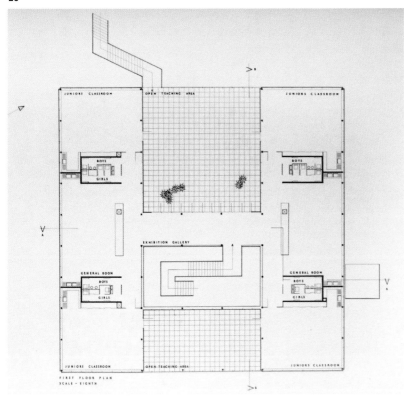

20

FIRST FLOOR PLAN
SCALE · EIGHTH

This group of fourth-year students applied the 3' 4" module adopted and promoted by the Ministry of Education to a primary school in a heavily built-up suburb of London. The limitations of the site and the desire to preserve as many trees as possible inspired a compact plan developed around a central assembly hall. All classrooms have access to dedicated outdoor play and teaching areas, with the first-floor ones sheltered by canvas blinds. The black steel frame and full glass cladding echoes Mies van der Rohe's Crown Hall, even though the coloured insulating panels which were placed behind the glass would have given the building a more serene look.

21

Primary School at Tulse Hill, London (Bryan Archer, Dennis Ball, David Oakley, Ernst Priefert, fourth year, 1951/52)

possible political motive behind his dismissal.[52] Yet within only two months another controversy brought the issue back to the fore, and while the row with Goddard was confined to the AA's inner circle, this one played out in full public view.

On 25 October 1950, AA President S. E. T. Cusdin delivered his inaugural address under the heading 'Fumbling in the Quiver', which involved his firing metaphorical arrows at a number of architectural 'targets', including the AA itself.[53] The speech prompted one member of the audience, Winston Walker, to invite Cusdin to aim another arrow at the communist members of staff, who, in his view, had been appointed for their political persuasion rather than their teaching ability.[54] Four weeks later, Walker repeated these accusations in a letter to the *Builder*, whose editors praised him for 'bringing into the open a matter which has been causing much uneasiness not only inside the Association but [. . .] in the outside world' and urged the AA council to carry through a purge of its staff to ensure that students 'are not taught in an atmosphere in which politics, and especially Communism, could be admixed with general or technical learning'.[55]

While the allegation that staff appointments were influenced by candidates' political affiliation seemed preposterous, the presence of staff with links to the CP was undeniable. They included the members of ACP, particularly Leo De Syllas, as well as Arthur Korn, Graeme Shankland and – above all – Colin Penn, a studio tutor and member of the ABT's executive committee, who harboured profound and, to many, rather alarming sympathies with the Soviet Union. At a time when James Richards championed the 'New Empiricism' as a middle path between an uncompromising functionalism (which lacked appeal to the 'common man') and a state-imposed architectural style along the lines of Zdhanov's socialist realism (which was philosophically and aesthetically reprehensible to most British architects),[56] Penn startled attendees at a meeting of the CP's architects' group by implicitly advocating the latter course. Asked whether the CP's cultural policy meant that architects would have to follow

the style cultivated in the USSR, Penn replied that 'this question of artistic style has not been settled yet',[57] which was, according to the *Builder*, 'itself a conclusive answer to everything that was asked'.[58]

Few, if any, at the AA shared these views (least of all Jordan himself), and even the ABT immediately distanced itself from 'Mr. Colin Penn's doctrines'.[59] Nonetheless, the presence of a devoted communist such as Penn seemed to confirm the suspicions of those who regarded the AA as infested with radical left-wing ideology. The council, alive to the potential damage such rumours could cause, considered legal proceedings against Walker, and AA member Ann MacEwen, a planner with the LCC, proposed to call a special general meeting with a view to expelling him from the association.[60] The AA's solicitor, however, advised against either course as Walker's statement did not qualify as 'slander' in a legal sense, nor could the AA 'expel a member merely because he was disliked'.[61]

Trying to avoid any controversial correspondence in the press, the council limited itself to a brief reply from President Cusdin to the *Builder*, in which he rejected Walker's allegations and confirmed that 'it is and will continue to be the practice of the AA to admit members, appoint staff and enrol students irrespective of their religious or political beliefs or of their nationality'.[62] Coming from within the suspect association, this letter had little prospect of changing the minds of those who shared Walker's concerns, and neither did a note in the *Architects' Journal* which, evoking the spectre of McCarthyism, criticised the *Builder* for appearing 'bent on carrying the American inquisitorial technique into the heart of English architectural education' and praised Cusdin for his 'brief, dignified, factual statement of AA policy'.[63] This was all the more the case as the controversy coincided unhappily with the eighth edition of *PLAN*, which contained an article giving detailed advice to students intending to register as conscientious objectors.[64] Deploring this 'curious pacifist propaganda', the *Builder* accused the AA council of a lack of control over its students,[65] and the *Empire News* surmised that the article might constitute a treasonable offence – a question which was eventually raised (and rejected) in parliament.[66] Meanwhile, the affair threatened to have financial repercussions for the AA as potential donors such as Banister Fletcher rejected an appeal for funds on the grounds 'that they were not prepared to give financial support to an association in which communism was apparently allowed to flourish'.[67] In fact, the council itself, while taking a united stand in public, was clearly divided over the issue. When A. R. F. Anderson, as the council member responsible for the hanging of pictures in AA premises, asked for his colleagues' support in having a print of Picasso's *Dove of Peace* removed because it had 'Communist association' and was, as such, 'a direct affront to the council', the motion was only defeated by a narrow margin.[68]

The controversy continued to put a strain on the AA throughout the first half of 1951. Eventually the relentless pressure proved too much for Jordan, who informed the council on 28 May 1951 that due to health reasons he had been 'advised to have some relief from his exacting duties'.[69] The council persuaded Jordan to carry on until the end of the summer term while looking for a suitable vice-principal. Yet within a few weeks, possibly triggered by the premature death of his older brother, Jordan suffered a nervous breakdown and was ordered to take four to five weeks' complete rest in the countryside by his physician. Ten days later, on 9 July 1951, he resigned with immediate effect.[70]

Unfinished Business

Jordan's sudden departure left important policy matters unresolved. In July 1949, the council's development subcommittee, instituted two years prior, had at long last concluded its deliberations.[71] These had revolved around the question of safeguarding the school's long-term independence or, if this proved impracticable, affiliation with either an existing university or the LCC, neither of which was deemed appealing nor pursued any further. Jordan had hoped to transform the AA into a government-funded national college akin to the

RCA, but the Ministry of Education dismissed this idea out of hand. In light of this, the development subcommittee sounded out the conditions for a reinstatement of the direct MOE grant but did not recommend this course of action to the council, largely because it was divided over the scope of the problem: Jordan predicted that, although the school was in a rare state of affluence at the time, with rising costs and the forthcoming cessation of FET grants, it was likely to face a deficit of nearly £6,000 in 1954/55 – an estimate which treasurer Anderson rejected, alleging that Jordan had purposely 'taken a pessimistic view in order to support a case for aid being put to the Ministry'.[72]

The final report of the development subcommittee was thus inconclusive. None the wiser, the council restated its intention to maintain the AA's educational and financial independence and agreed a gradual reduction of the school from currently more than 500 students to its pre-war size of 300, hoping that the resulting deficit might be cushioned by vacating some of the premises in Bedford Square and attracting a greater number of scholarships and grants. Based on this vague outline policy, the council discharged its subcommittee and delegated the task of preparing a 'carefully worked out educational scheme' for such a scaled-down school to its principal instead.[73] Embroiled in a controversy with his deputy, Jordan failed to make any progress with his assignment, and the question of financing, in particular, remained unanswered.

Equally in the balance was the AA's relationship with the RIBA's Board of Architectural Education. Jordan was conscious of – and entirely indifferent to – the fact that his pedagogical approach differed profoundly from the mainstream of architectural education at the time. Examining over a hundred portfolios of senior students wishing to transfer from their schools to the AA, he concluded drily:

Either what we are doing and intend to go on doing at the AA, in the way of experiment, freedom, site-work, et cetera, is wildly wrong, or else architectural education as administered under the Registration Act is wildly wrong. We are only too conscious of the hundreds of things to be put right at the AA, but it seems clear – for good or ill – that in our outlook at least (if not as yet in our actual work) we are no longer part of the national 'set-up' in architectural education.[74]

Accordingly, Jordan regarded the forthcoming visit of the RIBA's visiting board in June 1950 as little more than a nuisance. Though perhaps not quite as disparaging as the rather thin-skinned Jordan professed, the board's report did contain several criticisms.[75] It had reservations about the planning aspect of the second-year programme, which it thought too advanced for junior students (Fig.26; see also p.81). It also did not appreciate the close involvement of specialist lecturers such as Felix Samuely and Ove Arup, who were – as at Harvard, but singularly in Britain – seen as members of the studio staff and thus an integral part of the design teaching process. Most importantly, the board criticised the preponderance of group

working, which it wished to see 'confined to one or possibly two subjects in the course'.[76] In doing so, the board challenged the cornerstone of Jordan's pedagogical approach, and it is difficult to see how he could possibly have upheld it against the RIBA's objections.

Jordan's premature departure left this problem unresolved, and it occurred at a critical moment in the school's history. In 1951, the AA faced a future without FET-funded students and therefore without a secure source of funding. Worse still, it had isolated itself educationally and politically at just the moment when both the MOE and the RIBA began to play a more active role in guiding the affairs of the schools. How the council and its new principal tackled these challenges will be examined in Chapters 5, 6 and 7. Before that, however, it is worth revisiting the immediate postwar years to take a closer look at the students themselves and the wide-ranging educational (rather than political) activities that unfolded within and beyond the AA.

4 Chuzzlewit's Heirs (1945–1951)

Moth-Eaten Old Students and Noisy Little Schoolboys

From 1945, the school was invaded by a large number of service personnel whose training had been interrupted by the war. Ripened by their wartime experiences, these 'moth-eaten old students', as they were referred to by one of the year masters,[1] were serious, industrious and anxious to make up for lost time. Driven by idealism and a pronounced single-mindedness vis-à-vis the task at hand, they were neither in need of nor prepared to accept top-down instruction in a traditional sense, especially since many of their tutors were barely older than themselves and, not insignificantly at the time, often of lower or no military rank. The students, writes Saint, 'exuded the confidence of victory [and] came back to the AA with the marks and bearing of an officer class'.[2] Gordon Brown, to whom the same applied, was sympathetic to their general outlook and accorded them preferential treatment. A case in point was the supposedly mandatory entrance examination, which Brown, as one of his students remembered, only demanded from unwanted applicants, that is, non-service personnel:

> [It] was almost a joke. I found him, in the full uniform of a paratroop major sitting in his office. All I had to show him was a rather bad copy I had made of a portrait by Rembrandt of an old man. Gordon Brown said: 'Okay young man you are in

(looking at my subbies stripe).' I said: 'Isn't there an entrance examination?' He said: 'Oh yes, but we only give it to people we don't want.'[3]

Brown respected the maturity of his students and tried to accommodate their wish to play a more active role in the affairs of the school. Students, he felt, should be given 'a much greater part in determining the form and direction of [their] education',[4] and he met on a weekly basis with their representatives to discuss changes to the curriculum. Yet Brown's goodwill had its limits. While he certainly did not see architectural education as an 'extension of military discipline',[5] as one chronicler claimed, he was a self-confessed autocrat, who was prepared to give students a large part in defining the policy of the school so long as it was a 'consultant's part';[6] he clearly did not tolerate insubordination.

The case of fourth-year student and future RIBA gold medallist Joseph Rykwert may serve as an example. In the official account, in December 1946, Rykwert, an outspoken member of the students' committee, was asked to leave the school after councillors Hugh Casson and Hilton Wright had examined his portfolio and deemed it 'totally inadequate'.[7] According to Rykwert, who recalls the traumatic incident vividly, the original examiner had in fact been Casson's partner Christopher Nicholson, who was friendly and enthusiastic about his work.[8] Gordon Brown, who judged Rykwert's project unacceptable, had the portfolio re-examined by another member of council, S. E. T. Cusdin, who pointed out that there were drawings missing and insisted that Rykwert must replace them. It was at this point that Brown demanded that the council exclude him from the school for unspecified insubordination. In sharp contrast to the school committee minutes, Rykwert remembers that Casson and Hilton Wright had defended him on the council, and the fact that the latter immediately offered Rykwert a job in his office (which he accepted) seems to support this. Rykwert suggests that the minutes may have been doctored by H. L. Bromley, the school registrar, whom he also suspects of 'losing' his drawings:

> My position in this was conditioned by my being the secretary of the Architectural Students Association [see p.63], and we had ideas about how we were being taught. [. . .] I suspect the whole thing was meant as a warning to insubordinate students.[9]

The enlarged student body itself was initially a diverse group, and there appear to have been considerable tensions not just with the principal but between the different factions themselves. Apart from a growing contingent of ex-service personnel there was, immediately after the war, still a significant number of students who had started their course in the more relaxed and – both literally and metaphorically speaking – escapist atmosphere of suburban Barnet. Many of them had difficulties adapting to the new realities in Bedford Square and exhibited an 'attitude to their work [that] was casual and somewhat indifferent'[10] and, as such, markedly at odds with the work ethic of the homecomers.

As to these homecomers, it would be inaccurate to portray them as a coherent body. Most ex-service students had held assignments remote from the front lines or were – like future HKPA partners John Killick and Stanley Amis – still in training when the war ended. At the opposite end of the spectrum, however, were battle-hardened and highly decorated warriors such as Jacqueline Cromie, a lieutenant in the French army and recipient of the *Légion d'honneur* for bravery; Douglas Bailey, a lieutenant colonel with

the Royal Engineers and holder of the American Bronze Star; Paul Hamilton, an Austrian Jew, who had narrowly escaped the Holocaust and volunteered for highly perilous intelligence missions behind enemy lines; or Ralph Smorczewski, a Polish count, who had joined the armed resistance in his home country and participated in acts of sabotage and the elimination of SS units.[11] John Cordwell, an airman with RAF Bomber Command, was shot down over Belgium in 1941 and spent four years in the notorious Stalag Luft III prisoner-of-war camp, where he was involved in the failed tunnel escape famously commemorated in the 1963 film *The Great Escape*. Cordwell's recollections of his AA years resonate with contempt for fellow students whose upper-class backgrounds may have saved them from a similar fate by their having been placed in less hazardous branches:

> All my competition were all very aristocratic people. 'Johnny, I don't have a clue. I don't know what I am doing,' and they really didn't know what they were doing. [. . .] They were awfully nice people, you know, and they talked too much. All they could do was talk all the time in very affected accents.[12]

Though perhaps not representative of the majority of ex-service personnel, Cordwell's statement reflected the sentiments of a vocal group among them. This in turn complicated the position of the handful of teenagers who entered directly from school, completing the social makeup of the AA and giving further cause for irritation to some of the older students. When Brown – due to staff shortages – tried to involve the latter in the tutoring of first-year students by inviting them to act on juries, they outright refused to do so and the plan was dropped. In fact, supported by Brown they asked to be separated completely from the younger students, which, however, foundered on the resistance of year master John Brandon-Jones:

> I thought it ridiculous and wasn't prepared to run my second-year course like that, so I spoke to the students. I called them up – servicemen first, which were about three quarters if not more. Then I called up the schoolboys, and there were

about two, so I said: 'Well if you can't put up with two noisy little schoolboys, I don't think much of you.' So that settled it.[13]

With time the tensions between the different groups abated, not least because ex-service students came to be largely among their own as wartime students reached graduation and 'schoolboys' either managed to fit in or dropped out. The school thus became older, and – in stark contrast to the war years – it also became male-dominated. In order to fill the places in the school, the council had, for the duration of the war, agreed an intake quota of '50 per cent' women, which due to the earlier call-up for men, often resulted in a slight preponderance of women over men, most notably in the senior years.[14]

The co-existence of young women in their late teens or early twenties and a rapidly growing share of, at times, considerably older men returning from the war apparently caused problems, at least as far as Gordon Brown was concerned. In November 1945, he reported to the council that, 'as the work became more intense', he had a number of cases of young women who 'could not stand the strain, and had breakdowns'.[15] Brown asked the council in vain to raise the entry age of women from 17 to 19, and one month later he announced 'that in future only twenty per cent women students would be admitted, reverting to the pre-war arrangement'.[16] Due to slow demobilisation, Brown could only gradually decrease the intake of women, but from autumn 1946 there was a drop in absolute numbers. In September, the ratio between female and male students was 1:3, equivalent to the overall ratio at English universities, and one year later, by limiting the actual intake of women to approximately ten per cent, this figure was lowered to 1:4. That the AA, in spite of these efforts, never returned to its pre-war gender ratio of roughly 1:5 may suggest that the 'erosion of the male dominance' which, according to Lowe, had been a 'striking characteristic of earlier periods'[17] continued seamlessly after the Second World War; however, the fact that the council's policy was never officially rescinded and its implementation only stalled for financial reasons indicates that – at least at the AA – this 'erosion' was in fact slow in coming.[18]

Beyond the AA: The Architectural Students' Association

For lack of alternative amenities in a capital mired in austerity, the students' social life centred on Bedford Square, which explains the resurgence of the various student societies after the war, not least the political ones mentioned in the previous chapter. The students' main interest lay, of course, in architectural matters. In the summer of 1946, Hugh 'Sam' Scorer instigated the formation of the 'Foundation Society' as a restricted sub-section of the students' club aimed at giving 'a more organised and permanent form to the sort of general discussion about architecture [. . .] which goes on in the school'.[19] At the same time, the students' committee absorbed a different, if probably overlapping, group of students which had been organising informal lunch-time discussions on questions of architectural education and at Brown's suggestion reconstituted it as its official education subcommittee to liaise directly with the principal.[20]

This surge in student activism was by no means limited to the AA. Unlike many of its counterparts in other countries, the British National Union of Students (NUS) had not only upheld but expanded its activities during the war. In 1940, 500 students attended its largest annual congress to date; in the following year, the number more than doubled; and yet another year later, it tripled. Similarly to the role of MARS within CIAM, the NUS emerged from the war as the driving force behind an increasingly thriving international student movement. In November 1945, it organised a meeting of foreign students exiled in Britain at which a preparatory committee was entrusted with the task of formulating the constitution for a global student organisation. Nine months later, representatives of 38 countries ratified this document at the inaugural World Student Congress in Prague and established the International Union of Students (IUS), headquartered in the Czech capital.[21] The IUS was divided into different sections, one of which – the 'Architectural Faculty Bureau' (AFB), directed by Italian Giuseppe 'Bubi' Campos – sought to stimulate the formation of national

22

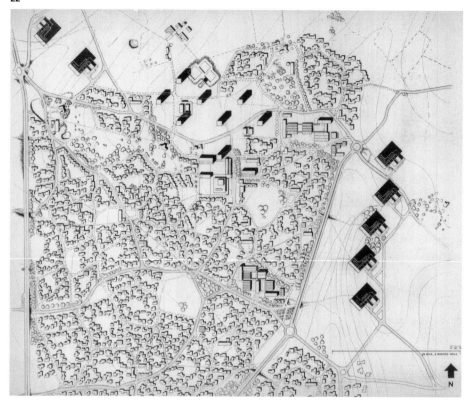

This scheme for Stevenage New Town shows the growing influence of Le Corbusier at the AA. The layout is partly inspired by the unrealised reconstruction plan for Saint-Dié of 1945. It combines single-storey houses with point-blocks, the larger of which – the so-called 'Big Towers' – have 27 floors and incorporate several features of the Unité d'habitation, *then nearing completion at Marseilles. These include communal services on the ninth and tenth floors, a public roof terrace and the reliance on structural elements regulated by the dimensional scales of Le Corbusier's* Modulor.

23

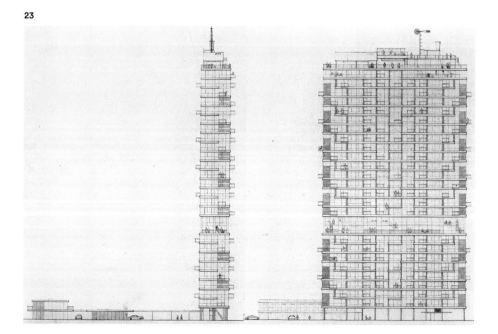

Pin Green, Stevenage (John Killick, Hugh Morris, Stephen Macfarlane, Bill Howell, Jill Sarson, thesis, 1949/50)

architectural students' organisations and coordinate their activities with a view to promoting reforms in architectural education.[22]

At the time the AFB was formed in May 1947, the United Kingdom was the only country in the world where such an organisation already existed. The Architectural Students' Association (ArchSA) had its origin in a congress of six northern schools of architecture at Manchester in February 1934, which gave birth to the bustling Northern Architectural Students' Association (NASA). The editors of *Focus*, who attended the annual NASA congress in Hull in 1939, were anxious to set up a southern branch, but the plan failed and the AA was conspicuously absent when, in April 1941, 11 schools of architecture from all parts of Britain met at Cambridge to transform the NASA into the countrywide ArchSA and launch *PLAN* as its trimestrial journal. The AA eventually joined the ArchSA in August 1943, when 13 AA students headed by John Beloff (later a leading authority on parapsychology at Edinburgh University) registered Mount House as the organising centre of its southern section. The AA council, which had not been informed of this undertaking, let alone asked for permission, reacted with irritation when the fact was eventually brought to its attention but sanctioned the affiliation retroactively.[23]

Beloff, though entitled, never served on the ArchSA council. It was under his successors John Kay, who was to become the chief architect to the Department of Education and Science under Margaret Thatcher, and Bruce Martin, soon to join the Hertfordshire schools programme, that the AA from 1945 onward began to play a more active part in the affairs of the association. In doing so, it increasingly clashed with the longer-standing northern factions (one of which – Newcastle – was at the time run by Peter Smithson and Jack Lynn). At a council meeting of the ArchSA in April 1946, Joseph Rykwert, one of the new AA delegates, incited a contentious debate about its strategic aims, which 'failed to achieve any measure of agreement'[24] and brought to the fore the tensions between the older groups and the new arrival. Determined to take command of the association and its journal, over

the course of the following months Michael Ventris, Graeme Shankland and Oliver Cox mobilised the support of fellow members on the AA students' committee and in April 1947 led a 14-strong delegation to the annual ArchSA congress: 'We went to Brighton for a conference and virtually [. . .] wrested the entire thing from Northern.'[25]

The Wonder Years

The formation of the education subcommittee and the takeover of the ArchSA secured AA students a voice within and without the confines of their school. They set the scene for what was with hindsight the *annus mirabilis* of the AA student movement as the new students' committee, elected in September 1947, persevered with, and indeed expanded, the activities of its predecessor body. Chaired by Bernard Feilden, later knighted for his conservation work, it constituted no fewer than seven different subcommittees. The only pre-existing one – the education subcommittee headed by Oliver Cox and Hugh Morris – was confirmed as a permanent and largely autonomous entity empowered to discuss pedagogical matters with the principal. In addition, the students' committee set up subcommittees to liaise directly with the two relevant national student organisations, namely the ArchSA and the NUS. Unlike other architectural schools, which were affiliated via their mother institutions, the AA as an independent school was directly represented on the NUS, and Feilden's students' committee saw this as an opportunity to inject itself into the broader national student discourse. More importantly, its strategic approach allowed the AA to consolidate its supremacy within the ArchSA. As Bubi Campos, the well-informed director of the AFB, noted:

> The students of the AA have begun to win the executive positions in the ArchSA and are gradually making of it a more active and progressive organisation. [. . .] In the space of a few months [. . .] the entire structure of the ArchSA will be changed.[26]

The students' committee underlined its ambitions by organising a separate programme of events in connection with the AA centenary celebrations in December 1947 and famously persuaded Le Corbusier, who had rejected an official invitation from the council, to give a talk to the students.[27] Le Corbusier's paper on the *Modulor* was but one item in a densely packed two-week schedule which included lectures by other distinguished architects such as Jaromír Krejcar from Czechoslovakia and Jens Dunker from Norway as well as a series of organised tours in London, each attended by 200 to 300 students. The programme closed with a symposium on the problem of adapting methods of architectural education to meet the requirements of a changed society. It brought together 16 student delegates from ten countries, who along with representatives from the AA and four other British schools passed a resolution promoting the creation of national unions of architectural students and their affiliation with the IUS, the arrangement of international exchange schemes, cooperation with CIAM in the field of architectural education, and the preparation of an international conference in the following year.[28] Sigfried Giedion responded by inviting students to take part in the discussions on architectural education at the forthcoming CIAM congress in Bergamo, which were attended by Joseph Rykwert along with two current AA students, Andrew Derbyshire and John Turner.[29]

Organised by the AA students' committee, the first 'World Conference of Architectural Students' eventually took place at the RIBA in April 1949, under the patronage of Patrick Abercrombie and with discussions chaired by Arthur Ling and Robert Furneaux Jordan. The four-day event, which despite visa difficulties was attended by over 60 delegates from 23 countries across the globe, stood under the theme 'Unite and Rebuild for Peace', and the *Architects' Journal* praised the students for their idealism:

> The theme [. . .] is a brave one, and at a time when post-war unity on any subject is fast disappearing it ill behoves anybody to

disparage this youthful attempt. [. . .] It is refreshing that students have avoided the cynicism and pretentiousness that in their elders could make such an endeavour futile [. . .].[30]

Yet the same magazine was less enthusiastic about the outcome, describing it as a 'strange affair – vague and inconclusive with its generalised clichés and its undertow of half-repressed political emotion'.[31] The *RIBA Journal* likewise deplored 'a certain laxity about the organisation of the conference, definition of purpose and the itinerary itself which left much to be desired'.[32] However, much the harshest criticism of the conference resolution – essentially an anti-war, anti-colonialism manifesto infused with the tenets of AA postwar pedagogy such as realism, site work and student participation[33] – arose from within the school itself. In May 1949, a general meeting of AA students passed a motion stating that 'in view of the politically biased nature of the main resolution of the International Architectural Students' Conference, the students of the Architectural Association desire to dissociate themselves from the political sentiments expressed therein [. . .]', indicating that in the increasingly polarised political climate of the late 1940s the left-wing radicalism of the students' committee ceased to reflect the views of the student body as a whole.[34]

Nonetheless, the dominance of the AA within the ArchSA itself remained unchallenged and reached its pinnacle at the annual congress in Oxford on 19 July 1949, to which its delegates submitted a 14-point circular as a basis for discussion.[35] The points (real sites and real clients, cross-year group working, experimental workshops, and so forth) reflected either current or envisaged AA practice and marked the penultimate step of a three-year effort initiated by Rykwert to redefine the aims of the ArchSA and align them with progressive AA thought. At the annual congress in Brighton in the following year, the participants passed a final resolution which incorporated key aspects of the 'Fourteen Points' and turned them thus into official ArchSA policy.[36]

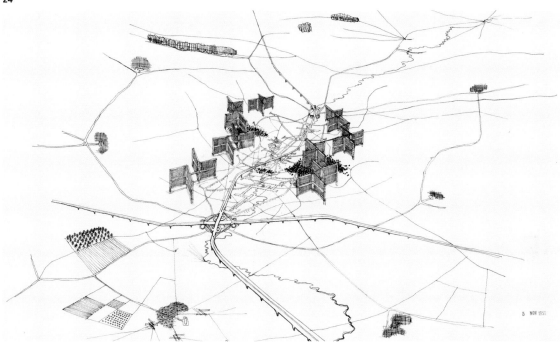

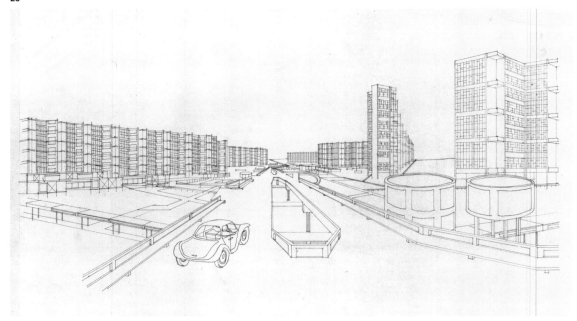

Zone (Pat Crooke, Andrew Derbyshire, John Voelcker, thesis, 1950–52)

The idea of a network of self-sufficient farming communities supporting an urban core was seen as a possible model for the reorganisation of the entire country. Mirroring the Smithsons' concurrent investigations into 'scales of association', the city housed 60,000 inhabitants and consisted of six neighbourhoods, which in turn split into smaller districts, streets, and ultimately 'doorsteps' of approximately 30 people each.

Cross-generational Links:
From *Focus* to *PLAN*

The 1950 resolution and the more idealistic of its 'Fourteen Points', such as the substitution of lectures by free discussion and the control of the school curriculum by joint staff-student committees, owed a manifest debt to the pre-war insurgents and recalled similar proposals in *Focus* and the Yellow Book. Oliver Cox, who had designed the covers of *Focus* as a second-year student before joining the war effort, remembered: 'We were welcomed back by the students as victors – not of the war – but victors over the old regime at the pre-war AA.'[37] The same applied to two of the editors of *Focus*, Leo De Syllas and Oliver's older brother Anthony, who returned to the school as members of the ACP teaching collective. Anthony Cox, in particular, soon rekindled his pre-war activism and from 1947 represented the MARS Group on the 'MARS/ArchSA Joint Committee on Architectural Education'. Chaired by Jane Drew, the joint committee had been formed in December 1945 to conduct a survey of architectural education but had not made any appreciable progress since. Along with AA student Graeme Shankland as ArchSA representative, Cox seized the initiative and drafted the committee's interim report, which was eventually issued in June 1948.[38]

The close AA involvement did not escape Douglas Jones, the head of the architectural school at Birmingham, who wrote:

> The authors of the report do not scatter many bouquets, but when they do praise one particular educational establishment – however right and sincere they may be – it is a pity that it happens to live in the same building from which the report was sent out [. . .].[39]

Jones's sneer notwithstanding, a distinct AA bias was barely perceptible, for the report did not specifically address the training in recognised schools: its key conclusion was that such training was, in fact, still the exception as a much larger proportion of students than previously presumed qualified by way of external examinations, the vast majority of them without any school training whatsoever. With its unconcealed criticism of the RIBA, which focused its attention on the recognised schools and played down the educational needs of external students as a 'special problem', the report attracted a great deal of publicity. In the end, though, it failed to make a lasting impact as the RIBA challenged its findings by publishing corrective statistics which exposed inaccuracies in the MARS/ArchSA figures.[40] The MARS Group discontinued its participation in the joint committee, and a final report was never produced.

The ArchSA/MARS interim report was the only tangible outcome of a direct collaboration between the pre-war and postwar generations of AA students, yet nowhere was the former's influence on the latter more evident than in *PLAN*. 'We decided that we must reproduce what my brother had done just before the war', recalled Oliver Cox, 'an architectural magazine for the students.'[41] *PLAN* replaced the *NASA Journal* following the inaugural ArchSA congress in 1941, but initially it remained 'a little newsletter, a broadsheet',[42] offering the expectable mixture of news items, illustrated school work and travel reports. The AA students' committee took charge of the journal at the 1947 Brighton congress and enlisted the help of the AA council to obtain more advertisement revenue for *PLAN* and thus enlarge the publication.[43] This was clearly successful, for when the first AA number was released, it comprised four times as many advertisements as the previous one, allowing for twice the number of editorial pages, which in turn justified a significantly higher price.

In form and content *PLAN* bore little resemblance to the unassuming leaflet which had preceded it, its layout design and spiral binding emulating the character of *Focus* instead. As opposed to the previous editions of the journal, which had been the result of individual efforts by students at Manchester and Liverpool, the AA's *PLAN* was a group enterprise from the outset – to the extent that in the final three numbers articles ceased to be attributable to individual writers. The high quality of the journal and its considerable impact on students at the AA owed much to the fact that the core of the continually changing editorial team consisted of some of the school's most admired students, notably the Stevenage and Zone thesis groups (see p.53). As with *Focus*, the editors envisaged *PLAN* as a medium facilitating the 'exchange of ideas between students and professional circles',[44] with ArchSA affairs increasingly edged to the sidelines. The attempt to broaden the readership through contributions of more general appeal, such as Michael Ventris's influential essay on Swedish architecture or Stephen Macfarlane's early report on Le Corbusier's *Unité d'habitation*, proved exceedingly successful, with *PLAN* growing its circulation from 600 to 2,500 during the AA's editorship.[45]

In January 1949, Gordon Brown resigned as principal of the school, and the five *PLAN* issues which were produced between 1949 and 1950 reflected the preoccupations of the school under his successor, Robert Furneaux Jordan. Dissatisfaction with the anticlimactic reality of New Town planning was a recurring theme, but the greatest bone of contention was the inefficiency of the building industry. The fifth issue, with its technical report on the new London Transport double-decker bus RT3, highlighted the superiority of industrial manufacturing in terms of prefabrication and dimensional precision, and in the same vein the eighth issue praised the achievements of the aviation industry as an inspiration for the development of new technologies.[46] In later numbers, the editors increasingly advocated a 'synthetic view' of architecture, exemplified by the ingeniously structured sixth issue, which examined the 'process of breakdown [. . .] in the fields of building, architecture, and education' and – while maintaining a profoundly pessimistic outlook – praised the Hertfordshire schools programme as a rare paragon of successful reintegration.[47] Jordan, who contributed regularly to *PLAN*, complimented the editors on their achievement: 'It is a magnificent effort in every way – a fine gesture against ineptitude in spite of its undercurrent of despair. Does it end there? What do we all do next?'[48]

PLAN embodied the self-confidence of a student generation whose standing was recognised within and beyond their own school and whose sense of mission and faith in the permanence of their contribution was not clouded by doubts. In this sense, the years 1949 to 1950 marked the climax of the AA student movement. By mid-1950, political controversies began to poison the climate within the AA and, perhaps inevitably, overshadow the 'intense practicality of outlook', which, according to Saint, had previously characterised *PLAN*.[49] With professional (and therefore educational) matters considered inseparable from their political context, a distinctive left-wing undercurrent had always run through the pages of *PLAN*. Yet appropriately enough, only the final issue published under the AA's editorship in the autumn of 1950 was overtly political in content, featuring an anti-war editorial, an open letter in support of a ban on nuclear weapons (signed by, among others, Cox and De Syllas) and, as mentioned in the previous chapter, a highly controversial guide for intending conscientious objectors.[50]

In early 1951, in compliance with ArchSA regulations, the AA students handed over *PLAN* to their colleagues at Birmingham, and only half a year later, Jordan resigned as principal of the school. Within the space of six months, the AA students lost both their mentor and their medium. Worse still, an ambitious but ill-conceived international 'Architectural Students' Festival', jointly organised by the London schools in connection with the Festival of Britain, left the ArchSA in discord and irrecoverable debt, which after two more numbers put an end to *PLAN* (and eventually, in 1953, the association itself).[51] These events dealt a blow to the students' aspirations, and simultaneous events in the wider world added to their growing sense of disillusionment. The implementation of building cuts meant that for the first time since the war there was a decline in building production and therefore employment prospects for young architects; and the victory of the Conservative Party in the general election seemed to seal the fate of the New Jerusalem, which had driven the ambitions of postwar students and provided a tremendous stimulus to their training. It was in this situation that the council faced the task of finding a new principal for the school.

5   The Battle of the Principal (1951–1956)

The Reluctant Principal

On 29 June 1951, shortly before the end of the spring term, Robert Furneaux Jordan took sick leave, and the council appointed Michael Pattrick, the most senior of the current members of staff, as acting head. When ten days later Jordan handed in his resignation, the council retained Pattrick as interim principal and, alarmed at the untimely departure of the two previous incumbents, decided to give careful consideration to its next appointment, possibly leaving the position vacant for up to a year in order to attract suitable candidates under contract elsewhere.

William Michael Thomas Pattrick was born in Norfolk in 1913 and from 1931 onward had a distinguished career as an AA student, winning annual travelling scholarships awarded to the best student in three of his five years at the school. After qualifying in 1936, he was briefly employed by George Grey Wornum before entering private practice and teaching at Cambridge and at Liverpool. During the war, Pattrick was in charge of various projects for the Ministries of Supply and Aircraft Production, and in 1945 he resumed his small practice, in later years often collaborating with his wife Jo, an interior designer, whose renown surpassed his. In September 1945, Pattrick joined the AA as a part-time tutor and began his rise through the ranks. As Gordon Brown's administrative assistant, Pattrick masterminded

the reorganisation of the school in the first half of 1946 and, once this work was completed, took charge of the third year before becoming, under Jordan, the director of technical studies.

Pattrick was thus well known and, by all accounts, rather unpopular with (at least the more vocal section of) students. This was in part due to his aloof disposition, which made him compare unfavourably with his approachable predecessor. Moreover, it was assumed that although Pattrick had been a member of Jordan's executive, he shared neither his pedagogical vision nor its underlying socio-political worldview. The choice of Pattrick as interim principal therefore caused great concern among the students, who feared that his permanent appointment and, by implication, the repeal of Jordan's educational system were a foregone conclusion. The students' committee acted at once and, on the first day of the new academic year, mobilised the student body in protest against Michael Pattrick. Peter Ahrends, one of the new first-year students, remembers:

No sooner were we settled into our places when some much older students came around the studio and said that there was a protest meeting in the hall downstairs about the new principal and told us to come down. It was more or less an order because these were older people, some of whom had gone through military service. So, we all went, as a body, filtered downstairs. [. . .] There was no sense that one was not to participate in this completely unforeseen, unheard-of activity. Within two hours on the day you arrived, you were part of this protest group which you knew nothing about. You didn't know about Pattrick or Jordan or what their politics were. There was a sense of excitation which was immediately inclusive.[1]

The council advertised the position in July 1951, and by closing date on 1 September, 25 candidates had applied, including – somewhat optimistically – David Goddard and Winston Walker. In addition to a dual background in teaching and architectural practice as the standard requirements for AA principals, the council, in light of the planned reduction of the school to pre-war numbers, searched for someone capable of overseeing this administrative transition. Only two applicants managed to impress the selection committee. Robert Paine, the youthful head of the recently established and already highly regarded architectural school at Canterbury, was perceived as being of 'strong character', but the committee felt that 'his ideas for the future did not seem large enough'.[2] Donald Reay, the Liverpool-trained chief architect and planning officer of the East Kilbride Development Corporation, too, had no teaching experience 'on the scale required at a school the size of the AA'.[3] Moreover, Reay not only made it a condition that he be allowed to continue working for his current employer but was unable to give an assurance that he would be staying at the AA, and the committee, which considered him a 'first-rate man', feared that he was likely to be attracted elsewhere.[4]

Unable to give either candidate its unanimous support, the selection committee eventually recommended Pattrick for the permanent position, even though it had initially thought of him as 'scarcely in the running' and Pattrick himself had assured the students that he did not intend to stand for principal.[5] Geoffrey Spyer, the chairman of the students' committee at the time, remained convinced that the dismissal of Jordan and the installation of Pattrick were the constituent parts of a plot hatched by a faction of the council led by

Hugh Casson.[6] The recollections of John Brandon-Jones, like Casson a friend of Pattrick's and member of the selection committee, seem to support the assertion: 'Michael Pattrick was persuaded to take the job on against his better judgment [. . .]. He would have liked to have been appointed vice-principal. He didn't really want to be the head.'[7]

The council, on the whole, welcomed the committee's suggestion, though some members raised questions about Pattrick's character. President Anthony Chitty, who supported Pattrick's candidature, nonetheless deplored a 'slight querulousness at times and a lack of tact'[8] on his part, and S. E. T. Cusdin wondered whether he 'carried sufficient weight and was an agreeable personality likely to recruit teaching staff'.[9] In spite of such concerns, the council appointed Pattrick on 7 November 1951, offering him an initial five-year contract with the stated intention to continue it for a further five-year period.[10]

Unpopular Measures

Pattrick's initial actions as principal seemed to confirm the fears of those who had seen his accession to office as spelling the end of Jordan's educational policy. On 29 June 1951, at his first meeting with the school committee as acting principal, Pattrick had been informed that the school was operating over budget, and the need to effect savings put an immediate end to the appointment of foreign teaching staff and lavish prize-giving ceremonies, both popular features of Jordan's tenure.[11] In addition to this, Pattrick was expected to implement the council's policy to reduce the numbers in the school, prompting him to relegate or expel weaker students, which had rarely happened under his predecessor.

Meanwhile, the RIBA, in a departure from previous practice, called on the AA to set out how it planned to address the suggestions and recommendations of the visiting board which had inspected the school in June 1950.[12] Jordan had rejected the board's criticisms, and so did

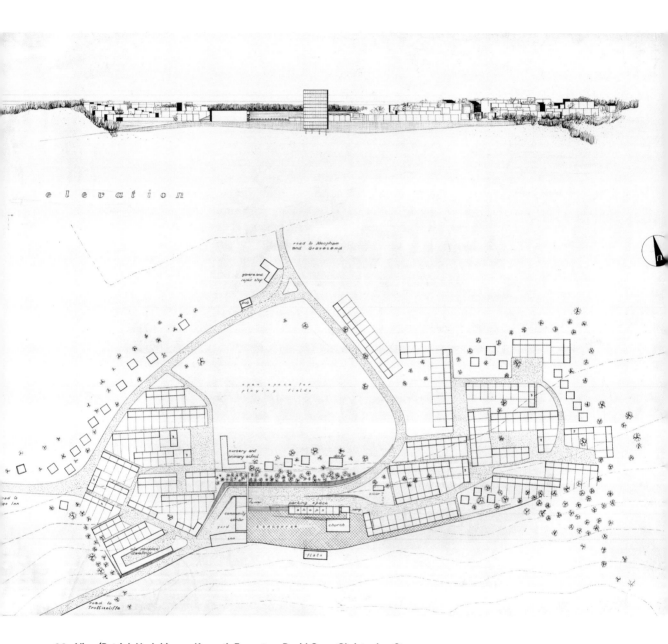

26 Vigo (Patrick Hodgkinson, Kenneth Frampton, David Gray, Christopher Stevens, Anna Tomlinson, second year, 1951/52)

The second-year village scheme was originally conceived by John Brandon-Jones and Arthur Korn in 1947. Students prepared a development plan for an existing village – in this case Vigo in Kent – and used this as the framework for individual buildings later in the year. The programme reflects Korn's unwavering desire to couple the teaching of architecture and planning, as well as a rekindled interest in the English countryside following the publication of Thomas Sharp's seminal survey The Anatomy of the Village *in 1946.*

Pattrick.[13] He therefore deferred fundamental changes to the inherited curriculum, though he did take steps to restrict group working – one of the key issues raised by the visiting board – partly to facilitate the individual assessment of students and partly because it was the only element of the course he could change without altering the curriculum itself. These steps brought Pattrick into conflict with some of the more influential students in the school, notably the Zone thesis group. Rumours that the RIBA might disqualify group work altogether, and the apparent disinclination of their principal to oppose this, placed the successful completion of the two-year project in serious jeopardy. According to Andrew Derbyshire, it was only due to the backing of their tutors Arthur Korn and Ernesto Rogers that the final thesis was eventually passed (helped, no doubt, by the fact that the lead external examiner happened to be John Madge, a leading figure in the emerging field of urban sociology, who had counselled the group when they started their project).[14]

Self-evidently, Pattrick's measures were not primarily aimed at such outstanding students but at preventing weaker students from being carried by a stronger team. Jordan himself had acknowledged this problem but thought it negligible, and Pattrick, in fairness, soon softened his stance. In fact, despite his stated intention to limit the scope of theses to the 'purely architectural side',[15] in the early 1950s, Zone inspired a succession of similarly ambitious town planning schemes, many of them completed as group exercises. They included Richard Hughes, Terence Powell and Harold Seward's 'Maragua', a development plan for an ideal town in Kenya; Michael Brawne and Gordon Sheere's 'Town as Home' on the North Sea coast; Gordon Collins, Brian Falk, Nigel Grimwade and Roger Waters's 'Daemonia', a new town in south-west England; Denise Scott Brown and Brian Smith's 'Maerdy', a low-rise housing development for a Welsh mining village; and Ronald Jones's futuristic 'Life Structure' (Figs 27–35; Plate 7). Even so, such collaborations were limited to selected thesis students and in the more junior years at least, Jordan's collectivism all but disappeared.

Relations between Pattrick and the students were dealt a further blow when the RIBA followed through with a controversial ruling on its requirements for office experience. Precipitated by reports suggesting that British architects (in comparison with their American counterparts) often lacked a proper grounding in practical knowledge and office procedure, the RIBA had, in November 1949, announced a requirement of 12 months' *postgraduate* office experience before the examination in professional practice could be taken and application for registration and associateship could be made – a directive which came into force in January 1951. At the AA, students were required to complete a year's practical experience *before* they could apply for their diploma, and the retrospectively applied RIBA regulations meant that for those graduating at the end of the 1950/1951 academic year the possibility of entering the profession and earning a living would be delayed by an additional year at just the moment when the postwar employment boom was drawing to an end. Worse still, the RIBA's refusal to set up tribunals to deal with cases of hardship left a sense of 'real bitterness' with AA students, who suspected the school authorities, and Michael Pattrick in particular, of under-representing them on the BAE.[16]

Constructive Proposals and Scathing Attacks

Leery of their principal and alarmed by the apparent monetary difficulties of the AA, which led to a substantial rise in school fees, in the summer of 1952, the students' committee pushed for a joint meeting with the council to 'discuss a number of matters concerning the association and its finances'.[17] Anxious to prevent any attempts by the students to circumvent him and undermine his authority, Pattrick used his influence with the council to ensure that no such meeting took place. Instead, on 8 October 1952, President A. R. F. Anderson invited Pattrick and representatives of the students' committee to join him on a new so-called 'council/staff/students' committee' – an unprecedented, if ultimately short-lived, panel bringing together the various stakeholders with the objective to bridge the 'split between the club and the school' and 'make the AA more of an association'.[18]

Though initially conducted in a constructive, almost amicable fashion, the meetings of the council/staff/students' committee could not dispel the students' mistrust and dislike of Pattrick, who appeared intent on changing the face of the school and who – true to the 'querulousness' which Chitty had attributed to him – aggravated matters by adopting a rather ruthless approach in his dealings with nonconformist students. Over the course of almost two years, the students' committee pursued an overt campaign initiated by Spyer and his vice-chairman, John Smith, to get Pattrick removed from office. Things eventually came to a head at a general meeting of students on 12 March 1953, called to debate a motion of censure on the principal. Just over half of all students attended the gathering and passed an almost unanimous vote of no confidence in the principal and a request to the council to consider a new appointment. The council took a resolute stance, reaffirming its 'complete confidence' in the principal and forbidding the students any further discussion about its employees.[19] Pattrick, who professed himself 'completely unaware [. . .] that something like this was brewing up',[20] hoped that, given his support on the council, he might be able to ease matters with the students. However, despite holding a series of weekly meetings with them during the Easter holidays, in May 1953 he conceded that he was 'not able to say that any common ground of agreement had been reached'.[21]

In fact, Pattrick underestimated the gravity of the situation. Drawing their inspiration from the Yellow Book, the students' committee had appointed a sub-committee to draft a 'Report on Recent Events in the School, and Suggestions Toward a New Policy', which it intended to circulate to the membership.[22] Completed in June 1953, the report was a peculiar hybrid of two wildly inconsistent parts. Its main body outlined the factors which had, in the

students' view, led to 'the present decline of the AA school' and put forward a number of 'constructive proposals' to improve the situation.[23] The majority of these concerned school policy, including the re-introduction of the unit system, the adoption of a liberal educational model and – triggered by recent events and somewhat quixotic – the possible foregoing of RIBA recognition to enable the AA to 'follow its own course unhindered'.[24] In addition, the report listed a number of suggestions relating to the association as a whole, notably the re-branding of the *AA Journal* as a proper architectural magazine run by an editorial board with student participation and – most importantly – the restoration of the student vote. In sharp contrast to these 'constructive proposals' in the main body of the report, the appendix, which gave a history of events over the previous two years, served no discernible purpose other than to launch a scathing attack on the principal and, to a lesser extent, the council itself. Predictably, neither of them was inclined to sanction the dissemination of such a document. On 9 June 1953, the council resolved that 'no lobbying of this nature be permitted',[25] and three days later Pattrick advised the students' committee that a 'deliberate disregard of the council's order' might result in the expulsion of those concerned.[26]

Pattrick rejected the students' justification of their conduct as being in keeping with a 'type of "unwritten" constitution'[27] and acted on the legally sound, if somewhat insensitive, premise that they had 'no constitutional rights whatever'.[28] Even so, he empathised with the students, whose recalcitrance he saw as an understandable reaction to the worsening employment prospects awaiting them upon qualification, and he stubbornly refused to take their attacks personally (even when they were meant to be). Indeed, in a memorandum to the school committee Pattrick asked its members to 'understand that however wild and illogical the students' proposals may be, they are, for the most part, entirely sincere, and therefore deserve serious consideration'.[29] Hugh Casson, who had taken over the presidency from Anderson, agreed and called a meeting of the council/staff/students' committee on 18 June 1953 to examine the report.

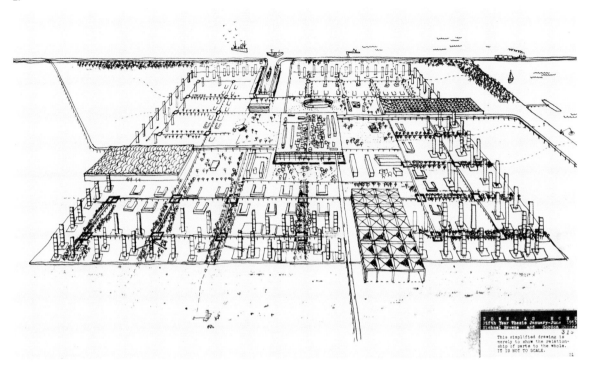

This seven-mile square grid town for 250,000 people on a reclaimed site in the Wash combines a carpet of single-storey courtyard housing with high-rise flats. The layout seems to reverse traditional notions of urbanism by placing the dense grouping of tower blocks along the edge of the site, opening up the centre for low-level civic functions. The thesis echoes current CIAM debates about the need for a 'fifth function' in the form of a civic core, as exemplified by Sert and Wiener's Motor City and Le Corbusier's plan for Saint-Dié. The 25-storey towers are perforated by private terraces for children's play areas overlooked by the flats.

Town as Home (Michael Brawne and Gordon Sheere, thesis, 1952/53)

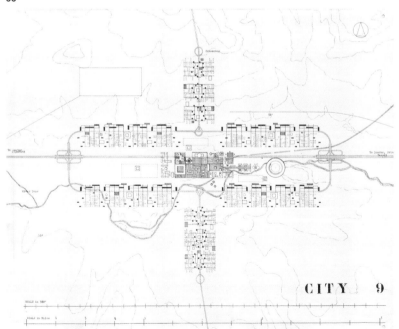

The new town of Daemonia was envisaged as a regional centre in south-west England. Residential tower blocks for 120,000 people were grouped around a new civic core, reflecting the same CIAM preoccupations with the 'heart of the city' that had been the basis of Brawne and Sheere's thesis of the previous year. The symmetrical layout of the scheme was highly unusual at the time and may have been inspired by an exhibition of Liverpool thesis designs at the AA in December 1953. According to the Architects' Journal (3 Dec 1953), the exhibition had displayed 'that curious post-war development, rudely referred to as Maniera Liverpudliana – rigidly symmetrical Beaux-Arts plans (with just the teeniest naughty deviations)'.

Daemonia (Gordon Collins, Brian Falk, Nigel Grimwade, Roger Waters, thesis, 1953/54)

The council representatives, though impressed with the students' constructive proposals, rejected the appendix as being detrimental to the interests of the association and – given the students' unwillingness to withdraw it – categorically refused to issue the report to the membership.[30] Casson warned the students that they might be excluded from the school should they proceed with their plans for publication, and Pattrick himself threatened to take legal action:

> You cannot surely in your wildest dreams imagine that I am going to agree to the circulation of this document on recent history. It would put me in a position of having to sue for damages [. . .]. I would certainly bring an action on it.[31]

Alarmed by indications that the report was being leaked to sympathetic sections of the membership, in the following week the council convened a special meeting to discuss the situation. Pattrick made it clear that he 'did not want to sack anybody',[32] but some members of the council were considerably less lenient. Brandon-Jones felt that 'the time has come now for something to be done',[33] and so did fellow councillor Richard Arthur de Yarburgh-Bateson, an architect with Hertfordshire County Council:

> Regarding what has become the Battle of the Principal, I think that the students should be informed as strongly as possible [. . .] that any student, who is dissatisfied with the way that the Principal is running the school, has the remedy in his own hands. He can seek his architectural education elsewhere.[34]

In spite of this, the council hoped that the discussion on the students' constructive proposals would be continued, and at the beginning of July 1953 Casson called further meetings of the council/staff/students' committee to this end. The student representatives, however, were not content with limiting the debate to their proposals and urged the council to rescind its directive banning any discussion of the association's employees, not least because it prevented the committee from examining their report in full.[35] Unwilling to expose his principal to the humiliation of having his position scrutinised by the students, Casson used a doctor's appointment as an excuse to cancel a follow-up meeting.[36]

The council meanwhile pursued the students' constructive proposals: it set up an 'AA Journal advisory group' (and eventually implemented its recommendation to create an editorial board with student participation), and at a meeting on 13 July 1953 it rather unceremoniously agreed to work towards a restoration of the student vote.[37] When in November 1953 the council/staff/students' committee reconvened once more, the council representatives urged the students to withdraw the appendix of their report, not least because it portrayed them as an irresponsible body and thus hurt their case before the membership. Brandon-Jones, who strongly supported their re-enfranchisement, warned the students that if the paper were leaked to the members it would 'stop all hope of the vote being returned'.[38] Fellow councillor Peter Shepheard, a distinguished architect and landscape designer, concurred:

> We do feel absolutely at the end of our tether. I think if you had any sense at all you would drop this thing and never bring it up again. It is a document which can only be described as childish and does you no good at all.[39]

To the council's incredulity, the students' committee valued its opposition to the principal higher than the implementation of any of its proposals and, on 1 December 1953, resigned en bloc.

The Return of the Student Vote

The plea for a restoration of their voting rights was the most momentous proposal contained in the students' report, and to fully understand the ensuing debate we need to briefly redirect our attention to the immediate postwar years. When the council relinquished its annual MOE grant in March 1946, it effectively removed the obstacle for

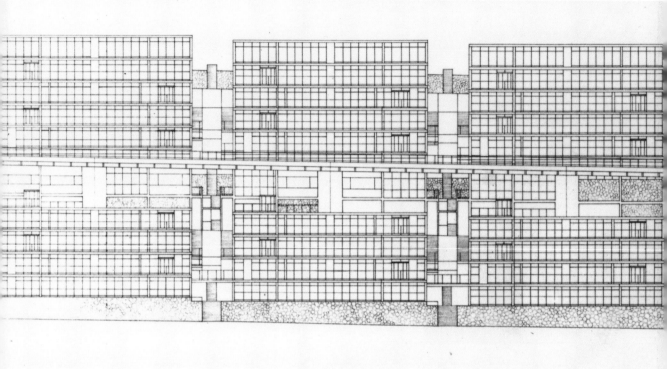

31

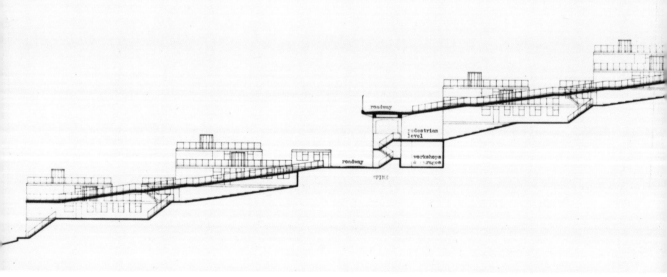

32

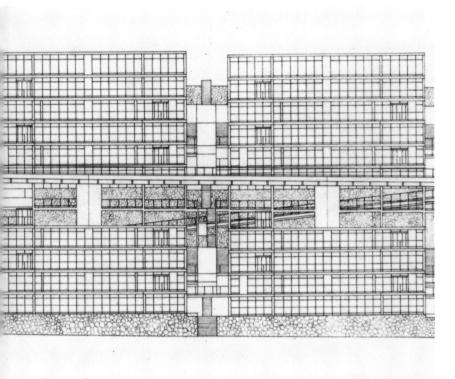

In the early 1950s, the decline of the Welsh mining valleys became increasingly apparent. This was one of two thesis projects in this year which sought to address the issue by modernising their building stock. Denise Scott Brown (née Lakofski) and Brian Smith proposed the extension of an existing village in the form of stepped two-storey housing. The layout of the 750 units has a family likeness with Ludwig Hilbersheimer's city plans and draws on Le Corbusier's low-rise schemes for rural locations such as Sainte-Baume and Roq et Rob.

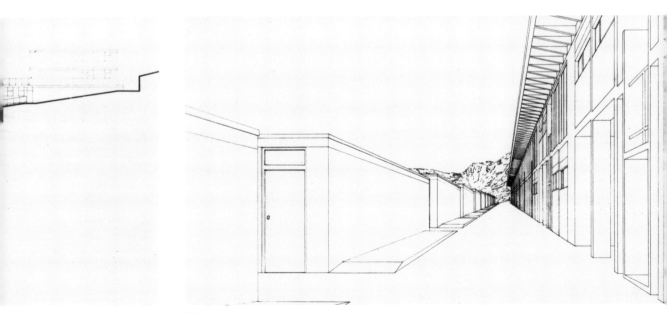

33

Maerdy, Rhondda Fach (Denise Lakofski and Brian Smith, thesis, 1953/54)

34

Life Structure, Year 1954 (Ronald Jones, thesis, 1953/54)

The assumption was that a century of exponential growth would change the concepts of civilisation and require new 'Life Structures' powered by thermal energy wells. Each 'Unit Metropolis' accommodated two million people and consisted of 'Unit Cities', which themselves grew from four monumental 'Unit Towns' linked by travelators. The cardboard model shows one such 'Unit Town' – 2,360 metres long, 560 metres high, and 200 metres wide. It was inspired by Le Corbusier's Unité d'habitation *but reduced the 'vast Marseilles building to the dimensions of a beach bungalow', as the* Times *wrote (22 July 1954).*

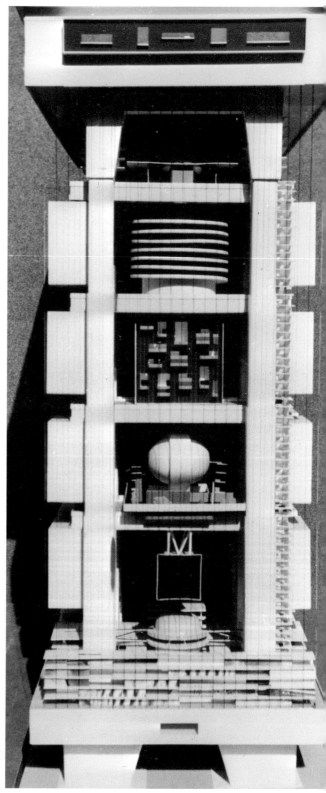

a reinstatement of the student vote. The students' committee soon woke up to this fact and, with Gordon Brown's support, repeatedly asked the council to address the matter. In January 1949, Jordan succeeded Brown as the head of the school, and though the question of the student vote never disappeared entirely from the students' agenda, the initial sense of urgency was clearly lost, presumably because Jordan involved them actively in the school's affairs and their lack of influence on council policy seemed therefore of lesser importance.

Michael Pattrick's appointment changed all this, and in the early 1950s the students' committee pressed the issue of the student vote with growing importunity. Alas, the council was meanwhile preoccupied with finding additional sources of income (see Chapter 7) and, while not in principle averse to the idea of reinstating the students' voting rights, sought to avoid any controversial issue which might jeopardise its negotiations with outside bodies, specifically the MOE. The council did make a tentative approach to Frederick Bray, the responsible under-secretary at the MOE, with the idea of granting limited voting rights to senior students. Bray, however, took an 'unfavourable view' of even a partial restoration of the student vote, and the council left the matter in abeyance.[40]

It was in this situation that in October 1952 President Anderson called the inaugural meeting of the council/staff/students' committee to discuss with the students means of establishing closer ties with the ordinary membership, but also to explain to them the financial predicament of the association and thus the council's hesitation in tackling the question of the student vote. From the students' point of view, the two issues were causally linked since the schism dividing the association evidently only existed because there were two separate classes of membership in the first place. While the students welcomed suggestions for greater cooperation with the membership, they saw these as interim provisions, subordinate to the restoration of the student vote (i.e. the abolition of probationary membership), which they consequently put forward as one of the proposals in their 1953 report.

The students demanded no less than full membership, including the right to elect student members to the council. Pattrick had no objections to students casting their votes for ordinary members, but he rejected any scenario which might result in 'a student in the school to sit on the council'.[41] The staff and council representatives on the council/staff/students' committee, all of whom supported the return of the student vote in some form, generally agreed that there would have to be safeguards to prevent students from controlling the policy of the school (which was, of course, precisely what they had in mind). Nonetheless, the committee advised the council to 'favourably consider the abolition of the probationary membership class and the awarding to students of complete parity of membership with entitlement to vote'.[42] The council duly did so at its meeting on 13 July 1953 though it remained 'confused as to exactly what had been agreed';[43] almost four months later it was, to Pattrick's growing despair, still 'divided in its view as to what form of vote it was intended to recommend the membership to restore'.[44]

The council eventually met on 23 November 1953 to clarify once and for all whether to advance complete parity for students or merely the granting of voting rights, that is, the abolition or the modification of the probationary class of membership. After lengthy debate the council agreed upon the latter course, and within days the AA's solicitor approached the Board of Trade (BOT) to request its (legally required) consent to the necessary alteration in the articles of the association.[45] The students' committee resigned shortly after, and the council/staff/students' committee was dissolved and never reconvened. The students thus forfeited the opportunity to obtain first-hand information of – and possibly contribute to – the protracted negotiations which began at the beginning of the following year, when the BOT – upon consultation with the MOE – declined the council's request.[46]

In a letter to the students' committee, Hugh Casson expressed the council's 'great disappointment' with the BOT's decision and promised to make representation 'at the highest level'.[47] At the end of April 1954, Casson led an AA delegation to meet with Bray, who told them that, as a matter of principle, the MOE considered it reprehensible that students should have control over the government of the school; however, if the AA felt strongly about it, he himself would not object to limited rights being given to students whereby they might vote for not more than two (out of a total of 18) members of the council.[48] While the AA's solicitor was working out a new proposal along these lines, the financial situation of the AA worsened (see p.101), and the council – in the process of approaching possible donors (including the MOE) – informed its advisory council in confidence that the student vote was now 'temporarily an academic question' which was not being considered 'as one of tremendous urgency'.[49]

It was not until November 1954 that the new president, Peter Shepheard, resumed negotiations with the MOE. On 13 December, Shepheard met with Bray to discuss the latest proposal whereby students would have the right to nominate as many candidates for the council as they wished, provided these were full (i.e. non-student) members, but would only be entitled to cast two votes (as opposed to full members, who could cast a maximum of ten votes, one for each ordinary member of the council, the eight officers being returned unopposed).[50] Bray considered this suggestion practicable, and the BOT eventually approved the intended alteration to the articles of association at the end of April 1955.[51] The fact that after protracted negotiations only this relatively mild compromise proved viable showed in all clarity that even at a time of financial self-sufficiency, the AA's room for manoeuvre was severely restricted, its independence largely a myth.

Predictably, when the proposed changes were put up for discussion at a general meeting of AA members on 7 December 1955, many of them expressed disappointment about the fact that they would not 'see the restoration of the 1938 situation'.[52] It was, however, generally accepted that under the circumstances it was the best outcome that could be achieved, and a motion to circulate the voting papers to the membership was passed. Peter Shepheard, due to whose initiative a workable compromise

had finally been manufactured, remained sceptical whether the general membership would actually agree to his proposal. His concerns proved unfounded, for when on 8 March 1956 the result of the postal ballot was announced an overwhelming majority had voted in favour of it. Two months later, the AA elected a new council and both Anthony Cox and Bill Howell, the two candidates put forward by the students' committee, obtained the necessary number of votes.

By the time the student vote was finally restored, the ex-service students, who had originally orchestrated the fight for re-enfranchisement and the dismissal of the principal, had mostly left the school. The last FET-grant-aided students had entered the AA in 1951, and one year later the average age in the first-year course dropped from 24 to 18. The student body in the mid-1950s was not only younger but – unaffected by the hopes and ambitions of the immediate postwar period – politically and socially considerably less enthused. John Miller, who started his course in 1950, when the first signs of this change were becoming evident, remembers being confronted by the promoters of the various political societies on his second day in school: 'We were bemused by these energetic and rather hairy men who came in and tried to ingratiate us into their clubs. I didn't join any of them, nor did any of my mates at the time.'[53] Four years later, Dennis Spencer Roberts, the chairman of the students' committee, expressed his regret about the changed mood among students:

> Symptomatic [. . .] is the virtual extinction of many of the clubs and societies which now exist only on paper, and some not even that. [. . .] I shall not bore you by dwelling too much on the old days, but the difference between 1948 and 1954 is only too apparent to anyone who knows the school.[54]

Peter Shepheard shared the sentiment but not the regret and welcomed that 'the students' committee now consisted much more of people who were level-headed and real leaders in the best sense rather than political leaders'.[55] Times had changed – the 1950s had arrived.

6 The AA School under Michael Pattrick (1951–1961)

New Curriculum

Michael Pattrick was still acting principal when, in October 1951, he recommended that the school revert to the year master system, which Robert Furneaux Jordan had abolished in favour of a division into preliminary, intermediate and final schools. The year master system spread the second-tier responsibility among five rather than three senior members of staff and thus curtailed the influence of the current directors Leonard Manasseh, Kenneth Capon and Henry Elder (who had succeeded David Goddard in the final school). Manasseh stayed on as first-year master until 1953, when he left for Malaya and was replaced by one of his tutors, interior designer Neville Ward. Capon took over the second year, Hilton Wright the third, and Fello Atkinson the fourth. Elder continued as fifth-year master but resigned after only two months in protest at the new principal. Pattrick struggled to fill the vacancy, and in July 1952 he eventually appointed Richard Eve, then working with Hertfordshire County Council, as Elder's successor.

In pedagogical terms the system change was initially of little consequence as Pattrick was reluctant to make changes to the course. It was not until the end of his first session as principal in June 1952 that he announced a revision of the curriculum to be gradually implemented over the following three years. Initial changes were largely limited to the second-year village scheme, which had been conceived by John Brandon-Jones and Arthur Korn in 1947 and expected students to collaborate on a master plan for an existing village as the contextual framework for a number of individual buildings (Fig.26). The RIBA visiting board had singled out this particular element of the curriculum for criticism – partly for the prevalence of group work, which over an extended period of the second year was effectively mandatory, but mostly for the planning aspect of the programme, which the board considered to be too advanced for junior students. Jordan had rejected the board's suggestion that students were asked to 'design a village' and stressed that the context of the village was merely given to introduce students at an early age to 'simultaneous thinking'.[1]

Pattrick concurred with this view: 'Our intention is to make students consider the cottage in its relation to the village as a whole; we do not look upon this programme as an essay in town planning.'[2] Nevertheless, he moved the village scheme to the later part of the third year and instituted a series of shorter and more controlled programmes relating to different basic types of structure in the second.

In the course of the following session, the reorganisation of the second year was complemented by a number of changes in other parts of the course, which together completed the transition to the so-called 'new curriculum' by the beginning of the academic year 1953/54. The common feature of the new subjects was their diminished scale, intended for individual rather than group work. The first part of the third year, for instance, was given to a detailed study of a small building as opposed to the 'first major building' stipulated in Jordan's curriculum (Fig.36). Under both Gordon Brown and Jordan, the fourth year had centred upon complex cultural and industrial schemes, almost always done as group exercises. Under Pattrick, the year became the domain of the 'London Type buildings' – larger structures in compliance with London bylaws, complete with structural calculations and full sets of working drawings – and was divided into one term each for housing, industry and commerce (Figs 37–39). Finally, the greater part of the fifth year was spent on the thesis. Yet while the first term had previously featured another large-scale planning problem, again usually done in groups, Pattrick – probably inspired by the much-debated competition for Coventry Cathedral – asked students to investigate a 'building whose symbolic character is of particular importance and is likely to dominate considerations of planning or structure'.[3] (Neave Brown chose an archaeological faculty (Fig.40); Cedric Price, characteristically, designed a pub (Plate 8).)

'Liberal Education' vs Unit System

The students' dismay about the perceived paradigm shift in the school's pedagogical approach was, as the previous chapter showed, at the heart of their agitation against their principal. In their report of June 1953 they requested that Jordan's popular policy of giving students the freedom to write their own programmes be revived and that the school adopt a 'liberal type of education, such as one gets at a university'.[4] At the same time, the students also called for a return of the unit system, and given the conflicting nature of these two demands, one is inclined to sympathise with Pattrick, who complained that the students 'don't know what they want, but they don't like what they have got'.[5] As Beak Adams, the students' strongest ally on the council and one who had started his course under the unit system and completed it under Jordan, pointed out:

If you have a liberal system with a tutor and you all do different things, then to me it seems to be entirely against the unit system of education where you have a small group of people working together and terribly closely with the man who is teaching them.[6]

Pattrick was ready to concede that 'one or two students might benefit from a completely free system' but adamant that for the majority of students this was not the case, especially now that their average age was dropping.[7] He was, moreover, convinced that the school had a responsibility to keep a close check on students and that failure to do so would be tantamount to forfeiting RIBA recognition, which in turn would almost certainly result in parents withdrawing their children from the school – a risk neither he nor the council was prepared to take.[8]

The students' plea for a reintroduction of the unit system found a more favourable reception. In its original form, the system had been based on 15 term-based units, each ideally numbering between 15 and 17 students. If one wished to avoid the administrative and pedagogical problems involved in organising several parallel units within terms, there was evidently a mathematical limit to the size of institution in which the unit system could be operated. Realising that the school would soon reach twice that size, Gordon Brown had abolished the unit system in 1945; tellingly, Jordan, who left little else in the school untouched, never tried to reinstate it. The reduction of the number of students to pre-war levels made the unit system once more a viable option, and contrary to the students' suspicions there was ample support for its reintroduction within the council.

Pattrick, who had studied under the unit system, appreciated its advantages but was conscious of its inherent drawbacks, specifically the problem of synchronising the annual lecture course with termly entry, which had driven Frederick Gibberd to despair. To tackle this issue, Pattrick revived the idea of a parallel unit system, whereby students would enter the school in September and work together as a 'year' before being split into parallel streams of

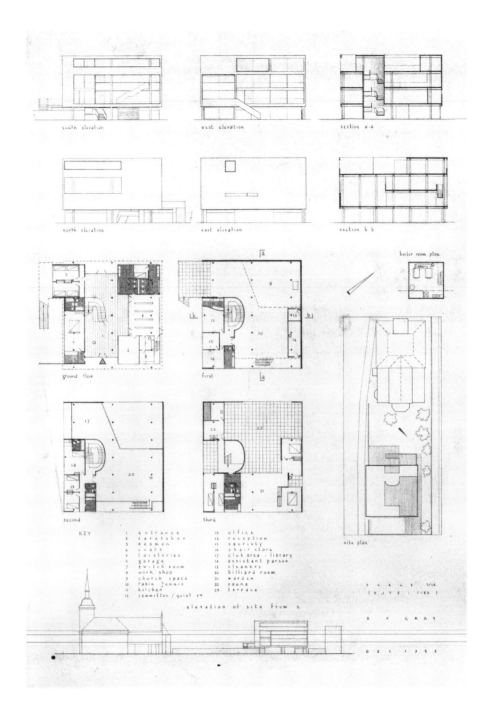

36 Finnish Seamen's Mission (David Gray, third year, 1952/53)

In the early 1950s, a close-knit group of students which included Neave Brown, David Gray, Kenneth Frampton, Patrick Hodgkinson, Ram Karmi and John Miller rediscovered the source material of early continental modernism. Gray's Seamen's Mission, with its grid of pilotis, horizontal windows and sheltered roof terrace, was evidently inspired by Le Corbusier's villas of the interwar years, notably the Villa Stein and the Villa Savoye. Much of this work was known through books and magazines, and the relative dryness of the students' plans and elevations emulated the lack of detail in drawings prepared for small-scale reproduction in black-and-white publications.

approximately 16 students each at the beginning of their second year. The chief advantage of this system was that it retained annual entry and therefore did not require changes to the lecture programme or the curriculum itself. Yet it was not without its downside in that the need to coordinate a greater number of unit masters instead of four-year masters would put a heavier administrative burden on the principal. More problematically, these senior members of staff would have to be paid accordingly. Treasurer Denis Clarke Hall resisted the scheme for months before succumbing to pressure from Pattrick and the school committee and offering to meet the inevitable deficit from the association's limited reserves.[9] On 22 March 1954, the council formally inaugurated the new unit system.[10]

Staff Recruitment under the Unit System

In October 1951, when considering Pattrick's candidature, S. E. T. Cusdin had wondered whether he carried sufficient weight and was an agreeable personality likely to recruit teaching staff. Cusdin's concerns soon appeared justified as Pattrick's initial staffing efforts looked uninspired when compared to his predecessor's. In part this was due to the council's policy of reducing the number of students, which often obviated the need to replace retiring staff. Yet even when vacancies arose, as was the case when Elder left, Pattrick struggled to attract applications, not least because unlike other schools the AA could neither afford to offer prospective teachers a pension plan nor pay them competitive salaries. For this reason, too, Pattrick was compelled to put an end to the engagement of foreign staff as the growing disparity between salaries in Britain and abroad (and in particular the United States) made any attempt at continuing the internationalism of previous years illusory. Unaware of his financial predicament, the students put the blame for the unsatisfactory personnel situation on their principal, alleging that his appointment had caused popular members of staff to resign.[11]

The claim was easily rebutted as only Elder had in fact left because of Pattrick and staff turnover was demonstrably slower than in previous years. Even so, Pattrick shared the students' dissatisfaction with the current staff makeup, and one reason why he pushed so vigorously for the reintroduction of the unit system was the fact that it would give him free rein to reshape it to his liking.

There were initially no major changes in those parts of the course which were not affected by the new system. Neville Ward stayed on as first-year master until March 1956, when he relinquished his position in favour of John Dennys, a postwar graduate of the AA best known for the modernist manor house he later built for the Duke of Westminster at Eaton Hall. The fifth year was ultimately not divided into units, and Richard Eve continued to run it until May 1957, when he was replaced by Peter Smithson, who had joined the staff in February 1955 as a tutor and then unit master in the fourth year. Pattrick approached 22 candidates to fill the new staff positions in the second, third and fourth years. Of the current year masters, who had a running contract and were therefore by default included in this list, Oliver Carey (second year) took over one of the second-year units, while the other two – Ronald Sims (third year) and Fello Atkinson (fourth year) – declined. Also approached were eight part-time members of staff, two of whom – Arthur Korn and Gordon Michell – were prepared to run a unit. In addition to these Denys Lasdun, John Killick and Peter Moro accepted Pattrick's offer, but not Donald Reay, Pattrick's rival for the principalship three years prior.

Given the vigour with which its members had campaigned for the unit system as students, there is a certain irony in the fact that the Architects' Co-Partnership was the prime casualty of its (partial) reintroduction. With the virtual abolition of teamwork in 1951 the group's collaborative approach had become somewhat anachronistic and following the revision of its second-year course, its influence in the school gradually diminished. In March 1952, the school committee expressed doubts whether the staffing arrangement with ACP was 'entirely satisfactory',[12] and when it was discussed in council, one member – Basil Ward of Connell, Ward and Lucas – objected against it in principle as he felt 'they would try to impose their views on architecture on the school'.[13] Although Pattrick defended the arrangement against repeated criticism from the council, in 1953 Capon lost his position as second-year master to Carey, and the group was broken up, with three of its seven members subsequently tutoring in Atkinson's fourth-year course. In May 1954, Pattrick offered two unit master positions to ACP, but they all declined.

Such rejections notwithstanding, the introduction of the unit system invigorated Pattrick's staffing efforts, presumably because the prospect of having sole responsibility for their teaching programmes without having to answer to a superior year master appealed to the more mission-conscious among the leading young architects.[14] To fill the remaining posts, Pattrick engaged Elizabeth Chesterton for the second year, and Stirling Craig for the third. Chesterton, an AA graduate and leading planning consultant, was the first woman to join the studio staff since 1946; Craig, formerly with the Stevenage Development Corporation, was currently setting up in private practice with his wife Margaret. An interesting novelty was the presence of David Jones, an architect with the Ministry of Works. Unlike Brown and Jordan, who had been equally eager to attach public architects to their teaching staff, Pattrick, in February 1954, succeeded in negotiating an agreement with Leslie Martin, the chief architect to the LCC, whereby members of his staff would be given a period of leave to teach full-time at the AA.[15] Martin was at first unable to release an architect from his staff, and Pattrick presented the scheme to other public offices, including the Ministry of Education and the Ministry of Works, both of which pledged their support. Thus, in the academic year 1954/55 David Jones joined the third year, followed one year later by future RMJM partner Hugh Morris, then an architect with the LCC, who took charge of a second-year unit.

The most far-reaching changes occurred in the fourth year, initially run by Killick, Korn and Lasdun. Though permitted to conduct the teaching and supervision of his unit from his office, Lasdun

resigned after only one term due to pressure of work, while Korn relinquished his position after two years and rejoined the fifth-year tutorial staff. Unlike many of his colleagues, Killick considered teaching a calling rather than a mere stopgap and prioritised it over his private work. His professional experience and predilection made him particularly suited to run a unit in the fourth year, which increasingly centred on urban renewal tasks. (Incidentally, the mere scope of these tasks made a return of group working almost inevitable – a development which Pattrick himself had anticipated.) Drawing on connections with his former employer, Killick always related his programmes to current LCC problems, be it a commercial development in the hotly debated St Paul's precinct or high-density housing for Paddington using the site of the controversial Kadleigh-Horsbrugh proposal (Figs 43–46), which not only raised their appeal for students but gave them relevance beyond the confines of the school. In October 1955, Leslie Martin exhibited the St Paul's proposals at County Hall and one year later *Architectural Design* featured a number of housing schemes from Killick's course alongside, and almost indistinguishable from, real-life projects by Chamberlin, Powell and Bon.[16] Killick hoped that some of these schemes 'may become pointers' for CIAM 10 and its discussion on the subject of 'habitat' in an urban context.[17] Closer to home, Killick used his influence to link student work into a broader architectural discourse when in January 1957 he became the editor of the *AA Journal* at the students' suggestion.

The Department of Tropical Architecture

Two novelties characterised Pattrick's course in the first half of the 1950s, neither of which resulted from his own initiative. The new curriculum, instituted in 1953, combined a number of measures necessitated by RIBA pressure, while the reintroduction of the unit system in the following year was the outcome of student agitation. Unlike Jordan, Pattrick was not

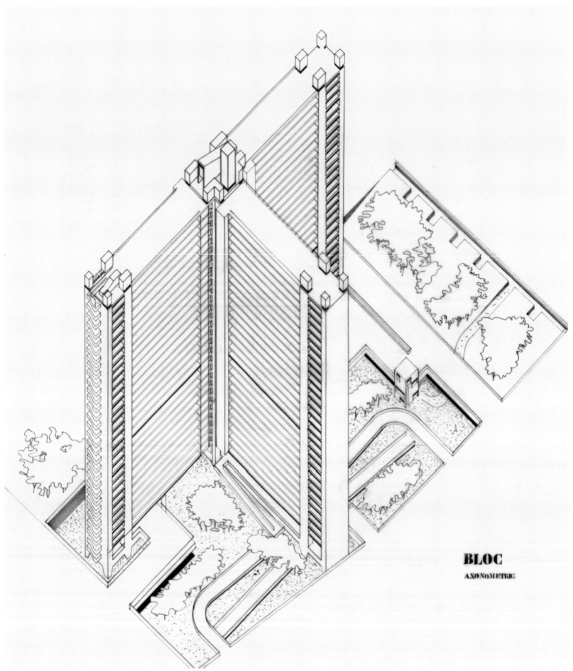

BLOC
AXONOMETRIC

Offices (Adrian Gale, fourth year, 1954/55)

Much of the student work in the senior years was marked by rigidly geometric planning and the pervasive – and often simultaneous – influence of Le Corbusier's Unité d'habitation *and Miesian office buildings such as Lever House. Adrian Gale's curtain-walled office block, with its tapering concrete columns and its sculptural roofscape, is a particularly striking example of this trend.*

38

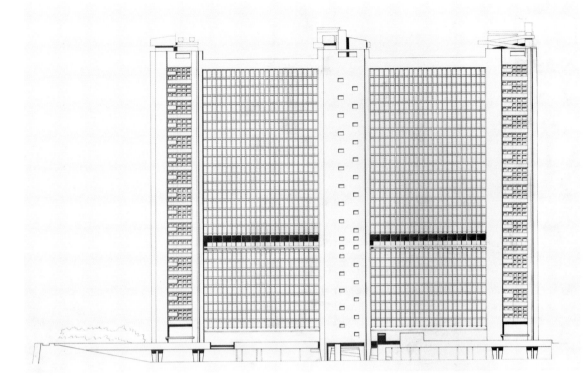

39

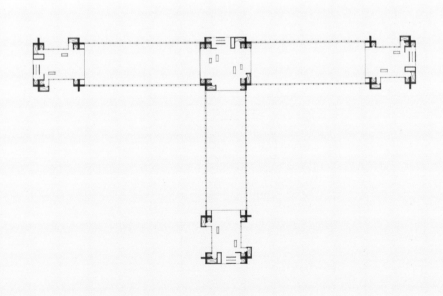

motivated by an overarching vision for the AA. He had no intention of revolutionising the pedagogical system of the school and was content with making specific adjustments if and when they were required. Pattrick sought to prepare his students for their work as practising architects by infusing the course with the utmost sense of realism, but he pursued this in a rather more pragmatic way than his predecessor. Questions as to how architects could maintain their role as leaders of the integrated building teams of the future were of secondary importance – Pattrick's main concern was with the here and now:

> However much [. . .] the students may desire radical changes in the building industry, we realise that these changes are not going to come about overnight. It is therefore our duty to train our students to take their place within the framework of the industry as it is today.[18]

Accordingly, Pattrick's most ambitious schemes aimed at maximising the students' job prospects under current conditions. Invited to submit evidence to the RIBA's McMorran Committee (see the next chapter), in January 1953 Pattrick drafted a letter on behalf of the AA which focused solely on the 'relationship between the training and the later employment of the architect' and put forward three proposals for consideration.[19] The first of these called for office training to become an essential part of any recognised course, while the other two revolved around the idea of a two-tier qualification for architects, with the higher level taking the form of postgraduate training confined to students of proven ability. The council agreed that these proposals were to form the basis of future policy, 'whether they were accepted by the [McMorran] Committee or not'.[20]

Both Brown and Jordan had advanced the idea of an 'office adoption scheme' but failed to implement it owing to lack of support from architectural practices. Equally eager to feed the 'better side of the pupillage system'[21] back into the school curriculum, Pattrick through most of the decade operated such a scheme for second-year students though his plan to

eventually expand it over the entire course faltered on the resistance of his staff, who criticised its disruptive effect on the curriculum.[22] By far the more important suggestion in Pattrick's submission to the McMorran Committee concerned provisions for postgraduate training, aimed at limiting the number of subjects in the syllabus and thus preserving – or even shortening – the length of the basic course at a time of increasingly demanding requirements for specialist knowledge within the profession. The list of potential subjects which the AA put forward included town planning, landscape architecture, structure, interior decoration, and industrial design; yet from July 1953 the idea of a course in tropical architecture took precedence.

The lack of information about the specific challenges involved in building in the tropics was a matter of growing concern in British architectural circles – Gordon Brown, now in Hong Kong, was one of many who complained about it in a letter to the *Architect and Building News* in May 1951.[23] In March 1953, University College London organised a one-week conference on tropical architecture, which brought together a small group of architects and scientists with expert knowledge in the matter and passed a five-point resolution calling, among other things, for 'improved educational facilities for students and architects interested in work in the tropics and particularly the establishment of permanent centres for the study of architecture and planning at ordinary and post-graduate level'.[24] Addressing a general meeting of the AA in the following month, George Atkinson, the colonial liaison officer to the Building Research Station and one of the conveners of the conference, reaffirmed the need to provide specialised training for the great number of British architects required for work in the tropics: 'Is there not room for at least one school to take a special interest in tropical architecture?'[25]

The AA, with its traditionally strong links to the colonies and dominions, seemed particularly well-suited for such an endeavour. By 1947, more than a hundred practising architects in the dominions had trained at the AA,[26] and in the immediate postwar period the school continued to attract a significant number of students from the developing world.

Many of these would have a profound impact on developments in their home countries, including Sri Lankan architects Minette de Silva, Geoffrey Bawa and Valentine Gunasekara; Chen Voon Fee and William Siew Wai Lim, founder-members of the ACP-inspired Malayan Architects Co-Partnership; and Shanghai-native Stanley Kwok, who practised in Hong Kong for 20 years (and then became a major real-estate developer in Vancouver). Moreover, the leading British practices operating in late-colonial Africa were largely composed of AA graduates. These included ACP and James Cubitt Partners (Fello Atkinson, Stefan Buzas and Dick Maitland), who worked across the continent, as well as Kenneth Scott Associates (Michael Willis and Geoffrey Spyer) in Ghana, Richard Hughes in Kenya, John Godwin and Gillian Hopwood in Nigeria, and John R. Harris in the Arabian Gulf.

When Otto Koenigsberger, a researcher at the London School of Hygiene and Tropical Medicine, approached the AA with a tentative proposal for a course in tropical architecture, Pattrick seized the opportunity.[27] In October 1953, he formed a committee consisting of Atkinson, Koenigsberger, Leo De Syllas and himself to consider how a self-supporting and largely autonomous 'Department of Tropical Architecture' might operate within the AA. Owing to Koenigsberger's preparatory work, it took the committee merely two months to work out a draft syllabus. Targeted primarily at British postgraduates but also open to overseas architects and selected fifth-year students of the AA, the six-month, full-time course was to comprise specialist lectures on climatology, tropical air-conditioning and socio-economic aspects, complemented by a series of design exercises related to different tropical conditions. On 4 January 1954, the council approved the report of the committee and inaugurated the DTA, the first non-planning related postgraduate department in any British school of architecture.[28]

Pattrick approached 43 organisations and government departments to secure the starting capital, and in April 1954, Maxwell Fry agreed to supervise the course, which was to commence in October. The number of applications was three times higher than anticipated, and instead of 12 the school eventually admitted 30 students (Figs 41–42; Plate 9). The quality and content of the course, however, fell short of the expectations of the first cohort of AA students, and their co-existence with international postgraduates was not without problems. Two AA students – David Gray and Neave Brown – caused annoyance with the DTA staff by refusing to collaborate with foreign students, and the school committee warned that 'in future if any student showed a similar uncooperative attitude towards the Course, he should be asked to leave it immediately'.[29] Hans Heyerdahl Hallen, a South African architect who spent a year at the AA as a postgraduate and attended DTA crits, remembers an air of prejudice:

> As a South African I was considered a 'Colonial', not worth listening to! Few thought that critiques from people who had experienced sub-tropical climates were worth listening to. Geoffrey Bawa and I, who grew up and practised in this sort of climate, were ignored. It gave us both a laugh.[30]

Even so, as far as the school authorities were concerned, the fact that in June 1955 the Tema Development Corporation in Accra announced the recruitment of five highly paid DTA graduates for its operations alone, justified a course intended to generate employment opportunities for its participants. Although the number of applications decreased, James McKay Spence, who had replaced Fry as the head of the department, had no difficulties filling the desired 15 places for the second instalment.[31] In spite of this, there were growing doubts regarding the future of the department. In June 1956, Fry, who had joined the DTA's advisory committee, predicted a decline in the demand for British architects with special expertise in tropical architecture and recommended that the course be dropped.[32] Spence announced his resignation, but the council – on Pattrick's insistence – committed to continuing the DTA for at least another two sessions and appointed Otto Koenigsberger as its new director.[33]

Koenigsberger's arrival in October 1957 proved beneficial for the DTA. Despite frequent absences

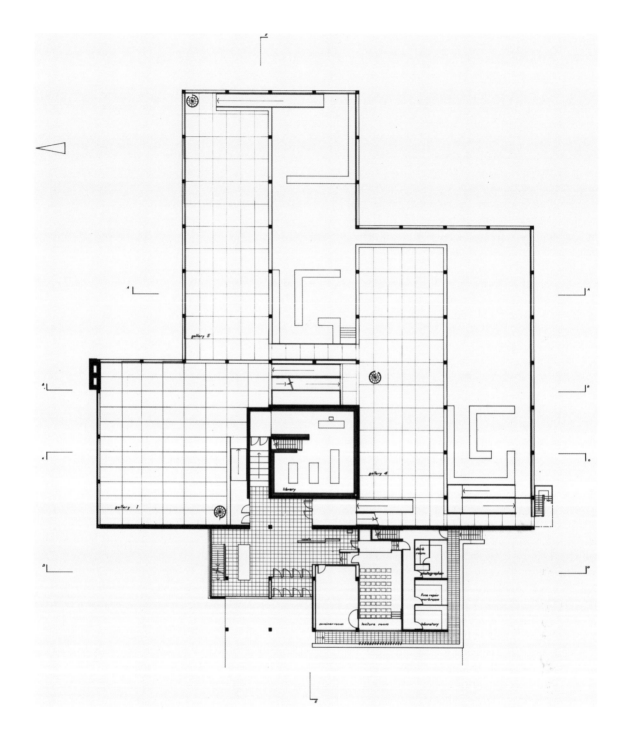

40   Library, Gallery and Faculty of Classical Archaeology (Neave Brown, thesis, 1954/55)

Neave Brown took two terms for his 'symbolic building' and turned it into his thesis project. Brown belonged to a group of students with firm Corbusian leanings but gradually expanded his formal repertoire and adopted a more intuitive approach inspired by Alvar Aalto. The pinwheel grouping of separate yet unarticulated volumes around a central circulation core was a characteristic feature of the work which he and fellow students such as John Miller and David Gray produced at that time.

as expert advisor overseas, Koenigsberger managed to run the department with great success at a time when its complexion changed rapidly. Fry's prediction had been vindicated sooner than expected as the interest of domestic students began to decline from the second session onward. Though intended as a further education and employment scheme for British architects, the DTA soon mutated into a finishing school for overseas professionals. Nineteen of the 30 participants of the inaugural course had been students or recent graduates of the AA, with the remaining third coming predominantly from developing countries. (The DTA never succeeded in attracting a significant number of non-AA British graduates.) As the British colonies attained independence, the number of AA students gradually dropped, and towards the end of the decade the DTA usually had around 20 participants and never more than one from within the AA. Instead, the course attracted predominantly civil servants from the newly independent countries, most but by no means all of them former British territories.[34]

Koenigsberger responded to the diverse educational backgrounds of his polyglot student body by devising a highly structured curriculum based on a lecture programme that was closely linked to the corresponding design subjects and incorporated feedback mechanisms to inform future instalments of the course.[35] For the same reason, too, the emphasis of the course lay on climatic (rather than social or economic) factors, which allowed Koenigsberger to bypass national specificities and focus on commonalities instead.[36] Ignoring precedent and with an unquestioned faith in the fundamental appropriateness of modern architecture underpinning the enquiry, Koenigsberger relied on building science to investigate climatic considerations and offer universally applicable strategies to deal with them.[37] It was this scientific bias, aimed at grasping 'fundamental principles' rather than relying on 'ready made recipes',[38] which distinguished Koenigsberger's course from his predecessors' and allowed it to make a seamless transition from the late-colonial job creation scheme, as originally conceived, to the unrivalled post-colonial

educational and research hub that it would subsequently become.

The DTA never trained a significant number of British architects for work in the tropics – the time for this had passed – but it did further the education of a large number of architects whose names might be less familiar to Western readers but who contributed significantly to the built environment in their home (or, in some cases, adopted) countries. These included architects in private practice such as Kamil Khan Mumtaz in Pakistan, Muzharul Islam in Bangladesh, Pheroze Kudianavala in India, and Israeli architect Zalman Enav, who worked extensively in Ethiopia in the 1960s. They also included official architects such as Joseph Ranford Jarrett-Yaskey and Alim Jallo-Jamboria, chief architects to the Sierra Leonean Ministry of Works; Gopal Singh Nandiwal, the chief town planner to the Government of Rajasthan; and Daniel Dunham and Kul Ratna Tuladhar, who both designed major infrastructure projects in their respective countries – the former in Bangladesh as chief architect to engineering consultants Berger, the latter as chief engineer of Nepal's Public Works Department.

The success of the DTA inspired proposals for a number of similar postgraduate schemes, the most important of which was the so-called 'Department of Building Management', which the AA pursued over a period of three years in conjunction with leading members of the building industry and which was eventually superseded by the MOE's plan for an integrated 'College of Building Technology' in 1957 (see the next chapter). Another scheme which preoccupied the AA in the second half of the 1950s was Graeme Shankland's proposal for a postgraduate department in urban design, which was abandoned in January 1958 after two years of planning as the AA found itself unable to cover the anticipated starting deficit. Unperturbed by these setbacks, Pattrick, who was convinced of the need to provide facilities for postgraduate specialisation, continued to advance similar projects, including separate departments for building services, landscape architecture and the 'care of old buildings'. Ultimately, though, all his attempts to emulate the success of the DTA failed.

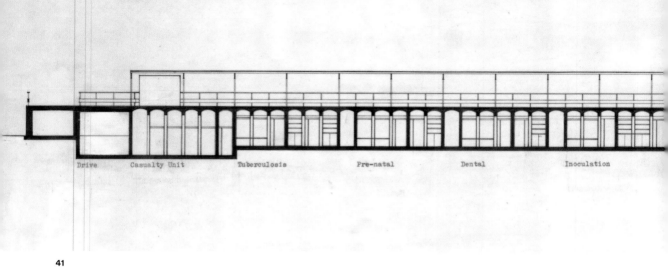

Drive   Casualty Unit   Tuberculosis   Pre-natal   Dental   Inoculation

41

Health Centre in Iraq (Kenneth Frampton and John Miller, DTA, 1954/55)

The Department of Tropical Architecture was initially popular with selected fifth-year students. There was a missionary element to this, but mostly the students joined with a view to seizing a slice of the job market in the colonies at a time when building production in the United Kingdom was low. This scheme for a health centre in Iraq is a fairly typical example of the work of the DTA in these early years. There was a strong belief in the universal rightness of modernist planning and technology, responses to the tropical context were largely limited to an acknowledgment of the prevailing wind and humidity conditions and to the occasional use of non-Western design features.

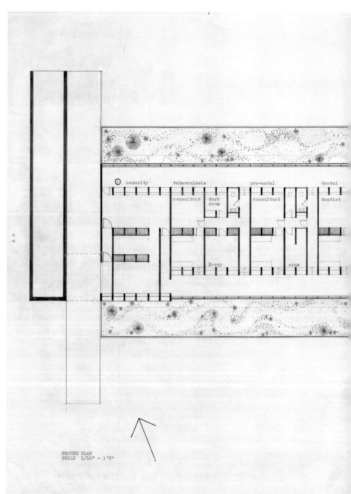

GROUND PLAN
SCALE 1/10" = 1'0"

42

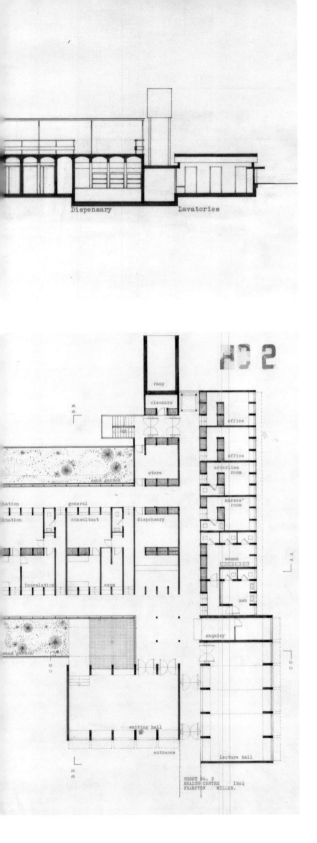

Dispensary   Lavatories

ramp

cleaners

up

store

office

office

orderlies room

nurses' room

women

men

...ation ...ination   general   consultant   dispensary

isoolation   exam

sand garden

enquiry

waiting hall

entrance   lecture hall

SHEET No. 2
HEALTH CENTRE   IRAQ
FRAMPTON   MILLER.

Brutalist Eclecticism

The unit system and the DTA revitalised the AA after the relative stalemate of the previous years and contributed to raising its international profile. From 1955, distinguished foreign visitors inspected the school on a regular basis, and an exhibition illustrating the AA's curriculum travelled to all corners of the globe. In July 1956, impressed with the work of its principal, the council reappointed him for another five-year period. In his second term in office, Pattrick assumed a more directorial role, similar to Brown's ten years prior: he involved himself more actively in the council's policy considerations, and he spent considerable time nurturing the AA's international contacts while leaving the day-to-day affairs in the hands of his trusted senior staff.

The heightened reputation of the AA in the second half of the 1950s owed much to the fact that it provided a home for the vanguard of British architecture, notably Peter Smithson and John Killick, at just the moment when, through their activities in CIAM and the agency of *Architectural Design*, they were thrust into the international limelight. In 1954, the Smithsons had completed their Miesian school at Hunstanton, while Killick and his future partners Howell, Partridge and Amis were designing the Alton West estate at Roehampton, the first large-scale adaptation of Le Corbusier's *Unité d'habitation*. Both schemes attracted international interest and are today seen as early examples of an architectural style – Brutalism – which from the late 1950s began to spread worldwide.

The use of the term 'Brutalism', nowadays indiscriminately applied to almost any building in exposed concrete, requires clarification. In 1966, Reyner Banham, in an attempt to claim British provenance for what was clearly an international phenomenon, proposed a differentiation between 'New Brutalism' as a distinctly British 'ethic' and 'Brutalism' as an internationally applied 'aesthetic'.[39] Despite the obvious difficulties involved in synthesising a definite relationship between the two, illustrated by Banham's failure to provide a coherent canon of buildings, historians such as Kenneth Frampton – who from the early 1980s onward established Brutalism as an integral part of the historiography of twentieth-century architecture – by and large adopted his line of argument.[40] More recent scholarship has done little to negotiate the dichotomy inherent in Banham's definition, with writers either situating Brutalism within the international Team 10 context of the late 1950s and early 1960s and thus to some degree downgrading the British contribution or, conversely, embedding it in the London art discourse of the early 1950s and divorcing it from subsequent architectural developments.

Banham's British bias was understandable since – while the Brutalist style derived from Le Corbusier's postwar oeuvre and had its parallels in other countries – the rhetoric surrounding the term 'Brutalism' (albeit not the term itself) was undeniably homegrown. The Smithsons first used it to describe their unbuilt project for a house in Soho in December 1953,[41] and their prominence among young British architects ensured that it triggered a sustained debate in the correspondence columns of the architectural press (and presumably many a social gathering).[42] It is noteworthy how closely this debate remained linked to the Smithsons' thinking. Independent views on Brutalism were conspicuously absent as contributors confined themselves to interpreting the possible meaning of the Smithsons' characteristically obscure statements, much like the ancient Greeks tried to make sense of Pythia's prophecies. Robin Middleton argued that Brutalism was essentially 'what [the Smithsons] said and did', and in the 1950s the two were indeed coextensive.[43]

The Smithsons themselves did little to clarify matters as their priorities shifted over time. Hunstanton, their Brutalist manifesto scheme ante litteram, was a major contribution to the postwar discourse on proportion; in January 1955, they published their first written statement on Brutalism, stressing its affinity to 'peasant dwelling forms', which provided the ideological backdrop for the MARS Group's village housing schemes for CIAM 10;[44] in the same year, Banham, in consultation

with the Smithsons, published his own take on Brutalism, introducing image memorability as one of its objectives and a-formalism based on topology as the methodological device to accomplish it;[45] finally, in 1959, the Smithsons linked their definition of Brutalism to their growing preoccupation with urbanism: 'The essential ethic of Brutalism is in town planning.'[46] In other words, the Smithsons' priorities changed, and so did their notion of Brutalism.

The one consistent thread running through the Smithsons' writings was a recall to first principles and a corresponding insistence on 'clear exhibition of structure' and 'valuation of materials "as found"', to use Banham's phrasing.[47] The Smithsons saw these as the core values of early modernism (i.e. prior to its being codified as an International Style and popularised for local consumption at the Festival of Britain) and called for a 're-evaluation of those advanced buildings of the twenties and thirties whose lessons [. . .] have been forgotten'.[48] There was just a little step from 're-evaluating' to emulating or even imitating these buildings, and in principle at least the Smithsons' approach differed little from the historicism of previous eras apart from the fact that their models stemmed from the more recent past. In its essence, Brutalism was, as Banham himself conceded, 'modern-movement historicism'.[49]

This notion resonated with AA students such as Robert Maguire, Neave Brown, David Gray, Patrick Hodgkinson and John Miller, who were equally disenchanted with the state of modern architecture in their country and sought their inspiration for a new formal expression in the 'heroic period' of continental modernism. As Miller recalled: 'It seemed in the early fifties that architecture had been diverted from its true antecedents and, in consequence, the source material of the 1920s and 1930s was exhumed after being neglected for over a decade.'[50] It seems worth pointing out in this context that these students' reaction against the Festival style in the form of a modern-movement revival was immediate and noticeable in third-year student work by, for instance, Gray and Hodgkinson as early as 1952 (Fig.36). It should therefore be seen as a largely independent process which, though echoing the Smithsons' activities, was not directly influenced by them and predated their first substantive writings.

While the derivative idiom of the Festival of Britain provided its most readily available target, the students' architectural insurrection was driven by a more deep-seated disillusionment with the postwar building programme and its lack of formal vigour. In a talk to the AA in April 1954, fourth-year student Colin Glennie acknowledged the high standard of housing and schools in the country but maintained that 'architecture is not simply the fulfilling of a social programme'.[51] Two months later, fellow student Neave Brown expressed the changing attitude in the school as follows:

> By the immediate post-war students the work was seen to have an enormous social importance to the community, far more than its particular aesthetic importance, but now we see around us the failure of so many schemes, and the student's sense of responsibility has become more introverted, and he considers how his work is an aesthetic contribution to what may be called Western culture.[52]

A mystified Lewis Mumford urged the AA's students not to follow Mies and Le Corbusier into the 'bottomless pit [. . .] of purely formal and aesthetic solutions'.[53] Yet, with Killick emerging as the dominant force in the fourth year and Smithson taking charge of the fifth, the students' preoccupation with matters of style gathered momentum. Smithson was clear about his intentions:

> Style is a problem that I think has been completely neglected since the days of William Morris. [. . .] In the key year of 1913 there were the beginnings of four distinct architectural styles: Constructivism, de Stijl, Purism and Bauhaus. Each of these movements had an attitude and a complete, comprehensive, plastic system, that is what used to be known as style. The schools and institutes, the academies of today, do not teach style. They make no approach to the problem of architecture; they make an approach to

technology, to technique, but the central problem of creating an actual architecture they ignore.[54]

Smithson's impact was felt throughout the AA. In a series of packed-out lectures to the entire school, he drew upon Banham's research into the early history of modern architecture to direct the students' attention to its 'major minor figures'[55] (notably the futurists and expressionists), thus expanding the catalogue of possible precedents and placing 'modern-movement historicism' on a much broader basis. In doing so, Smithson was chiefly responsible for the Brutalist eclecticism which took hold of the AA in the late 1950s. Discussing the annual exhibition of student work in 1957, the *Architects' Journal* noted that 'one can pick one's style according to one's taste, particularly if it is early 20th Century',[56] and according to Cook, Killick alone absorbed a year consisting of 'five Christian Weirdies, two Bowellists, half a dozen proto-Neo-Futurists, recherché Edwardians and various persons of no particular persuasion at all'.[57]

Smithson and Killick's own work at the time reflected the changing mood. In 1956, they prepared a sculpturally bold scheme for the Sydney Opera competition consisting of two asymmetrical auditoria cantilevered from a central tower, with the exteriors covered in mosaic and the interiors lined with a tortoise-like shell made of lacquered scarlet and crimson. Peter Cook felt that Smithson and Killick's joint submission was 'the link back to the student work carried out under their wing',[58] and the students' creative efforts more than matched their masters' formal audacity (Figs 45–58). According to the *Architects' Journal*, the AA was 'losing its Miesian calm',[59] and Michael Pattrick observed a predilection for 'the irregular, the severe, the brooding and sometimes the convulsive', which he suspected 'might come as a disagreeable surprise [to] architects who have spent the last twenty years lightening and refining every detail over their buildings'.[60]

Though both Killick and Smithson nurtured this formal exuberance, their tolerance of eccentric deviators had its limits, particularly when they resorted to pre-modern precedents. Killick, for instance, fiercely opposed the work of the 'Christian Weirdies', a group including Andrew Anderson, Malcolm Higgs and Quinlan Terry, whose quest for originality found its stimulus in Arts and Crafts models (Plate 10).[61] According to John Outram – one of the 'Bowellists' and later a pioneering figure in British postmodernism – by the time Smithson left the AA in the autumn of 1960 he too had become increasingly uncomfortable about his part in inspiring the extreme eclecticism in his students' work: 'Smithson said he regretted giving these lectures because they had created this enormous outburst of strange buildings, but it was too late by then.'[62]

Smithsonian Curriculum

Though the AA witnessed a recognisable drive towards Brutalism, in the mid-1950s it still co-existed with other tendencies. The second year, for instance, remained firmly in the hands of the 'Festival generation' (mainly Oliver Carey and Elizabeth Chesterton); in the third there was James Gowan, who was in the process of building the canonically Brutalist Ham Common flats, but there was also Stirling Craig, who had been responsible for the displays exhibited in the Festival of Britain's Dome of Discovery; the fourth year had John Killick, whose hard-edged housing estate was going up in Roehampton, but it also had Leonard Manasseh, who had designed the cheerful '51 Bar for the Festival and continued to pursue a mild-mannered form of modernism. Not surprisingly, there was growing consensus among students and staff that the school's lack of a guiding philosophy was making it difficult to discern what precisely its aims and objectives were.

Pattrick shared this assessment, but he saw the school's eclecticism as an appropriate reflection of a British architectural landscape marked by factional disputes and the absence of a unifying theory, and he deliberately reinforced it through his staffing policy. While fundamentally opposed to imposing his own views on the school, Pattrick saw it as the duty of his tutors to advocate theirs with conviction:

[The architectural teacher] cannot just stand aside and wait for somebody to produce an argument which has universal acceptance. He is expected to offer guidance and criticism. He must have a point of view and establish in his own mind a basis for criticism. The fact that his theory is an individual one rather than universal may be his misfortune, but in the present circumstances it is certainly not his fault.[63]

When in the second half of the decade a 'theory' – Brutalism – appeared to gain 'universal' appeal, Pattrick's eclecticism was beginning to look out of touch with the mood in the school. In May 1957, he therefore approved the formation of a panel consisting of students and staff to review his curriculum. Chaired by fifth-year student and future RMJM partner Francis Baden-Powell, the so-called 'curriculum working party' issued its report in February 1958, covering both the educational system of the school, specifically the organisation of the teaching staff, and the curriculum itself, that is, the teaching contents of the various years and their linkage with each other.[64]

The working party took the view that, on balance, the drawbacks of the unit system in terms of maintaining consistent standards and the 'continuity of the teaching aim' over parallel units outweighed its advantages – a somewhat surprising verdict given how zealously the students had advocated the return of this system and how short a trial it had been given. To remedy its flaws, the working party recommended the appointment of 'co-ordinators' from within the ranks of the unit masters. Year masters in anything but title, these co-ordinators would synchronise their year's programmes in compliance with its overall teaching objective, with unit masters themselves retaining the responsibility for the detailed setting and handling of the studio briefs.

As to the course itself, the working party put its recommendations forward in the form of a model curriculum.[65] It attached great value to the series of second-year studio projects related to a particular material and recommended that the idea be extended. Thus, the final term of the first year

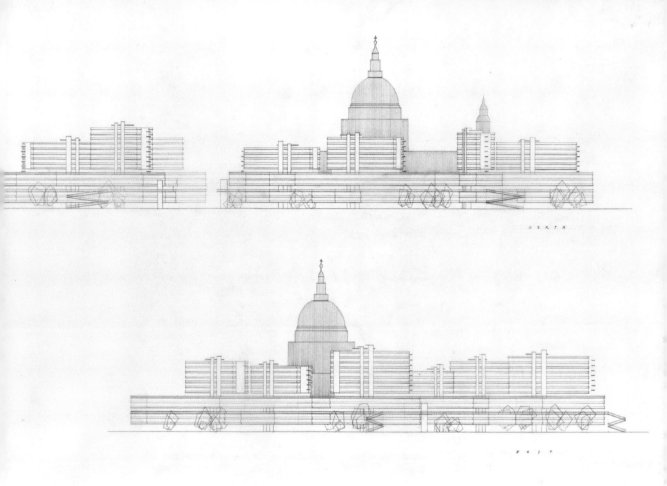

43

Ahrends, Burton and Koralek met as first-year students and collaborated closely throughout their course of study. An early and unfashionable interest in Frank Lloyd Wright's Prairie Houses was soon enriched by influences from Aalto and Le Corbusier, and by the time they graduated they had arrived at a collective and highly idiosyncratic style which defied easy categorisation. For their St Paul's development, the students arranged the main accommodation in two distinct layers along a ribbon, the upper level providing large open-plan offices, the lower one self-contained offices with separate entrances. Projecting branches for clubs, restaurants and a small hotel break up and vary the outside space, and the roof line of the superstructure aligns with the lower cornice of the cathedral to preserve the view of the dome. William Holford, who reviewed the project with members of the LCC (AAJ, Feb 1956), was doubtful whether it would achieve the desired effect: 'The scheme is set in a landscape in which there is a kind of ruined temple as part of the prospect.'

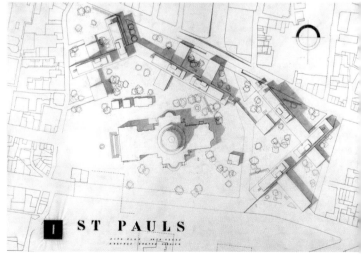

44

St Paul's (Peter Ahrends, Richard Burton, Paul Koralek, fourth year, 1954/55)

would feature a first, 'primitive' building in timber, followed by masonry, steel and in-situ concrete in the second, and precast concrete and synthetics in the third. Another element of the existing course which found the working party's approval was the village scheme, which provided the context for the design subjects in the third year – an approach which, in the eyes of the working party, could be developed throughout the course. Following the preparatory first year, all major programmes in the following years were to be linked to a specific gradation of architectural scale: the village in the second year, the town in the third, the city sector in the fourth, and the city in the fifth. Each year would include an initial period of group research into the conditions and growth of the chosen area, resulting in a redevelopment plan which would form the basis of the subsequent design projects.[66]

According to Gowan, the student members of the working party had reviewed the lecture course, Killick the staffing system, and he and Craig the curriculum itself.[67] However, in both constituent parts the new curriculum reflected the intellectual leadership of Peter Smithson even though he was not himself a member of the curriculum working party. The sequence of building studies in the lower years presupposed materiality to be a decisive factor in architectural design, and the contextual framework of the proposed curriculum echoed the Team 10 approach to urban planning based on different 'scales of association'. In other words, with its dual emphasis on materiality and context as the prime determinants of architectural form, the report of the curriculum working party drew together the two theoretical strands which pervaded the Smithsons' writings in the 1950s.

Given how tenaciously Pattrick had asserted his authority against the students in his early years in office, it may seem out of character for him to consent to a working party reviewing his curriculum. Yet Pattrick welcomed the input of staff and students so long as the proper procedures were followed, and – having participated in its preliminary discussions – he probably anticipated, and generally agreed with, the line the curriculum working party was likely to take. The proximity of

its recommendations to his own views certainly explains why Pattrick implemented them almost at once. The new curriculum, in operation from the autumn of 1958, retained the succession of tightly controlled single-material studies he had introduced six years prior, and it related design tasks to a progressive order of scales, which, in his view, promised to promote a visual and contextual approach in keeping with 'townscape' principles.[68] The fact that the curriculum also involved a broad return of group working and town planning (the latter being its very essence as far as Smithson was concerned)[69] suggests that Pattrick, having secured a second term in office, felt sufficiently empowered to ignore the RIBA's reservations, which, presumably, he did not share in the first place.

Pattrick also welcomed the reintroduction of year masters, which relieved him from administrative duties and allowed him to delegate much of the running of the school to his senior staff, whom he vested with great authority and sheltered from interference by the council. According to fifth-year tutor John Partridge, Pattrick held his staff 'like puppets on a string',[70] and James Gowan recalled:

[He] was in charge of the school and he ran it much like a ship, as if any minor deviation in the crew's behaviour could, and probably would, result in an immediate titanic disaster. In the regalia of full authority, he stared out from the bridge, ever alert for the enemy, the marauding flotilla of the council.[71]

Pattrick appointed Robert Maxwell and David Oakley as co-ordinators for, respectively, the second and third years.[72] Yet he departed from the working party's recommendations with regard to the fourth year, where he dropped the division into units, giving Killick the same scope of powers as fifth-year master Smithson. This decision had a profound effect on the staffing situation as Killick and Gowan, whom he chose as his assistant year master, surrounded themselves with tutors who shared their outlook, notably Bill Howell, John Voelcker and Peter Chamberlin. (Incidentally, Smithson's selection was less one-sided: in addition to his second-in-command Arthur Korn, who embodied the sought-after link to the heroic period of modernism, Smithson's 'tutors' included like-minded colleagues such as Alan Colquhoun, Theo Crosby and John Partridge, but also Eric Lyons and John Weeks.)[73]

Key members of staff left the AA in quick succession at the closing of the decade. Gowan resigned in October 1959 due to pressure of work following Stirling's invitation to teach at Yale, and Killick left half a year later when his deteriorating health made it impossible for him to continue his teaching.[74] Peter Smithson followed them in December 1960 to focus his full attention on designing the Economist building, and Michael Pattrick left one year later. The curriculum of 1958 survived the departure of its instigators into the mid-1960s. It was their educational legacy.

7   In Search of a New Policy (1951–1961)

Financial Crisis

The last FET-grant-aided students entered the AA school in 1951. In anticipation of this, two years prior the council had decided to gradually shrink the total number of students in the school from more than 500 in 1949/50 to approximately 300 from 1953/54 onward. Unlike Robert Furneaux Jordan, who had expected the school to incur a substantial deficit owing to the lack of income through student fees, the council had downplayed the financial implications of its policy, assuming that expenditures could be scaled down in tandem with the size of the school and that any potential shortfall could be compensated by attracting more industry-sponsored scholarships and local authority grants. This assumption proved fundamentally flawed as it overestimated the school's capacity to reduce overheads while at the same time underestimating the effect of rising costs. When in June 1951 Michael Pattrick took over as acting principal, the AA school was already in dire financial straits.

Pattrick vehemently opposed further cuts to school expenditure, especially staff salaries. The only solution therefore was to either find a new source of income or to alter the AA's educational model altogether. The then president, A. R. F. Anderson, preferred the latter course. Unable to keep in step with the university schools and the polytechnics, both generously funded by the government, Anderson suggested that the AA return to its roots as a part-time evening school running an atelier scheme for a limited number of postgraduate students.[1] Though there was some support for this view, specifically from Hugh Casson, in its majority the council rejected any radical departure from the AA's current setup and hoped to raise additional revenue by attracting donations from the building industry. By December 1953 the limitations of this approach became evident, and one month later councillor Walter Atkinson expressed the view that 'if no financial aid was forthcoming, the council should consider at the end of the current financial year the termination of the existing school course of five years'.[2]

In this desperate situation the council was prepared to sacrifice the school's treasured independence by attaching it to a larger academic institution. Negotiations about a possible amalgamation with the University of Cambridge, in particular, reached an advanced stage. The AA had traditionally strong links with Cambridge, which at the time only offered a course up to intermediate level and fed many of its students into the senior years of the AA to complete their studies. Pattrick considered their prior training deficient, and in 1952 he had instituted an annual five-week summer course to bring them up to the required AA standard, thus enabling them to enter directly into the fourth year without having to repeat the third. In light of this, Pattrick, who devised the merger scheme with Cambridge, was palpably resentful when in March 1954 the university turned it down 'on the grounds that what we had to offer was not, in their view, worth the money they would have to pay'.[3]

With all other options exhausted, the AA council in a last-ditch attempt to secure the needed funding applied to the MOE for a resumption of its annual grant, which it had relinquished in 1946, at a time of abnormally high student numbers financed almost exclusively through the FET scheme. In doing so, the AA had effectively substituted a recurring, long-term government subsidy with a temporary one, and this, with hindsight, turned out to be a myopic and costly miscalculation. In April 1954, the MOE announced that it was not prepared, either now or in the foreseeable future, to add to the number of establishments on its direct grant list and advised the AA council to approach the LCC instead.[4] This, however, proved equally unavailing.

The failure, over a period of almost three years, to raise sufficient funds to guarantee the future of the school left the AA in a state of crisis. Several members of the council's advisory committee shared Henry Braddock's feeling that the school 'had really finished its job [and] should run down and close'.[5] At the end of the 1953/54 session, the financial situation was such that the council felt it improper to issue a prospectus advertising a five-year course. Dismissing, as Peter Shepheard put it, the 'madman's course' of draining the AA's meagre reserves 'until we run into a blank wall',[6] the council decided to set its student fees at £150 p.a., which was the actual cost of training an architectural student in Britain at the time but four times more than rival schools were charging. It did so with the greatest reluctance as it feared (rightly) that some local authorities, already hesitant to support students wishing to attend the AA, would simply refuse to do so – a worrying prospect at a time when 60 per cent of applicants depended on such grants.

The problem was not only the quantity of students but also – and equally alarmingly – their quality. Any increase in fees automatically enlarged the group of those whose parents were too wealthy to qualify for local authority grants but not wealthy enough to cover the costs themselves. This was precisely the section of the populace which was assumed to be a particularly fruitful one from which to recruit architectural students, not least because it included the majority of architects. 'Thus', wrote the *Architect and Building News*, 'we have the paradox of a school of architecture set up and run independently for a hundred years by architects whose professional descendants cannot now afford to send their sons to the school but must have them trained elsewhere.'[7]

The AA and 'The Other Place'

Ongoing financial difficulties were not the only reason why the AA felt it necessary to reconsider its long-term policy as from the early 1950s onward the RIBA – often referred to as 'the other place' in AA debates – took an increasingly direct interest in the workings of the schools. The late 1940s had seen architectural education in a state of flux. This was in part due to the specific circumstances after the war, particularly the surge of student numbers and the realignment of the profession in the context of the nascent welfare state, but it was also because the deadlock between modernisers and traditionalists on the RIBA's Board of Architectural Education paralysed its ability to agree upon a coherent policy. Though the BAE as a whole began to recognise the need to reform architectural education, its members were divided about the manner in which this should be done. This changed in the early 1950s, and the previous chapter showed how Michael Pattrick, at the beginning of his term in office, felt compelled to modify the course in compliance with the wishes of the RIBA's visiting board. Crinson and Lubbock describe the BAE's policy at the time as 'one of gentlemanly persuasion',[8] yet to many at the AA it represented an unacceptable degree of interference. The authors of the 1953 student report went so far as to suggest that the 'possibility of foregoing RIBA recognition should at least be considered, as it would leave the school free to follow its own course unhindered',[9] and there was considerable support for this view, not least from President Anderson, who felt that 'the only logical conclusion [. . .] is to break away from the RIBA'.[10]

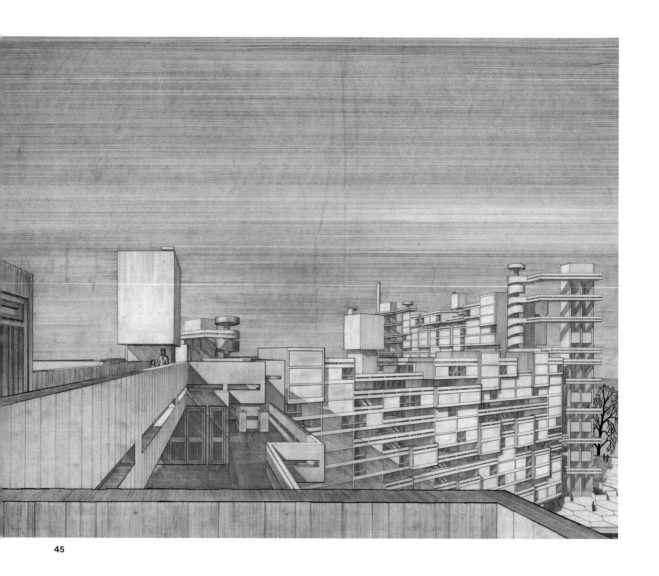

45

High-density Housing, Paddington (John Dalton, Anthony Eardley,
Ian Fraser, Robert Knott, fourth year, 1956/57)

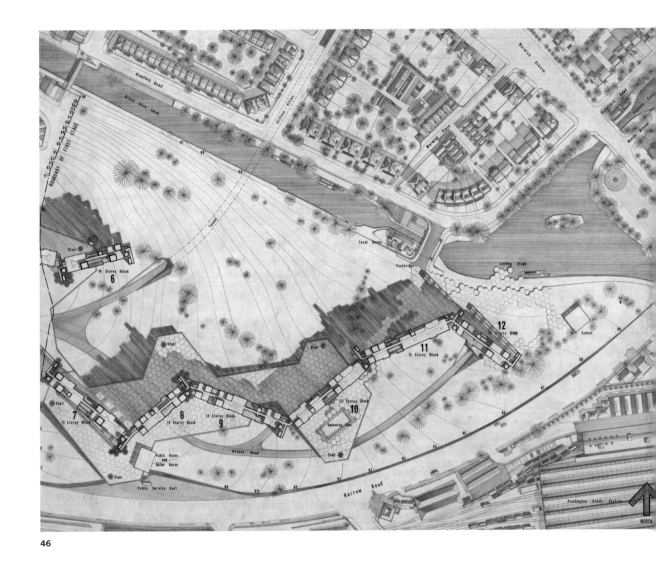

This low-cost housing project was devised in compliance with current LCC standards and regulations. With its loosely linear configuration along a meandering circulation path it links the Smithsons' seminal Golden Lane competition scheme to later adaptations such as Candilis-Josić-Woods's Toulouse-le-Mirail and Jack Lynn and Ivor Smith's Park Hill Estate in Sheffield. The design of the housing units is modelled on the Unité d'habitation, *with main access levels running through the building at every third level, giving access to five different types of dual-aspect and mostly double-storey dwellings. The rugged skyline and clear articulation of the concrete box frames, on the other hand, seems Constructivist rather than Corbusian and anticipates much of the Brutalist architecture of the following decade, notably HKPA's Weston Rise and George Finch's Lambeth Towers. The plan shows the first phase of the development. Once slum clearance of the site was completed, it was to be followed by a second phase providing a neighbourhood centre with communal amenities as well as a second string of blocks to the west.*

Even so, the majority of the council agreed with Pattrick, who argued that this course of action, while offering the desired freedom in the short term, would ultimately defeat its object as students would before long demand to be coached for the RIBA's external examinations, thus forcing the AA to conform to the very system it so firmly rejected. Avoiding direct confrontation with the RIBA, Pattrick's strategy was to build coalitions with colleagues who were thought to be in sympathy with the AA's approach.[11] Yet, with growing pressure for a more coherent educational system, there appeared to exist little goodwill towards the AA and its independent streak. On the contrary, Hugh Casson suspected that, though not a matter of AA policy, 'the removal of recognition might easily be considered as the RIBA's policy',[12] and Peter Shepheard asserted that there were 'many people gunning for the AA in the RIBA [and] ready to demote [it]'.[13]

Given the strained relations between the two organisations, it came as no surprise that when, in April 1952, the RIBA formed a committee under Donald McMorran to examine the current setup of architectural education in Britain, AA Principal Pattrick, though nominated, was not elected and only invited to join when one of his colleagues withdrew.[14] A private practitioner in the traditional vein and openly disdainful of school-based training, McMorran aimed the work of his committee at defining uniform examination standards and uniform lists of examination subjects for full-time and part-time courses, thus creating greater parity between the two and making the latter suitable for RIBA recognition. With the backing of the MOE, which predicted a growing demand for part-time facilities following the end of FET grants, 'the forces of the anti-school brigade [were] gathering strength', as a dismayed editor of the *Architects' Journal* observed.[15]

Unlike the university schools, to which the idea of part-time training was anathema, the AA was not opposed to it on principle. On the contrary, from January 1954 Pattrick organised free evening classes for junior assistants who had passed the RIBA intermediate but could not afford to attend any school of architecture.[16] He was equally alive to the shortcomings of his own students as newly qualified assistants, putting forward the integration of office and school training as one of the key objectives in his report to the McMorran Committee (see p.88). However, Pattrick's ideas centred on so-called 'sandwich' courses, that is, alternating periods of school and office training, and he took the view that any scheme leading to recognition of part-time courses would have to be run under the auspices of already recognised full-time schools. While there was thus some common ground, however shaky, between Pattrick and McMorran in terms of part-time training, they were poles apart in every other respect, as illustrated by the fact that the committee deemed the other two aspects of Pattrick's report – two-tier qualification and postgraduate specialisation – outside its terms of reference and refused to discuss them.[17]

Pattrick was suspicious of McMorran's intention to align the training of internal and external students and fought any interference with the AA's methods. He was, however, regularly outvoted by a committee on which he felt completely isolated:

Somehow I found myself always in that minority who are listened to, often without question, but chiefly because there was no possibility of our proposals being taken up seriously. On some issues, after endless delay, I was getting slightly petulant, and I suspected that I was becoming the sort of person whose note of apology for absence brings a moment of happiness into the life of the chairman and secretary alike.[18]

Not surprisingly, Pattrick welcomed the arrival of potential allies such as Robert Gardner-Medwin and Robert Matthew, who joined the schools committee in 1953 as the new heads of, respectively, Liverpool and Edinburgh. Supported by Douglas Jones, his counterpart at Birmingham, Pattrick succeeded in getting Gardner-Medwin appointed to the McMorran Committee. Gardner-Medwin shared Pattrick's views on architectural education, and together they managed to muster sufficient support to force McMorran to redraft

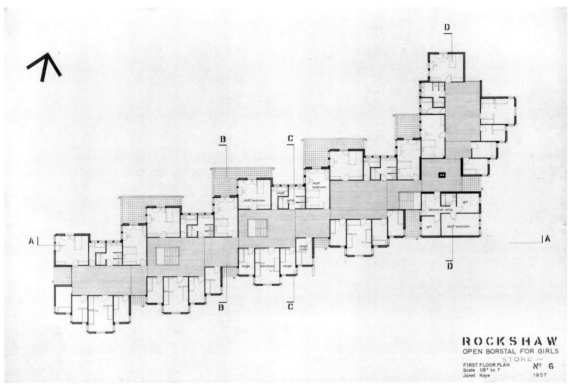

47

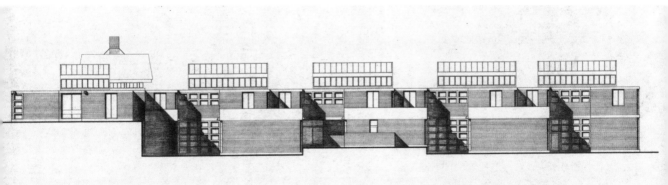

48

Rockshaw – Open Borstal for Girls (Janet Kaye, thesis, 1956/57)

The combination of brick walls and exposed concrete slabs was a Brutalist period feature, inspired by Le Corbusier's Maisons Jaoul *and – closer to home – Stirling and Gowan's Ham Common flats. Equally prevalent was the tendency to fragment the appearance of the building by expressing cellular spatial units in both plan and elevation. In the case of this borstal for girls, the approach was driven by the wish to help the rehabilitation of its residents by strengthening their sense of individuality through architectural means. So-called 'family groups', consisting of six girls and two staff, are grouped around a common living area; staircases give access to communal facilities on the floor beneath. Janet Jack (née Kaye) was one of the star students at the time and later became the first female partner at the Building Design Partnership.*

49   Concert Hall (Aalon Aaron Lee, Paul Drake, Edward Reynolds, fourth year, 1956/57)

*Edward Reynolds, who died when still a student, is regarded as one of the most
original talents the AA has ever produced. He generated the facetted envelope
of this concert hall in Trafalgar Square by devising a fan-shaped plan for the
auditorium, to which he attached a series of lateral stair towers. The emergence
of expressive and profoundly a-formal designs owed much to Banham's
rediscovery of previously ignored modernist groupings, be it the Italian Futurists,
the Russian Constructivists or – as in this case – the German Expressionists.*

entire paragraphs of the final report before submitting it to the BAE.[19] Most importantly, they persuaded the committee to express a firm commitment to full-time education by including a recommendation stating that a minimum of two years' full-time training in a recognised school should be made compulsory for all students of architecture.[20]

The balance of power was shifting. As a result, not only did it take almost a year to redraft the final report, but it also left experts profoundly unimpressed when it was finally published in February 1955.[21] 'What *could* it be that kept them arguing for nearly three years?' wondered the *Architects' Journal*, and *Architectural Design* declared: 'After several years of stormy backstage intrigue, the surprisingly mild McMorran report has emerged from the RIBA. [. . .] It has contributed little.'[22] Indeed, the work of the McMorran Committee was of little consequence to the recognised schools, which, given its initial part-time bias, was an altogether successful outcome. The RIBA council, where a group of public-sector modernists had meanwhile taken up the controlling positions, adopted its recommendations but agreed with Pattrick that it had failed to address the most pressing issue – the question of postgraduate training – and decided that a conference on architectural education should be held 'to discuss points of principle not covered by the Report'.[23]

Originally scheduled for early 1956, the three-day conference eventually took place in April 1958 at Magdalen College in Oxford. Chaired by Cambridge professor Leslie Martin and with an attendance limited to 50 carefully selected participants, it passed six resolutions:

(1) that 'the present minimum standard of entry into training (five passes at 'O' level) is far too low and [. . .] should be raised to a minimum of two passes at 'A' level';

(2) that 'courses based on Testimonies of Study and the RIBA External Examinations [. . .] should be progressively abolished';

(3) that 'all schools capable of providing the high standard of training envisaged should be "recognised" and situated in universities or institutions where courses of comparable standard can be conducted';

(4) that 'courses [. . .] should be either full-time or, on an experimental basis, combined or sandwich courses in which periods of training in a school alternate with periods of training in an office';

(5) that 'these raised standards of education [may] make desirable other forms of training not leading to an architectural qualification';

(6) that 'it regards postgraduate work as an essential part of architectural education [and] endorses the policy of developing postgraduate courses [. . .].'[24]

Pattrick, who had served on the organising committee of the conference, rallied the AA council in support of these resolutions, which he saw – with some justification – as the culmination of years of campaigning on his part and 'the only significant move towards improving the status and training of the architect that has been made since the recognised schools were started fifty years ago'.[25]

Pattrick's enthusiasm was understandable, considering how closely the RIBA's new outline policy resembled his own long-held views on architectural education. His 1953 report to the McMorran Committee, ignored at the time, had anticipated the need to acknowledge and cater to a two-tier profession and make provisions for postgraduate specialisation. Pattrick's advocacy of A-level standards may at first seem more surprising since it contradicted the system in place at his school. The AA at the time admitted almost all applicants subject to their possessing the minimal academic qualifications for RIBA probationership (i.e. O-levels in five subjects), but with a first year regarded as strictly probationary. Pattrick was satisfied with this system, and though he conceded that 'whatever other qualities we may possess as a body of men, we certainly are not very brainy',[26] he generally did not believe academic qualifications to be a reliable guide for future architectural proficiency. As an isolated measure he would therefore likely have resisted the introduction of higher entry standards. Yet Pattrick – and with him most participants of the Oxford Conference – saw A-levels and the creation of a two-tier education enriched by postgraduate studies as complementary measures.[27] The AA council had, in March 1958, reaffirmed its belief in a basic division of the profession into architects and assistants and decided that the school would only train the former.[28] Evidently, to justify the higher status of this select group, their education would need to be of a correspondingly higher intellectual order, which would in turn necessitate higher academic qualifications. Remarkably, the fact that at the time less than ten per cent of applicants to the AA had the required A-levels seemed no cause for concern.

The remaining resolutions were likely to strengthen the position of all recognised full-time schools, including the AA. The fourth resolution concerned the type of course and reflected both the universities' preference for full-time and the MOE's preference for sandwich courses.[29] The third resolution, on the other hand, concerned the type of institution in which training ought to take place. The Oxford Conference was unambiguous in its preference for university education but pressured by the MOE, it conceded that an education of such nature might be provided in 'institutions of a comparable character'. It was a concession to the leading polytechnics as well as the AA, which had no reason to believe that its singular status as an independent school was in any doubt, not least because it had so clearly anticipated and shaped the new RIBA policy. Moreover, at the time of the Oxford Conference the AA was involved in negotiations with the MOE regarding the creation of a new educational establishment which was to be the exemplar of such an 'institution of comparable character', offering an alternative model of higher education outside the university system. It is this scheme which will concern us in the following section.

Integrated Education: The Scheme for a College of Architecture and Building

The call for a closer integration of the building team based on joint training schemes was a live issue in the postwar years, promoted by architects, builders and progressive educationalists alike. At the AA, the idea fell on particularly fertile soil as the anti-Beaux-Arts line taken by the influential *Focus* generation had triggered an abiding interest in alternative, non-academic teaching methods. Lethabite ideals of integrating architecture and building training had informed a series of experimental schemes, from Douglas Jones's Bauhaus-inspired live projects before the war to Gordon Brown's practical training site and Robert Furneaux Jordan's factory and site work ventures, and it is worth pointing out that under both postwar principals a period of practical training remained a condition for the AA diploma even though the RIBA itself temporarily dropped it as a requirement for associateship. Michael Pattrick was intent on continuing this tradition: he arranged practical demonstrations for his students at the LCC's building schools of Brixton and Hammersmith, and he approached Leslie Martin, then the chief architect to the LCC, with the idea to initiate a programme of live projects akin to that currently being pioneered at Birmingham – a scheme which despite Martin's support eventually failed to materialise.[30]

It was against this backdrop that in June 1954 the AA received a proposition from the building industry which offered an opportunity 'to translate into practical form the current theory [of] joint education [as] the next logical step forward in improving building in the country'.[31] Conceived in all likelihood by David Woodbine Parish, the influential past-president of the London Master Builders' Association, the key objective of the designated 'Department of Building Management' (DBM) was to attract more desirable candidates to the executive branches of the building industry. The AA appeared ideally placed to host such an undertaking since the major universities were disinclined to offer a degree course for builders while the technical

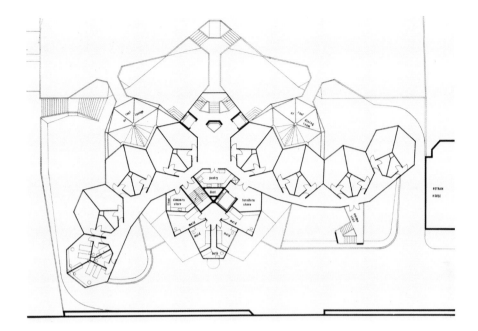

50

51

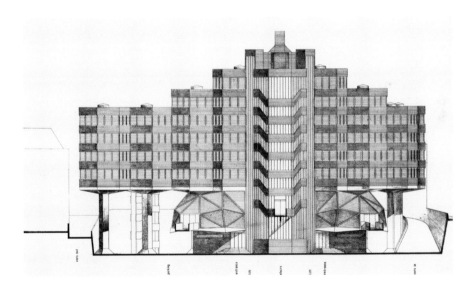

Richmond Hotel (John Outram, third year, 1957/58)

The main access is from a low-level towpath along the River Thames; the two entrances are underneath two fully glazed public rooms, which double as canopies and are themselves suspended from the mass of the hotel. A strictly symmetrical circulation core gives access to a string of Buckminster Fuller-inspired heptagonal hotel pods. The rooms are grouped around rhomboidal concrete trunks, which carry the loads of the building and contain its services. With its counterintuitive inversion of mass and glazing, and with the contrasting use of crystalline features against a stark brick exterior more generally, Outram's hotel is almost without precedent, though it has a certain affinity with Stirling and Gowan's Leicester Engineering Building, which was then in an early design stage.

By the late 1950s, the idea of the linear city gradually took on a more compact, megastructural form, with circulation and service spines 'feeding' the various neighbourhoods. The main difference to previous town planning concepts lay in the fact that the spine itself was architecturally articulated and eventually became the determining feature of the urban landscape. This development plan for Westminster by a group of fourth-year students, which incorporates a travelator as its prime generator, was an early example of this emerging pattern. It echoed (and possibly predated) Kenzo Tange's Boston Harbour scheme at MIT and, with its layering of commercial and residential districts, anticipates van den Broek and Bakema's much larger schemes of the following decade, notably the Pampusplan.

52 City of Westminster Redevelopment
(Robert Boot, Tim Tinker, John Thompson, fourth year, 1958/59)

colleges lacked the required academic standing. Over the following months, the council conducted negotiations with leading members of the building industry, and in December 1955 Pattrick presented a draft syllabus for a combined first-year course for approximately 20 students.[32] Both Leslie Wallis, the president of the Institute of Builders (IOB), and Antony Part, the under-secretary for further education at the MOE, appeared supportive of the pilot project. Negotiations stalled, however, as the parties found themselves in a conundrum: the MOE would not endorse the scheme until the funding was secured, and the IOB would not finance it until it had the MOE's approval.[33]

While the AA continued to seek the backing of the building industry for its DBM, Part himself began to pursue a much grander scheme. A government white paper, issued in February 1956, announced a substantial programme of capital development aimed at expanding and upgrading technical education by means of designated Colleges of Advanced Technology (CAT).[34] Part envisaged the creation of such a college in central London to provide advanced-level training for all major building trades centred upon a 'strong architectural element', that is, a fully recognised school.[35] Though not entirely convinced by the AA's DBM proposal, he acknowledged it as a 'genuine and [financially] disinterested attempt to make progress'[36] and had little confidence in the builders' ability to make a worthwhile contribution to the question of integrated training:

> [The] Architectural Association are potentially closer to the ground with a proposal than anybody else, and I think that, if necessary, we should have to take a bit of a chance on their being able to attract students of a kind who would not normally go to [. . .], say, Brixton.[37]

In January 1957, Part initiated talks with the AA council, which in turn abandoned its negotiations with the building industry. The council was sympathetic to the ideals which inspired Part's scheme, but the question of financial – and therefore ultimate – control over the proposed

college proved to be a major obstacle, particularly since Part was adamant that the MOE itself would not be prepared to fund the new college directly. As the AA had neither the space nor the financial means to establish the college on its own, the only practicable solution seemed to be an alliance with the LCC, which, apart from being sufficiently funded, was the legitimate authority to administrate educational institutions on its territory and, through its powers of compulsory purchase, ideally suited to find and develop a site in central London. The council, however, remained unconvinced by Part's repeated assurances that the AA's influence and independence would be adequately safeguarded and, with more than a touch of class hauteur, deplored the idea of turning its school into a 'better Brixton School of Building'.[38]

In June 1957, the AA elected a new council, and headed by its new president, John Brandon-Jones, who was overtly dismissive of any scheme involving the LCC, it took an increasingly uncompromising stance. Brandon-Jones doubted whether the college would achieve the desired academic standard – a rather absurd contention given that the proposed entry level was higher than that required by the AA at the time. However, his chief concern was that the AA would not have sufficient control over its school, while the division into separate departments would prevent a proper integration of the college as a whole. Oblivious to the conflicting nature of these claims, the council adopted them as the official position of the AA.[39]

On 4 November 1957, a palpably irritated Part terminated negotiations with the AA,[40] and over the coming months he tried to position either the Northern Polytechnic or the Regent Street Polytechnic – both run by the LCC and fully recognised by the RIBA – as the possible nucleus for the new college. In July 1958, he approached the AA anew, and the council, now headed by Denis Clarke Hall, accepted his offer to re-open discussions as it considered itself in a stronger bargaining position – not only because Part's quest for an alternative partnering school had evidently failed, but also because it felt that the resolutions passed at the recent Oxford Conference (which Part had attended) might have 'converted him more to the AA's point of view on architectural education'.[41]

Indeed, by the beginning of 1959 there appeared to be broad agreement between the AA, the MOE and the LCC. The main stumbling block remained the AA's fear of sacrificing its independence to a governing body on which it would constitute the single largest contingent, but which was itself presumed to be at the financial mercy of the LCC. Pattrick – at first critical but now 'wholeheartedly in favour' of the scheme – argued that

> the possibilities of improving our educational standards are far greater in a College of Advanced Technology than they could ever be by preserving a sort of haughty independence – an independence, incidentally, which is largely illusory, as there are few things more restricting than an acute lack of money.[42]

Although resentment toward the LCC pervaded the deliberations of the AA council, most members seemed inclined to agree with Pattrick. Clarke Hall at least was taken by surprise when, at the end of a council meeting on 8 April 1959, James Richards moved – and a majority concurred – that 'the AA should not continue negotiations for a college of architecture and building if this involved association with the LCC'.[43] Six weeks later, the outgoing council called an informal meeting of the association to report on the course and failure of its negotiations. The post-mortem left no doubt that its decision to abandon the talks did not reflect the general feeling of members and students, the vast majority of whom supported the scheme.[44] Encouraged by this, Clarke Hall urged his new colleagues to rescind the previous council's resolution when they met two weeks later to inaugurate the academic session.[45] His motion passed with a comfortable majority, but the LCC rejected the AA's request to re-open the discussions for a third time and half a year later announced its intention to proceed with the Regent Street Polytechnic instead.

Looking at it with the benefit of hindsight, it is easy to dismiss the proposal for an integrated college of architecture and building as just another

in a series of ambitious AA projects which, for one reason or the other, did not quite make it over the finish line. Yet at the time, students, members and observers alike lamented its failure as a missed opportunity to change the nature of architectural education along the lines predicted by the Bauhaus. An editorial in the *Architects' Journal* expressed the general sentiment:

> The present AA Council has behaved with an irresponsibility which must shake everyone's confidence in the leadership of this once progressive institution. For four years the AA Council has formally been considering integrated training with other members of the building industry, and during the last two years it has twice been discussing such a venture with the LCC. [. . .] No one can pretend that the LCC is the perfect partner for such an educational venture (one might ask: is the AA?) but it is only through local government that this integrated school is possible, and as a local authority the LCC is second to none. [. . .] The LCC has the material resources and the enterprise to make a success of integrated training – the training which has been wanted so long now by forward-thinking members of the building industry. [. . .] It is sadly ironical that the AA, which has pioneered so much in the past, has now, apparently, lost its nerve.[46]

Future Policy: The AA Working Party and the End of Pattrick's Reign

In the second half of the 1950s, the AA exhibited a renewed sense of confidence, both in its dealings with the RIBA and particularly in its negotiations with the MOE and the LCC. This was helped by the fact that, contrary to expectation, the recent rise in student fees (see p.101) had not affected the number of candidates applying for admission to the school. In part this may have been the consequence of educational changes, specifically the introduction of the parallel unit system, and the stimulus they gave to the school. It is worth pointing out that the

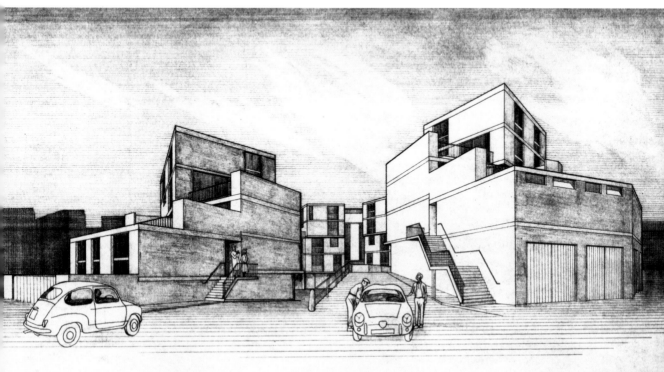

C A S T L E   C O M P L E X

53   Castle Complex, Great Westminster (Robert Boot, Tim Tinker, John Thompson, fourth year, 1958/59)

*The Castle Complex is a housing estate in one of the neighbourhoods proposed in the students' redevelopment plan for Westminster (see previous figure) and reflects Brutalism's preoccupation with, what Banham called, its 'memorability as an image' (*AR*, Dec 1955). The complex consists of 30 maisonettes, organised into an outer and an inner ring divided by a circular access corridor. The choice of a castle imagery for luxury housing evokes the notion of a gated community even though in this case it seems little more than a formal device: all units open towards the surrounding area, most of them through generous terraces, while the keep as the heart of the 'castle' remains strangely underutilised.*

The seductive quality of student drawings – a perennial feature of AA student work – made it difficult for less competent draughtspeople to make themselves noticed. According to Bryan Appleyard (*Richard Rogers*, London, 1986, pp 74, 84–8), the quality of Richard Rogers's student work escaped his tutors until his final years at the school. At the time, Rogers was enthused by the contextual modernism of Milan-based practice BBPR. Rogers's sympathetic fourth-year essay about his famous cousin, BBPR partner Ernesto Rogers, irritated Peter Smithson, and so presumably did his top-heavy hotel, which bore more than a passing resemblance to BBPR's Torre Velasca. Even so, in Bill Howell's view (*AAJ*, Sep/Oct 1960), 'Rogers' hotel was a better building than he was letting on and once one could build up a mental picture from the rather thin drawings it seemed to be a good scheme.'

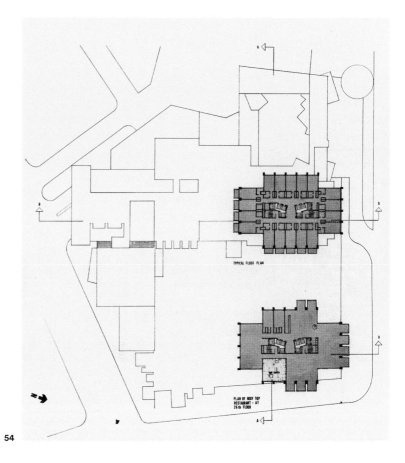

54

55

Hotel, Hyde Park Corner (Richard Rogers, fifth year, 1959/60)

council had approved the new system, which was inevitably going to involve additional expenditure, in March 1954, at a time when the AA school was facing imminent insolvency. This may seem paradoxical, but the council felt that the only way for the school to attract students in spite of its high and incessantly rising student fees was by continuing to provide a unique educational model. As Peter Shepheard stated:

> If I were to try to put the council's feelings into words, I would say that the answer is not to cut one's coat according to one's cloth but to expand, to go on improving the AA's services and its education, adding postgraduate research to its commitments, and so try to make [. . .] what we have to sell worth buying.[47]

It is impossible to assess whether or not this was indeed a contributing factor. It seems likely that the main reason for the unexpected change of fortune was a ruling by the MOE which from late 1954 obliged local authority schools to levy higher fees to 'out-county scholars' (that is, students holding a scholarship from a local authority other than the one where the school was located), who were now expected to cover 87 per cent of the total cost of their training rather than 70 per cent, as had previously been the case.[48] The AA as an independent school was not bound by this directive. Though it remained expensive for Londoners, the fees it charged to students from other parts of the country (which made up 70 per cent of the student body) were, for the time being, the same or even lower than in other schools, meaning that local education authorities (other than the LCC) were more inclined to grant awards to intending AA students.[49] As a result, applications to enter the school for the 1955/56 session went up rather than down, and the AA's financial situation improved considerably. The principal was pleased to announce that 'the uncertain outlook of twelve months ago has now changed into something much more cheerful'.[50]

This more 'cheerful' outlook left the council – albeit not Pattrick himself – unmindful of outside events which had the potential to harm the school.

The most significant of these was a change in the RIBA's policy on recognising schools, henceforth based solely on merit rather than on geographical location. Considering the AA drew a large proportion of its senior students from intermediate schools such as Cambridge, which were expected to attain full recognition for their five-year courses, this was a development which threatened to cut off a significant source of revenue.[51] Pattrick's concern that the newly recognised schools would attract more students and that, in addition, local education authorities would be less inclined to transfer grants from one school to another if they both offered the same qualification proved accurate. The consequences, however, were negligible as the government's decision in April 1957 to abolish compulsory national service sparked off a large increase in the number of applications, which allowed Pattrick to fill the school to – and beyond – capacity.

The prospective sea change in architectural education heralded by the Oxford Conference brought broader policy considerations back to the fore, particularly as a closer evaluation of the new A-level requirement indicated that it was likely to entail severe financial consequences for the AA. Pattrick predicted a temporary slump in student numbers in 1961/62, when the new standard would first be applied, but took the view that after 1963/64 the effect on the so-called 'facilities' schools (that is, schools which only gave part-time instruction to intending architects) would be such that most of their potential students would instead apply to the AA or other recognised schools.[52] The BAE did not share Pattrick's optimism, and neither did his finance committee, which professed itself unable to produce accurate budgets for the three or four years following the introduction of the new entry standards.[53]

Changes in the RIBA's organisational setup were likely to put additional pressure on the AA. In October 1959, the RIBA council decided to reconstitute its somewhat cumbersome BAE as a much smaller executive committee consisting of 12 to 15 members drawn from the, now purely advisory, predecessor body. Ironically, Pattrick had been a driving force behind this, expecting no doubt that the AA would retain its traditional representation on the new BAE.[54] This, however, was only granted after AA President Jim Cadbury-Brown intervened personally with the RIBA.[55] Moreover, the constitutional reform of the RIBA itself cost the AA its seat on its council, which put an end to the privileged status it had enjoyed since its inception and was bound to significantly diminish its influence. 'This is a sad blow', bemoaned the *Architects' Journal*, 'gradually, bit by bit, the AA seems to be losing its status in the profession.'[56]

It was in this climate of change that in November 1959 the students' committee called on the council to form a committee to consider the future of the AA.[57] The appointment of the so-called 'AA working party' – which was to be composed of an independent chairman, two ordinary members, two students, one representative each from council and staff, and Pattrick as a non-voting advisor – proved unexpectedly difficult as the council's top three choices for both chair and ordinary membership all refused the offer. Anthony Pott, the chief architect to the Ministry of Education, and Cleeve Barr, his counterpart at the Ministry of Housing and Local Government, declined due to pressure of work; Oliver Cox was willing to serve on condition that Pattrick be excluded as 'the students might find his presence inhibiting'.[58] Alexander Killick, the director of the Royal Institution of Chartered Surveyors (and John Killick's father), likewise rejected the invitation, and the council eventually nominated Peter Chamberlin as chairman, and Neville Conder and Robert Furneaux Jordan as ordinary members.[59]

It was amid the early consultations of the working party that, in February 1960, the final attempt to revive the negotiations with the LCC fell through. Maybe it was the realisation that – at a critical time when the future of the AA was in the balance – it had wasted two years on a futile endeavour which prompted the council to take a sudden and far-reaching personnel decision. At an informal and unminuted discussion on 28 March 1960, the council decided not to renew Michael Pattrick's appointment for another five-year term when it expired in November 1961. The records state no specific reason for this decision apart from the general view that 'the post of principal was one which would [*sic*] be changed from time to time'.[60]

The fact that an outgoing council would, almost on its last day in office, make such a momentous decision, and the conspiratorial fashion in which it did it, does raise questions. Over the past few years, many of Pattrick's supporters had left the council, most notably Hugh Casson, Peter Shepheard and John Brandon-Jones. Newer members included Jordan's long-time allies Leo De Syllas and Anthony Cox, as well as their practice partner John Smith, a leading figure in the students' committee of the early 1950s and Pattrick's nemesis ever since. In a letter to the *AA Journal* in the summer of 1959, Smith had launched a barely concealed attack on the principal:

> Right through our leadership the second-rate [. . .] is tolerated either because no-one can think of an alternative or because we cannot afford anything better. [. . .] Sooner or later it must be realised that an element of sincerity coupled with a certain administrative efficiency are insufficient compensation for the conspicuous lack of imagination and ideas in those ultimately responsible for the direction of the Association and its School. [. . .] The future is far from black; it is the present that is not too rosy. Some basic rethinking may be necessary, and a certain amount of reshuffling in high places perhaps inevitable.[61]

Edward Playne, one of the vice-presidents at the time, remembered 'subversive talk undermining [Pattrick's] position',[62] and it is tempting to interpret Pattrick's dismissal and Jordan's appointment to a working party considering the future of the AA as correlated events – belated retaliation by a younger generation of council members who were perhaps critical of the former and certainly sympathetic to the latter.

Pattrick's ten-year reign had lasted longer than that of any other principal before him and, in fact, longer than those of his four predecessors combined. Though he remained a divisive figure

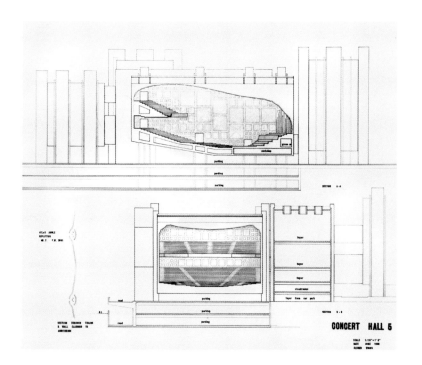

56 Concert Hall (Eldred Evans, fourth year, 1959/60)

Eldred Evans was seen as the outstanding talent of the class of '56, itself an unusually distinguished student cohort. Her concert hall, with its highly articulated floor plans, its distinction into serving and servant spaces, and not least its incredible toughness, was a typical example of her work – 'a giant Lou Kahn folly', as Peter Cook found (Arena, Dec 1966), 'but uninhibited and in the powerful monumental tradition'. A comparison with Reynolds's concert hall (Fig.49) illustrates the range of expressions which existed within the Brutalist canon.

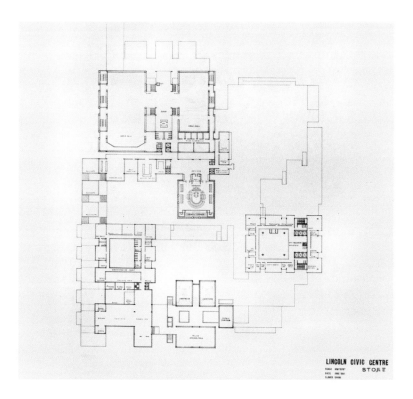

57 Civic Centre, Lincoln (Eldred Evans, thesis, 1960/61)

Like Rogers in the year ahead of her, Evans did not dazzle her jurors with her drawings. Bill Howell (AAJ, Sep/Oct 1960) was disdainful of her 'throw-away presentation', and James Gowan (AAJ, Sep/Oct 1961) criticised her drawings for failing to 'convey a sense of scale or material'. The quality of her work, however, was clearly exceptional. For her thesis, Evans resolved the challenging brief for the forthcoming Lincoln Civic Centre competition into a clustered plan arranged over a complex system of levels. A serial prize winner at the AA, she eventually prevailed over several established practices (and – aged 24 and still living with her parents – invested her prize money in a Rolls-Royce).

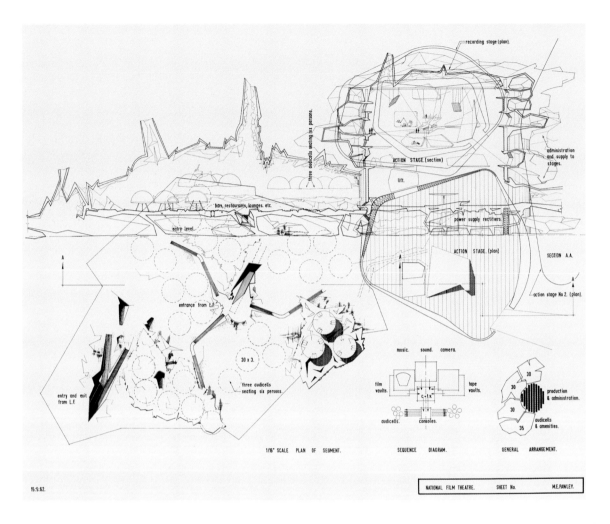

Labels within the image:
recording stage (plan).
three audicells seating six persons.
ACTION STAGE. (section)
administration and supply to stages.
lift.
bars, restaurants, lounges. etc.
entry level.
power supply rectifiers.
ACTION STAGE. (plan)
SECTION A.A.
entrance from L.F.
action stage No 2. (plan).
30 x 3.
three audicells seating six persons.
entry and exit from L.F.
music. sound. camera.
film vaults.
tape vaults.
C-t.x.
audicells. consoles.
production & administration.
audicells & amenities.
1/16" SCALE PLAN OF SEGMENT.
SEQUENCE DIAGRAM.
GENERAL ARRANGEMENT.
15:5:62.
NATIONAL FILM THEATRE. SHEET No. M.E.PAWLEY.

58   National Film Theatre (Martin Pawley, fourth year, 1961/62)

By 1961, Smithson and Killick had left the AA and the time for formal excesses had passed. Depending on one's viewpoint, Pawley's National Film Theatre of 1962 can thus be seen as the parting shot of a dying era or, as Peter Cook argued ('Electric Decade', p.137), 'a spark of fire in a grey atmosphere' – first stirrings of a new joyful exuberance which through the agency of Archigram would come to permeate the AA in the second half of the decade. Pawley proposed 700 bubble-shaped viewing cubicles for two people each, fed by video tape, which allowed each pair of visitors to watch the film of its choosing at the time of its choosing. The cubicles were distributed into four sections and arranged in a semi-circle around a central administration and production core, all of it supported and serviced by a massive megastructural platform.

within the AA, his success as the head of its school was widely acknowledged: in November 1961 he transferred seamlessly to the prestigious Central School of Art and Design (now Central St Martins), which he would direct until his retirement in 1978. Pattrick's impact on architectural education in this country was profound, if entirely unacknowledged. He was a member of all three committees which in the 1950s shaped the educational framework on behalf of the BAE: the McMorran Committee, the organising committee of the Oxford Conference and the influential Oxford Conference Committee tasked with recommending ways of implementing the conference resolutions. In these capacities

he promoted, with remarkable consistency and initially against considerable opposition, a view of architectural education – based on higher entry standards and carried out exclusively in recognised full-time schools at university level – which by the end of the decade became the official policy of the RIBA. According to Crinson and Lubbock, who do not discuss Pattrick's contribution in their standard reference on British architectural education, this new policy was the result of a campaign orchestrated by a group of public architects in the mid-1950s, and they consequently term it the 'Official System' – it could with some justification be called the 'Pattrick System'.

8   William Allen and the 'Art/Science Tension' (1961–1965)

A New Order

Michael Pattrick's departure and the forthcoming retirement of senior administrative staff offered the opportunity for a reorganisation of the AA's executive structure. This involved the creation of the new post of director of the association (in addition to the principal of the school). The AA had in the past experimented with the combination of director and principal – successfully with Robert Atkinson and Howard Robertson in the 1920s, less so with Harry Goodhart-Rendel and E. A. A. Rowse in the 1930s. However, both Atkinson and Goodhart-Rendel had served as directors of studies, concerned with the school rather than the association, whereas the chief task of the new director would be to 'increase the closeness of the link'[1] between the two. The council had no difficulties finding the right man for the job and appointed Edward ('Bobby') Carter, from 1930 to 1946 librarian of the RIBA and subsequently for 11 years head of UNESCO's libraries division in Paris.

A rather more difficult matter was the selection of a new principal. Discussing suggestions for possible candidates at the end of the 1960/61 session, the council was unable to agree whether or not to consider the appointment of an architect with a strong individual design attitude, generally referred to as a 'prima donna'. Most members of council rejected the idea and wished to keep to the AA's tradition of choosing a practising but not overly eminent or busy architect with a background in teaching. Denys Lasdun, for instance, felt that rather than a single-minded 'prima donna' the AA required a respected 'father figure' with a 'liberal, but serious attitude to architecture' – a trait he saw in Arthur Korn, Ernö Goldfinger or Ove Arup.[2] However, there were exceptions: James Cubitt took the view that the 'prima-donna system' should be tried as an experiment and favoured Anthony Cox or Peter Smithson, possibly in tandem.[3]

Divided over the issue, the council advertised the position in October 1960, and though the number of applicants was lower than expected, their quality was higher than on previous occasions. They included Birmingham principal Douglas Jones along with the heads of various other, comparatively minor British schools; Frederic Lasserre, who had worked with Tecton before becoming the inaugural director of the architectural school at the University of British Columbia; and former fifth-year master Henry Elder, now a professor at Cornell. Remarkably, apart from Douglas Jones none of these applicants was seriously considered. Instead, on 20 February 1961, the council appointed a man who was neither an educator nor in fact a practising architect – 'prima donna' or otherwise.

Born in Winnipeg in 1914, William Allen had left post-Depression Canada shortly after qualifying as an architect in 1936. Eager to pursue postgraduate

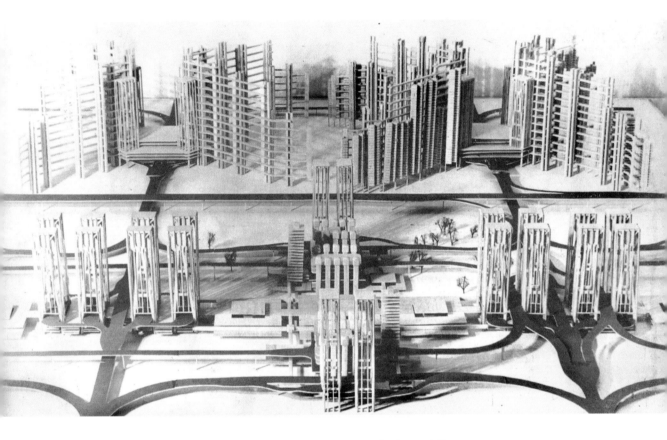

59   Euroway (Digby Bridges, Richard Farrow, John Martin, Harry Moon, thesis, 1961/62)

This group thesis illustrates the scope of ambition and unquestioned faith in the remit of architect-planners in the early 1960s. The students proposed no less than a complete redevelopment of the entire country, based on wide-ranging research and worked out in astonishing detail. Euroway is a two-mile wide, highly urbanised and industrialised land reservation accommodating a national power and transportation network connecting seven main entry ports (one of them a Channel bridge providing a direct link with the European continent following the United Kingdom's entry into the Common Market). The image shows one of numerous new 'urban units' of 500,000 residents each, which were to be established along this vast megastructural spine to prevent further urban sprawl in the Midlands and the South-East and halt the decline of deindustrialised towns elsewhere.

**Hook Housing
(Martyn Haxworth, James Hodges,
Christopher Woodward, thesis,
1961/62)**

*Working under the tutelage of Alan
Colquhoun, the students redesigned
one of the proposed housing areas in
the recently published master plan
for the LCC's New Town at Hook. At
the heart of the highly rationalised
scheme is a megastructural spine
containing five-storey apartment
blocks hovering above a multi-level
access deck. Branching off to either
side are further pedestrian decks,
the so-called 'spine routes', which
lead to parallel rows of two-storey
terraces and additional amenities
such as schools and youth clubs. To
the west, the spine routes bridge an
elevated motorway to give access
to a number of detached houses
overlooking the lake. Figure 60 shows
a perspective view of a spine route
(top) and the overall layout (bottom);
Figure 61 shows a section through
the spine (top), the garden elevation
of the terrace housing (middle), and
a section through one of the spine
routes, with part of the main spine
seen in elevation (bottom).*

studies but unable to find a university which offered any such programme, Allen worked with Louis de Soissons on plans for Welwyn Garden City before finding an opening at the government's pioneering Building Research Station (BRS) in Watford. During the war, when the AA school was based in nearby Barnet, Allen lectured regularly to students and organised visits to the BRS. Frederick Gibberd was anxious to appoint him to the teaching staff, and in the late 1940s the council put him forward for election on three different occasions. In 1953, Allen became the founding director of the architectural division of the BRS and as such the leading light in the emerging field of architectural science; one year later, he was elected to the RIBA council, on which he served continuously until 1971 (and again from 1982 to 1989). According to Crinson and Lubbock, Allen belonged to the breed of young public-authority modernists who came to dominate the RIBA,[4] and as a member of several influential committees of the BAE, including the ones entrusted with organising the Oxford Conference and implementing its resolutions, he was instrumental in shaping the policies which were to guide architectural education in the 1960s.

The professional press welcomed the AA's intention to embrace a more academic attitude in its approach to architectural education. The *Architects' Journal* praised the council for the 'considerable wisdom in its choice for its appointments',[5] and the *Architectural Review* considered that 'speculations about a new order at the Architectural Association [. . .] have been answered in a more drastic manner than had been expected, and a more promising one'.[6] The key figure in this was Leo De Syllas, who had worked at the BRS during the war and who together with his ACP partner Anthony Cox lobbied his fellow councillors to strengthen 'the scientific and social aspects of our work' by offering the principalship to his former colleague.[7] Allen, who was 46 at the time, at first rejected the offer as the usual incumbency of AA principals was likely to leave him 'out of my main job at an awkward age'.[8] The council only managed to persuade him by giving him the verbal assurance of tenure until

the age of 60, subject to his appointment being confirmed after an initial trial period of three years – an arrangement which would give cause for controversy.

Proposed Merger with the Imperial College of Science and Technology

In May 1961, three months after the council had appointed the school's new leadership, Peter Chamberlin finally issued the report of his working party on the future of the AA.[9] The so-called Chamberlin Report, 15 months in the making, was a comprehensive survey of the AA school, with particular emphasis on its precarious reliance on continually rising student fees and – to justify these – the corresponding need for a unique form of architectural education ('unique in the sense of being experimental and adventurous').[10] Broad in scope but light on detail, the report offered 13 recommendations, two of which proved significant. First, it called on the council to forcefully pursue the expansion of postgraduate facilities. At a time of growing control of school curricula through the RIBA, this was the one field where 'being experimental and adventurous' was in fact still possible and where consequently the AA could still distinguish itself from its competitors. Second, and most importantly, the working party, which mourned the missed opportunity of an integrated college with the LCC, urged the council to seek affiliation with another institution, preferably one which would offer both academic and financial advantages to the AA.

The council supported this view not least because in the early 1960s the RIBA began to actively pursue its agenda of moving architecture schools into universities. This agenda, an outcome of the Oxford Conference, was in keeping with current government policy. In February 1961, Prime Minister Harold Macmillan had appointed a committee under Lord Robbins to advise on the future pattern of higher education in Britain. It advanced the principle that 'all who are qualified to pursue full-time higher education should have the opportunity of doing so'.[11] To this end, it recommended the granting of university status to CATs as well as the development of three existing colleges – one of them the Imperial College of Science and Technology (ICST) – into 'Special Institutions for Scientific and Technological Education and Research' (SISTERs).[12] Though the Robbins Committee did not publish its report until October 1963, one would suspect that its members – notably Patrick Linstead, the rector of the ICST – had a clear idea of the line it might be taking. In 1953, the ICST had initiated a vast expansion programme aimed at transforming it into a 'London Institute of Technology' (i.e. a SISTER ante litteram), severed from London University and modelled on highly regarded international institutions such as the MIT, ETH Zurich and TU Delft. All of these centred upon thriving schools of architecture, which explains why, in April 1961, Linstead informed the AA of his interest to attach its school as a constituent college to the ICST.[13] The council welcomed the opportunity to make amends for its poor handling of the LCC negotiations, and in December 1961 it authorised its president, Michael Austin-Smith, to enter formal talks.[14]

Besides Austin-Smith, Bobby Carter and senior council members Anthony Cox and Leo De Syllas (both supporters of the previous LCC scheme) emerged as the chief promoters of the merger plan, though the council as a whole was unanimous in its enthusiasm and intent to bring the negotiations to a successful conclusion. In the substantial body of records documenting the initial stages of the plan there is not a hint of doubt that it would eventually materialise. The question, in the eyes of the council, was not if, but when. Accordingly, it exhibited a rare sense of purpose in its dealings with the ICST, treating controversial issues such as the necessary relocation from Bloomsbury to the less convenient South Kensington or the inevitable loss of control over the school – a deal-breaker only a couple of years prior – as matters of detail rather than principle. The process was facilitated by the fact that Linstead in particular appeared genuinely eager to preserve the AA's 'peculiar flavour'.[15] As

a result, negotiations proceeded smoothly: by May 1962, the AA and the ICST had established a constitutional committee tasked with drawing up a 'treaty' between the two schools; by December 1962, its heads of agreement had been approved by both governing bodies; and by May 1963, both senate and court of London University had formally accepted them as the basis for further negotiations and an approach to the University Grants Committee.

Though legally entitled to authorise the merger without their consent, the council felt a 'moral obligation' to consult the members of the association on their views.[16] From the beginning, it pursued its plan with the utmost transparency, organising a series of 'information meetings' to avoid provoking allegations of secrecy such as had been levelled against it in the wake of the LCC negotiations. In March 1964, in preparation for a referendum on the matter, the council issued the so-called 'Grey Book', a 44-page pamphlet setting out its arguments in favour of the merger.[17] Chief among these was, of course, the prospect of UGC funding; yet the council was equally anxious to highlight the perceived educational merits of the merger, notably the benefits derived from the expected cross-fertilisation with other fields of study.

At the outset, the general membership appears to have been supportive of the scheme. Diana Lee-Smith and Christopher Cross, respectively the secretary and chairman of the 1962/63 students' committee, were among the first who voiced their objections to the merger, defending the school's independent governance as 'an ideal principle we weren't going to go back on'.[18] It became the default position of the overwhelming majority of student leaders during the remainder of the decade – most forcefully expressed by Cross's successor Michael Glickman, a 'Christ-like figure rallying virtually the whole student body to state in no uncertain terms their attitude to the IC merger', as Peter Cook recalled.[19] In the run-up to the referendum, opposition to the merger scheme gained momentum among students and sections of the staff, driven by a growing sense of dissatisfaction with developments in the school (see p.129). John Smith, now the editor of the *AA Journal*, added

TRAINING
COLLEGE
SWINDON

SCALE 1/32" to 1' 21
NORTH WEST AXONOMETRIC

62 Teachers' Training College, Swindon (Edward Jones, Paul Simpson, thesis, 1962/63)

Edward Jones was a member of the so-called 'Grunt Group', which in the early 1960s produced a series of ultra-rational projects based on a thorough analysis of complex programme requirements. Jones and Simpson's thesis for a teachers' training college – one of four on this subject in that particular year – was a response to the Ministry of Education's recently announced policy to establish such colleges for a thousand students each, two-thirds of them being in residence. Unusually, the students placed their college on an urban site in the centre of Swindon. The spatial restrictions prompted a compact arrangement consisting of two distinct parts – a binuclear block for teaching and communal facilities organised into two interlocking squares, and a slab extending up a slope for student and staff accommodation. The main access level of the teaching block is on the second floor, which connects via a pedestrian bridge to the circulation tower of the residential slab.

63 Secondary School for 1,200, Wandsworth (Jeremy Dixon, thesis, 1963/64)

Dixon's thesis for a secondary school in Wandsworth is another typical example of the cool and systematic style of the Grunt Group. The main thrust of the project was to examine the impact of computer-organised group teaching. It attempted to reconcile current Ministry of Education schedules with novel American pedagogical theories calling for subjects (and therefore classrooms) to be clustered into so-called 'centres of interest'. The tight LCC site in Wandsworth inspired a two-storey building with outdoor facilities on the roof, disciplined by a rigid square grid, which determines the dimensions of all its major components. The no-frills presentation recalls functionalist drawings of the 1920s such as Hannes Meyer's competition project for Petersschule in Basel.

fuel to the debate, and in March 1964 councillor James Gowan withdrew his candidature for the forthcoming election in protest and resigned his AA membership.[20]

Meanwhile, general meetings became increasingly contentious, not least because the council's unreserved advocacy of the scheme raised suspicions: 'In selling the scheme so vigorously they have sown seeds of doubt in the minds of many of us.'[21]

By the time the referendum took place on 27 July 1964, the AA council had lost much of its confidence in a positive outcome, indicated by the fact that it was deliberately vague as to what precisely it would consider to be such an outcome.[22] In the event, the referendum delivered a comfortable majority, with 691 members voting in favour and 422 against.[23] However, a closer analysis of the figures exposed two major caveats which boded ill for the future of the scheme. For one, there was a sharp discrepancy between ordinary and probationary members: while the former supported the plan with a two-thirds majority, the students opposed it with an even greater one. Equally alarmingly, less than a third of the total membership had voted at all, showing a widespread lack of interest in a question of vital importance to the future of the AA. In spite of this, the council concluded that the result gave it a mandate to proceed with its plan of transferring the school to the ICST.[24] The students' committee grudgingly accepted this verdict – for the time being.

'Growth Points' – Allen's Vision for the AA School

Contrary to a persistent myth in AA circles, William Allen was not appointed to prepare the school for the ICST merger. His arrival predated the initial contact between the two institutions, and while broadly supportive of the scheme and intimately involved in the negotiations, he was neither its originator nor a driving force behind it. Instead, Allen's appointment and the ICST scheme were masterminded by the same influential group of council members and inspired by the same

technocratic worldview. The previous chapter traced the events leading up to the Oxford Conference, which rejected the traditional notion of architectural education as a vocational field of study and, with its twin drive for higher entry standards and postgraduate research, turned this worldview into official RIBA policy. The AA had been instrumental in framing this policy, but despite the success of its pioneering DTA all attempts to establish similar schemes had proved abortive. The real strides towards a more academic pedagogical model had been made by the leading university schools, where public-sector architects had taken up key positions, intent on transforming them into centres of architectural research. Leading the way at the time of the conference were Edinburgh's Robert Matthew and Liverpool's Robert Gardner-Medwin, who in 1955 had established the country's first chair of building science (and offered it to Allen). In 1956, Leslie Martin had left the LCC to move to Cambridge, where he strengthened postgraduate studies in history and urban reconstruction, and in 1960, Richard Llewelyn Davies took over the Bartlett, replacing its diploma course and Beaux-Arts methods with a science-based curriculum divided into a three-year degree and a two-year postgraduate course. These developments challenged the AA's standing as a pacesetter in British architectural education, and William Allen, one of the leading architectural scientists in the world, seemed the right person to restore its tarnished reputation.

The new principal expounded his pedagogical vision in his inaugural lecture on 28 February 1962, half a year after taking office.[25] To Allen, the key obstacle impeding the progress of the profession was its inherent 'art/science tension'.[26] Architects, he observed, were prepared to acknowledge the practical usefulness of science for their work but struggled to grasp the fundamental nature of its outlook, and the only way to overcome this was by making it an integral part of their training. Allen argued that this scientific outlook would neither replace nor limit the students' creativity, but would instead improve it since the quality of intuitive acts, including the creation of architecture, was predetermined by a person's prior knowledge, which in turn was best acquired through scientific methods.[27] More importantly, it would enable them to fulfil their obligation to society, which, in Allen's view, exceeded their traditional role as designers and required them as strategists and policy-makers to assume responsibility for the physical environment as a whole: 'Our concern must be not only for individual buildings but for the nation's building.'[28]

According to Allen, training for any profession involved the acquisition of knowledge and the necessary skill in applying this knowledge, that is, both 'education' and 'training'.[29] In sharp contrast to Martin and Llewelyn Davies, who advocated a clear distinction between the two, Allen considered the traditional setup of British schools of architecture – with its parallel arrangement of education (in the form of lecture courses) and training (in the form of studio work) – 'absolutely sound' and called for more, not less, integration.[30] The question was how to modify the elements of the course to accomplish this closer integration. Allen never really managed to offer a convincing answer and was particularly vague with respect to the studio teaching, which he more or less bypassed as 'a big subject on its own [. . .] which must at some time be tackled'.[31]

Unsurprisingly, Allen's ideas on the intellectual content of the course were rather more developed and centred on a reinterpretation and regrouping of specialist subjects. Faced with the fact that (with the exception of history) none of these was 'an academic discipline in itself which we can lift "straight" from somewhere else', Allen considered it to be the school's primary task to combine the 'borrowings' and process them for their specific use in the architectural course.[32] To achieve this, he hoped to consolidate the various technical subjects into a comprehensive technology department, which – equipped with state-of-the-art facilities and staffed with highly qualified personnel on long-term contracts – would advance them from a specifically architectural viewpoint and provide opportunities for postgraduate

research. Eventually, Allen envisaged the school to be departmentalised into four 'major areas of advanced study': the 'general practice of architecture' (i.e. studio-based design teaching), tropical studies, science and technology, and – as an additional 'growth point' requiring immediate attention – urban design.[33]

The prototype for these new departments was the DTA, which – renamed the Department of Tropical Studies (DTS) – continued to flourish and expand under Allen, providing the model for similar establishments throughout Europe and North America. Mirroring the regular school course, the emphasis of the DTS lay on the intellectual content of the work, with data compilation and research reports taking precedence over the actual design process (Plates 11–12).[34] Climate was increasingly studied in relation to human physiology (lighting, air flow, noise control and so forth) – a development which was clearly indebted to Allen, who had pioneered such work at the BRS. School programmes themselves were frequently linked to the sought-after consultancy service which the DTS provided to governments and organisations in the developing world.[35] It was due to the high reputation of the DTS that in September 1962 representatives of the Kwame Nkruma University of Science and Technology (KNUST) at Kumasi in Ghana approached Allen with a request to advise the university on the reorganisation of its faculty for architecture, planning and building, to appoint a temporary head and to take over its quality control.[36] The council ratified the agreement with KNUST in April 1963 and, at Allen's suggestion, nominated former first-year master John Lloyd as the dean of the faculty.[37]

The establishment of additional DTS-inspired departments involved considerable expenditure, which in turn necessitated an increase in student numbers. With full employment in the building industry and a sharp rise in the number of school leavers gaining two or more A-levels, Pattrick's prediction that the recognised schools would remain unaffected by the introduction of higher entry standards proved accurate. In fact, at all

Mahaddie's thesis project for a hotel in Bournemouth was unusual, not just in its choice of topic – commercial rather than social – but also in its apparently unsystematised and intuitive handling of structure and plan. Alan Colquhoun (AAJ, Sep/Oct 1963) was slightly bemused by the seemingly wilful and over-complicated scheme but impressed by the confidence with which its author tackled it. The contrast between Mahaddie's idiosyncratic design approach and the detached rationalism then prevalent in the school seemed to indicate a confusion of direction. According to Colquhoun, 'a pattern seems to have developed in which there are two poles of activity each representing a radically opposed definition of architecture'.

64 Hotel, Bournemouth (Andrew Mahaddie, thesis, 1962/63)

major schools the number of applications was far in excess of the number of available places; any expansion of the AA school was therefore limited solely by administrative considerations and a lack of space.[38] Yet despite the fact that the school was filled to capacity at any given time in the early 1960s, finances remained tight. In June 1962, only four months after Allen had outlined his ambitious development programme and identified specific 'growth points' for the school, the council urged its new principal to 'look closely at the budget to see if any savings could be made'.[39]

Allen received help from two different sources. First, the government, in passing the 1962 Education Act, made it compulsory for local education authorities to fund all full-time students in higher education. This meant that, unlike in previous years, the AA could set the level of its fees uninhibited by the fear of losing their goodwill. To offset the anticipated deficit incurred through Allen's development programme, in March 1964 the council thus raised the school fees to £325, roughly five times the amount payable at comparable schools.[40] Second, the Leverhulme Trust offered to finance both of Allen's two 'growth points'.[41] The first of these – the so-called Department of Science and Technology – was headed by services lecturer Peter Burberry, who was given the overriding responsibility for *all* technical lecture courses and thereby emerged as a powerful figure at the school. The second – the Department of Urban and Regional Design – satisfied a long-held ambition to fill a perceived void in planning education left by the closure of Rowse's SPRND in 1953 and thus secure architects a foothold in their turf wars with other professions vying for control over planning matters. When the Leverhulme Trust announced its grant in May 1963, Arthur Korn, who embodied the planning bias of the postwar AA, set up a one-year pilot scheme to prepare a group of fifth-year students for the final examinations of both the RIBA and the Town Planning Institute.[42] In December 1963, the council appointed Hugh Wilson, formerly the chief architect and planning officer for Cumbernauld, as the head of the department, which was formally inaugurated in

September 1964. Wilson resigned one year later to take up a government appointment and was succeeded by Leslie Ginsburg, an AA and SPRND graduate and for the past seven years head of the planning school at Birmingham.

The Beginning of the End

Allen dismissed the idea of architectural education as a 'studio activity with lecture courses as a kind of running commentary' and was intent on readjusting the balance between education and training.[43] His attempts at strengthening the formal education of his students by combining the technical subjects into a separate, fully funded department implied a certain neglect of the studio teaching and effectively, if unintentionally, reversed the traditional hierarchy underpinning the AA's educational system. Allen barely concerned himself with the nature and succession of studio programmes, around which much of the debates in previous years had revolved. Though disdainful of the existing curriculum, whose gradation of scales and succession of material studies he thought naïve and superficial,[44] he considered it of minor importance within his broader educational vision and retained it (Plates 13–17). While the curricular framework remained thus largely intact, the nature of the course changed profoundly as Allen, to the growing irritation of the design teachers, encouraged his specialists to interfere directly with their programmes and use the studio as 'an effective demonstration room or laboratory for the lecture programme'.[45]

The cumulative effect of such piecemeal and uncoordinated interventions was a gradual loss of coherence in the course. This had an impact on the morale of staff and students alike, in the latter case aggravated by the fact that the changeover to the new lecture courses was poorly managed. Specialist staff had trouble translating Allen's vision of a specifically 'architectural' approach to their subjects into practice – the structures course, for instance, saw a change in leadership (and method) on an almost annual basis. Moreover, the rearrangement of lecture courses evidently necessitated an accordingly modified examination system. The phased transition from the old system to the new one was not completed until March 1966, and in the meantime some students had to sit exams in subjects in which they had not yet been taught (and in some cases would never be taught at all) – with the corresponding rate of failures.[46] The students' reaction to the emerging problems in the school was almost instantaneous. Initially enthused about the new educational outlook, in February 1962 the students' committee circulated a critical report on the school, and by the end of the academic year it concluded drily that as far as education was concerned the students had 'stopped admiring Mr Allen's comprehension of this subject'.[47]

With the school in difficulties, the time was particularly inopportune for the RIBA's visiting board to announce its first inspection since 1950. Over the past four years the reconstituted BAE had developed its visiting board into the main instrument through which it exerted its influence on the schools. Although the board's visit in October 1963 was therefore anything but a formality, there seemed to be little cause for worry. Unlike Robert Furneaux Jordan, who had run the school with conscious disregard for the prevailing educational orthodoxies, the current principal was eager to align it with the RIBA's 'Official System'. The AA council had therefore every reason to believe that the visiting board would see the development of the school in a favourable light. Yet, while welcoming the thinking which inspired the changes to the lecture syllabus and the expansion of research facilities, the board declared itself 'very disturbed' by the high rate of failures in examinations and criticised both the system itself and the 'lackadaisical attitude' of staff and students towards it.[48] It was equally dissatisfied with the quality of studio work, in which a logical progression of projects seemed lacking and the 'policy of integration with the lecture course [. . .] not apparent'.[49] Though the visiting board appreciated that the school was in a transitional phase, its overall verdict was damning: 'If the

school was assessed on "promise" it would rate very highly but on present performance the school falls short in a number of ways.'[50]

Allen was taken aback by the findings of the board, and so was the council, which – having ignored all signs to the contrary – was under the impression that the school was 'thriving under [Allen's] influence'.[51] The report of the visiting board, issued in March 1964, put any such thoughts to rest. At a council meeting on 16 March, Tim Tinker, who was working for the Smithsons at the time, expressed 'strong doubts' about Allen's priorities (i.e. his emphasis on technology). One month later, a group of councillors including Tinker, Jane Drew and Francis Baden-Powell triggered a discussion on his suitability as principal – to the consternation of Allen himself, whose confidence was 'deeply shaken'.[52] The council's deliberations continued for several months; it was not until November 1964 that it eventually renewed Allen's contract, expressing its 'warmest appreciation' of his work but warning him that, with the enlargement of the technical departments, there was a 'special need [. . .] to strengthen and clarify the teaching of architectural design in the school'.[53]

The System Boys *vs* the One-off Boys

By 1964, opposition to Allen's direction of the school was building up both within the council and, exacerbated by the outcome of the ICST referendum, the student body. Worse still, Allen's undeterred pursuit of his development plan with its implicit technological bias increased tensions between himself and his studio staff. To understand the root cause of the latter's discontent, we need to consider their traditional position within the AA's educational system. As we saw in previous chapters, studio staff lacked job security and were grossly underpaid, which on the face of it made teaching at the AA a relatively unappealing prospect, particularly in times of full employment. On the other hand, shielded

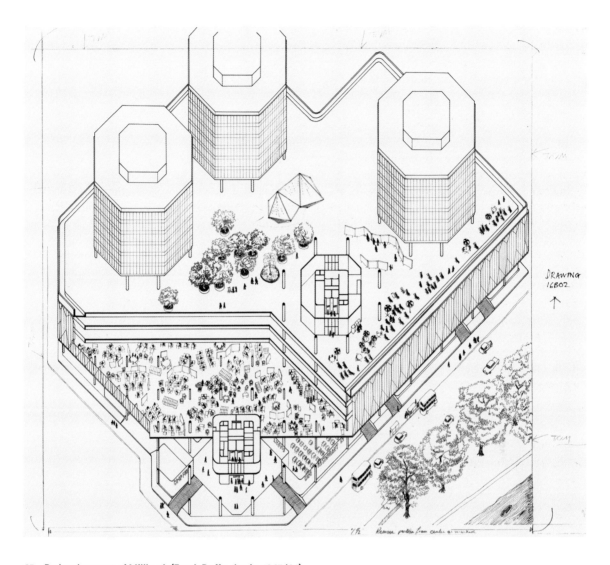

DRAWING 16B02

65 Redevelopment of Millbank (Frank Duffy, thesis, 1963/64)

The building consists of an arcade ground floor with shops, restaurants and banks; three floors of open-plan offices for Imperial Chemical Industries modelled on German Bürolandschaft *principles; a roof deck for sports and recreation; and five octagonal towers for speculative offices suitable for small firms. Duffy, who became an internationally leading figure in office planning, was critical of his first effort in this field (*AAJ, *May 1965). The relation between towers and base, he felt, was never resolved, and major decisions – great open floors, huge areas of glazing – had been made 'without really considering the effect on the poor people using the building'.*

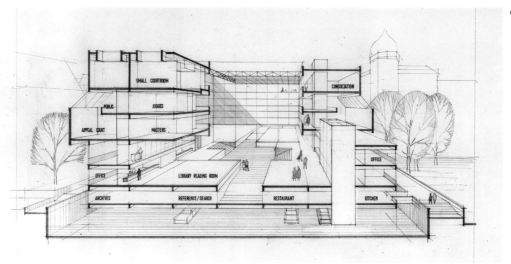

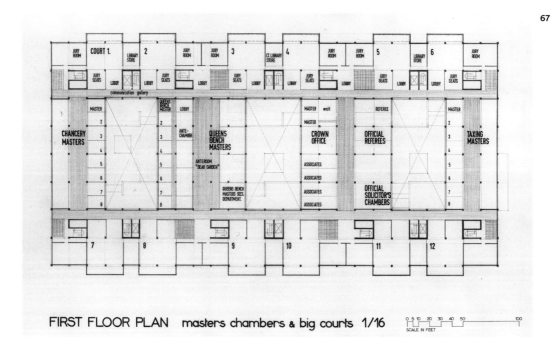

FIRST FLOOR PLAN masters chambers & big courts 1/16

Royal Courts of Justice (Simon Pepper, fourth year, 1964/65)

In 1964, Alvin Boyarksy succeeded John Winter as the fourth-year master. The choice of a one-off building – and one which implicitly asked for a formal and monumental expression – was a conscious decision to steer his students away from the school's current obsession with system-building. Boyarsky enlisted the support of leading legal experts such as Jack Jacob and Louis Blom-Cooper to advise his students on the minutiae of court proceedings and assist them in their research. Simon Pepper proposed a symmetrical layout consisting of an atrium sandwiched between two lateral layers accommodating the various courts. Bridges containing judges' and masters' offices span the public concourse, which negotiates the slope of the site via a succession of terraces.

from outside interference by the principal, studio masters had wide-ranging liberties in devising their programmes, which throughout the AA's history – and never more so than under Allen's predecessor – enticed enterprising young members of the profession to its teaching staff. The incremental loss of their authority over the design process to the specialist teachers not only curbed their enthusiasm, it also seemed to give them a glimpse of their future working conditions in a university setup marked by departmental infighting.

Indeed, opposition to the ICST merger was the common denominator of a diverse group of staff who began to take a stand against their principal, whom they saw – understandably if unfairly – as the spearhead of this undesirable endeavour. Third-year unit staff Cedric Price, Roy Landau and Michael Pearson saw the removal of Allen as a prerequisite to stopping a plan they rejected as running counter to the AA's ethos. They objected to the strictures of university governance, particularly the idea of permanent staff appointments, and they rejected Allen's alleged architecture-by-numbers approach even though they were not on principle opposed to the scientific outlook he sought to inject into the school.[54] To others, however, the developments at the AA raised architectural as much as educational concerns. Though their curriculum survived into the mid-1960s, stylistically the Brutalists' spell at the AA had been a short-lived affair. Reflecting Allen's vision of the architect-planner controlling the built environment in its totality, student schemes were generally vast in scope and scale but characterised, as Edward Jones put it, by a 'distrust of the private will to form [and a] general neutrality of expression'.[55] Their lack of formal bravado betrayed the influence of major American practices such as SOM and Gropius's TAC, where several AA tutors (including year masters Roy Landau and John Winter) had previously worked; yet it also recalled student work under Jordan and, like then, was the product of an educational model which prioritised social purpose over self-expression, technology over design (Figs 59–65).

Allen's school was consumed by the quarrels between the 'one-off boys versus the system boys',

to use Manasseh's memorable phrase.[56] His fiercest opposition came from the former, and specifically from a group of staff who looked to Colin Rowe as their spiritus rector. Rowe's formalism had been a major source of inspiration for the early Brutalists, and as a member of the so-called Texas Rangers at the University of Texas at Austin in the mid-1950s he had pioneered a curriculum which emphasised precedent and reflected his profound scepticism regarding the ahistorical outlook and scientific determinism of modern architecture. After brief stints at the Cooper Union and at Cornell, Rowe had returned to England in 1958 to take up a dispiriting teaching appointment at Cambridge, where Leslie Martin championed the very 'scientism' he abhorred. In 1962, Allen intended to appoint Rowe as history lecturer but was apparently vetoed by Cox and De Syllas:

> The Marxist establishment is quite opposed to having me around the place. [. . .] The ACP is a very powerful little group. Allen wants me. The ACP does not. Allen doesn't want to offend the ACP.[57]

Though himself persona non grata, Rowe had a significant following on the AA staff, which included fifth-year tutor Alan Colquhoun, history lecturer Thomas ('Sam') Stevens and first-year master Anthony Eardley. The key figure among Rowe's disciples was his former student and close friend Alvin Boyarsky, a Canadian architect who was working for Yorke Rosenberg Mardall at the time. Boyarsky joined the fourth-year unit staff in 1963 and one year later succeeded Winter as year master. He took charge of a complex exchange programme with various American and Scandinavian schools, and he cunningly reduced the required attendance of his unit masters, which even at a time of frenetic building activity enabled him to assemble an extraordinarily distinguished staff comprising David Allford (Yorke Rosenberg Mardall), Warren Chalk (Archigram), David Gray (Lyons Israel Ellis), Hal Higgins (Higgins and Ney) and David Shalev (Evans and Shalev) (Figs 66–67). Bustling and charismatic, Boyarsky soon emerged as an influential figure at the AA – and one who had, as Eardley remembers, a 'very thinly disguised contempt for Allen'.[58]

In the course of the 1964/65 academic year discontent turned into active resistance. In October 1964, three weeks into the session, Allen dismissed Richard Hobin, the new structures lecturer (and previously a popular second-year tutor), who was not prepared to tailor his course to the demands of his immediate superior, Peter Burberry. The year masters voiced their objection, and the students' committee apparently hired Hobin back as an evening lecturer and doubled his salary – to the embarrassment of the school committee, which felt compelled to reappoint him.[59] Meanwhile, relations between Boyarsky and both Allen and Burberry were taking a turn for the worse. In fact, 'Alvin's war on Peter'[60] (likely a mutual affair) reached a point where all communication between the two ceased – to the detriment of fourth-year students, who thus missed out on all but the most basic technical advice.[61]

With Boyarsky and likeminded studio teachers actively obstructing the work of the specialist staff, in April 1965 Allen introduced 'block teaching', which bundled individual lecture courses into several blocks lasting up to ten weeks during which time no studio work was permitted to take place. Though Allen continued to stress that he expected the 'integration [of lectures and studio teaching] to be practised as intensively as possible',[62] block teaching was effectively an admission that this integration had failed, and it further infuriated the studio staff, whose programmes were curtailed at short notice. Oddly, it was not until the end of the academic year that the full extent of the studio teachers' frustration became evident to Allen. On 25 May 1965, he issued an 11-page memorandum to his staff in which he acknowledged the need to 're-study and re-construct our curriculum' and itemised the various problems of the 'confused and fragmented' course.[63] The paper – short of solutions and written in an uncharacteristically vague, almost platitudinous manner – reflects a sense of helplessness in the face of overwhelming difficulties, and Boyarsky's annotations on his personal copy – 'CRAP [. . .] MORE CRAP' – indicate

how much support Allen could at this stage expect from his alienated staff.[64]

The controversy reached its climax during the summer break. On 29 June 1965, the students' committee approached James Cubitt, the new president, with a written statement deploring the 'prevailing atmosphere of aimless confusion' in the school and concluding that 'the running of a school of architecture of the AA's size and potential requires qualities of its principal which Mr. Allen, unfortunately, does not have'.[65] One week later, 19 unit masters followed suit by expressing their 'feeling of deep concern with the present educational policy of the school'.[66] In light of this, the council agreed that the following academic year should be regarded as an 'interregnum' and that a deputy principal should be appointed with special responsibilities for studio work. Cubitt tried to shield his principal by assigning the blame for the sorry state of the school to himself and his colleagues, who had neglected their oversight responsibilities and whose liaison machinery with the school had failed: 'It is we, the Council, who have done this. No one else has.'[67]

Cubitt's attempt to protect Allen was in vain. Over the past two years, Allen's power base had gradually eroded as the majority of those who had once supported his appointment had meanwhile left the council, including Michael Austin-Smith, Anthony Cox and, most importantly, Allen's proposer and president-designate Leo De Syllas, who died in 1964. Many of those who filled the vacant positions – mostly postwar graduates such as Tim Tinker, Peter Ahrends, Patrick de Saulles and John Dennys – were critical of the direction in which the school was steering. Thus, on 13 July 1965, the council decided to call a halt to the proceedings:

> The President was requested to convey to Mr. Allen the Council's wish that he should offer his resignation from the Principalship [and] the Council's hope that he would be able to continue his membership of the senior academic staff of the School in some role more closely related to his interest in the scientific and technological aspects of architecture.[68]

Allen accepted the council's decision and agreed to continue until a successor could be found, which was expected to happen towards the end of the 1965/66 session. He was in no doubt as to who had triggered the chain of events leading to his dismissal, and on 15 July 1965 he enlisted the support of his remaining allies on the council – Cubitt and his two vice-presidents Hugh Morris and John Eastwick-Field – to terminate the appointments of Alvin Boyarsky and fifth-year master George Balcombe.[69]

It was the last initiative Allen was allowed to take as he was increasingly sidelined in the decision-making process. On 19 July 1965, the council appointed John Voelcker as senior master with overriding responsibility for the fourth and fifth years (i.e. as deputy principal in anything but name).[70] Voelcker was the quintessential 'one-off' architect, who deplored specialisation and ran his practice in rural Kent as the equivalent of a country doctor's surgery. In July 1964, he had resigned from the editorial board of the *AA Journal* in protest at the council's merger plan with the ICST, not least because he rejected the idea of technology as being anything other than a useful tool at the service of the creative designer.[71] In other words, he was the antithesis to Allen, and the collaboration between the two was anything but cordial.

The council itself formed a so-called 'vacation committee', which assisted Allen in planning the curriculum for the forthcoming session. In spite (or perhaps because) of the shortage of time, Allen and the committee managed to arrive at a compromise which retained the existing lecture syllabus but gave greater powers to the studio staff and had the general support of specialists and design teachers.[72] Its implementation, however, foundered on the resistance of the students' committee. On 25 October 1965, following a meeting with its new chairwoman, Marie-Josée Pearson, the council unanimously agreed to relieve the principal of his duties at the end of the current term – to the bitter disappointment of an incredulous and disillusioned Allen:

When the terms of my contract were devised I was asked if I wanted a ten-year run, rather like Pattrick. I said this would put me out at 57 when it might be difficult to pick up other significant work. It was agreed therefore that we would have a 3-year trial – my suggestion – and if I was then confirmed my contract would be assumed to run 10 years to age 60. This was the only basis on which I was willing to move from BRS. [. . .] Now we have a position in which even 12 months is not envisaged, and not a soul has hinted at a sign of the slightest regret that the whole original intention of the contract has been set aside as if it never existed. [. . .] I have been pretty reasonable to the Council over this business, [. . .] and I am not very impressed.[73]

William Allen's headship ended on 17 December 1965, and he never taught at the AA again. Disillusioned with the state of architectural education in general, he turned his attention to the practice he had founded with his former BRS colleague John Bickerdike in 1962 and developed it beyond its core competencies in acoustics and lighting into a world-leading consultancy on building defects and litigation.

Allen's ill-fated attempt at merging formal education and design training – science and art – left the AA school in disarray. Perhaps a 'noble failure', as Andrew Derbyshire thought, but a failure nonetheless.[74] In part, the reason for Allen's troubles lay in his background. He was the first principal since Gibberd who had not studied at the school, and the AA's self-perpetuating cliquishness with its peculiar council-staff-students dynamic remained impenetrable to him. A more fundamental issue affecting Allen's principalship was generational. He belonged to a group of pre-war modernists to whom the postwar welfare state offered the long-awaited opportunity to realise their ideal of a social-minded, science-based and state-run architectural profession. Those who had set the agenda at the AA at the beginning of the decade embodied this vision, which found its expression in the Oxford Conference resolutions and the drive to integrate the AA into the higher education system. In December 1962, Robert Furneaux Jordan had noted with delight that 'in Bobby Carter, Bill Allen and Anthony Cox, we have a group of people who represent that continuity of the AA back into the past [. . .] in whose hands the future is absolutely secure'.[75] This 'continuity into the past', however, held little appeal for a new generation of students and staff whose worldview was not conditioned by the anxieties of the immediate postwar years, but by the relative carefreeness and affluence of the more recent past and present. As Michael Glickman wrote at the height of the ICST controversy:

'Before the war a group of rebellious students [. . .] fought to have their views recognised. [. . .] They are now the Architectural Establishment, although they still feel themselves to be the Avant-Garde. The president of the AA [. . .], with his generation, cannot accept that history, as always, has passed them by; that their particular battle was fought and (thank heavens!) won in the fifties and that it is the job of another generation (ours) to carry on as we see fit.'[76]

9 Epilogue: Beyond the Sixties (1965–1990)

Inspiration through the Letter Box – The Question of Allen's Succession

William Allen's departure did not resolve the tensions within the school as the council continued to pursue its existing policies and the student body continued to oppose them. The council put Otto Koenigsberger, who had deputised for Allen during his absences abroad, in charge of the school while considering the appointment of a new principal. Koenigsberger was popular with students, and together with Bobby Carter he managed to 'pilot the ship of the AA through stormy and difficult waters.'[1] However, the students' unease about the teaching arrangements persisted, and supported by councillor John Smith they began to push for a reinstatement of their full membership rights.[2]

The council, divided as ever, had difficulties agreeing on the selection criteria for the new principal. The job advertisement, in response to Allen's perceived shortcomings, stipulated 'a positive theory and knowledge of architecture', 'an awareness of the ideas and working of the AA' and 'assured academic ability' as the desired qualifications. Yet to fifth-year student (and future Liverpool professor) Simon Pepper, it seemed obvious that the council was 'reduced to waiting for inspiration through the letter box'.[3] Indeed, only one of those who were seriously considered – John Lloyd – could claim to tick all the boxes, and the fact that the group also included applicants of as varied a persuasion as Colin Rowe, Dutch architect Aldo van Eyck and AA graduate Peter Manning, who headed a research unit at Liverpool's Department of Building Science, indicates a lack of conviction underlying the selection process.

Manning's bid for the principalship apparently failed due to a poor reference from his colleague and quasi-superior Robert Gardner-Medwin.[4] Rowe, meanwhile at Cornell again, provided references from Leslie Martin and James Stirling and gathered a 60-strong 'lobby' to back his candidature.[5] Alas, Koenigsberger's vitriolic interview notes – 'a shifty character [. . .] evades all attempts to nail him down to a course of action [. . .] trembling, very nervous [. . .] does he drink [. . .] syphilis nose [. . .] no thanks' – leave little doubt that Rowe was still persona non grata at the AA.[6] Both remaining candidates had strong support on the council, and the records suggest that van Eyck would likely have won the race; he was, however, not prepared to give up his practice in Holland and withdrew his application despite repeated attempts to persuade him otherwise.[7]

This left only John Lloyd, the candidate of the council's selection committee. According to Columbia adjunct professor Grahame Shane, then a member of the students' committee, 'Lloyd had the backing of the old AA dynasty [but] presented a softer face [and was] seen as more design-oriented and less technocratic than Allen. It was a gesture to the students.'[8] Indeed, John Lloyd had been a popular first-year master and was known to be in

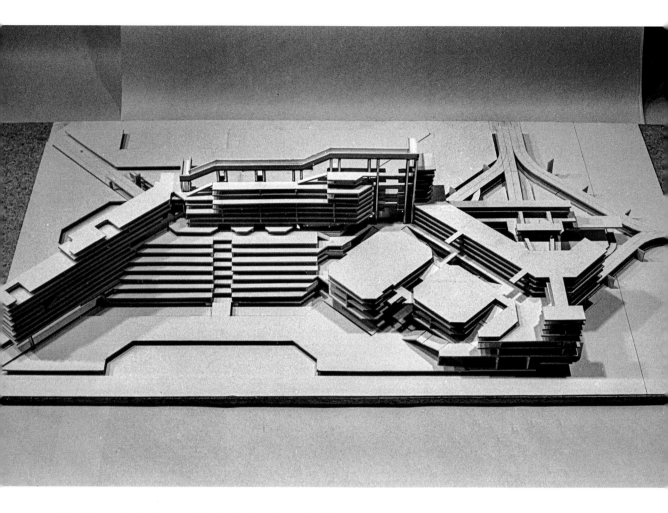

68   Battersea Redevelopment (Martin Godfrey, thesis, 1964/65)

*Boyarsky's formalism was a passing phenomenon, and so was the calm rationality of the Grunt Group. By the mid-1960s, the AA had come under the spell of the Archigram group. Martin Godfrey's megastructural redevelopment scheme for Battersea is a particularly striking example of the emerging trend. The aim was to develop an open-ended morphology of different urban situations which could be freely combined and extended in step with the demolition of the existing building stock. The image shows one of the new city sectors. According to Simon Sadler (*Archigram: Architecture Without Architecture*, p.162), Godfrey's scheme was, 'in effect, a solidified, monumental Plug-In City with "picturesque" massing and vertebral joints in its plan'.*

sympathy with the students' desire to control their own education – 'a man who reflects, faithfully and pleasantly, the AA's ethos', as the *Architects' Journal* found.[9] On the other hand, he was a close friend of William Allen's and shared his technocratic view of the architect as a strategist, whose responsibility as 'solution programmer and synthesiser' for the physical environment as a whole went far beyond their 'obsessional' role as 'form giver, the creator of contemporary fetishes'.[10] Worse still, having successfully headed his architectural faculty at Kumasi in a setup modelled on Imperial College, Lloyd was fiercely supportive of the council's merger plans and only applied for the position on the understanding that it would lead to a tenured university chair. Unsurprisingly, the council's decision to appoint him was far from unanimous: four members abstained and two of them – Tim Tinker and Peter Rich – resigned in protest.[11]

Lloyd's Vertical Unit System

Lloyd's principalship, which began in the autumn of 1966, was marked by such ambiguity. He was a transitional figure, though not an insubstantial one as he devised a pedagogical model which, in essence, survives to the present day. Like Robert Furneaux Jordan, under whom he had trained, Lloyd set up a tripartite framework of three separate 'schools' – in his case by combining the second, third and fourth years into a 'middle school' bookended by the first and fifth years – and like Jordan, he rejected the idea of a unified curriculum and gave students the freedom to develop their own pattern of courses and projects. On entering the middle school, students were asked to draft a 'statement of intent' and outline the contents of individual programmes for the following three-year period, while in the fifth year they opted for one of several topical streams.[12]

Lloyd's most significant intervention concerned the middle school, which he organised into nine units, each containing students from the second, third and fourth years. Unlike Pattrick's 'parallel unit system', in operation since 1954, the new system

abandoned the idea of a year-based curricular framework; unlike Rowse's original unit system of the late 1930s, it allowed students to choose their units and integrated them vertically through the years. John Smith had suggested a system of this kind as early as 1960,[13] but it was Lloyd (rather than Alvin Boyarsky, as is often mistakenly claimed) who established the vertical unit system as the core of an educational model which was to spread globally over the following decades.

The so-called vertical unit system and the renewed curricular permissiveness appealed to the architectural avant-garde of the day. Cedric Price would have been the students' preferred choice as Allen's successor and remained their guiding spirit, not least because he shared most passionately their distaste for the ICST merger scheme (and temporarily resigned his teaching post on the grounds that he 'would rather be tossed into a vat of crazed elephants than join the University structure').[14] However, it was the work of Archigram, the architectural figureheads of the 'Swinging Sixties', which more than any other captivated the mood of a generation disenchanted with the formulaic certainties bequeathed to them by their modernist elders. Archigram's particular brand of design subculture had begun to leave its mark on AA student work in the early 1960s, but its full impact did not manifest itself until the second half of the decade (Figs 68–71; Plates 18–19). By 1967, all members of Archigram had joined fifth-year master Peter Cook on the teaching staff, and student work echoed the group's preoccupation with impermanence and mobility – conveyed through seductive imagery and underpinned by a boundless faith in cutting-edge technology in the form of Fulleresque geodesic domes, pneumatic structures and movable dwelling units (Figs 72–74; Plates 20–21).[15]

Pearl Harbor, Vietnam . . . Imperial College

All the while, negotiations between the AA and the ICST continued even if the momentum had passed. With the death of Patrick Linstead in September 1966 and the retirement of Bobby Carter two months later the scheme lost its chief proponents, and the UCG's reluctance to finance it stalled progress for months. It was not until July 1967 that the UCG agreed to make recurrent grants available, provided that the AA itself would contribute half a million pounds to build its new headquarters. Although a public appeal raised little more than £200,000, the AA advertised a two-stage competition for the building, and in early 1970, AA President Jane Drew embarked on an extensive mission to the United States to raise the missing funds.

In the meantime, resistance against the merger within the AA grew and, mirroring events in the wider world, turned increasingly contentious. Richard Hobin, who reputedly supplied structural calculations for the Vietcong tunnel system, briefly joined the Bartlett but was sacked when he led an anti-war rally on the American Embassy in March 1968 and soon returned to the AA's teaching staff.[16] In general, though, any affinity with left-wing militancy occurred on a purely rhetorical level. Unlike the politically motivated upheavals in other institutions of higher education, the AA insurgency remained a characteristically private matter (albeit – equally characteristically – publicly aired). The students' club adopted the more combative title 'students' union', and in early 1968 a loose group of anti-ICST activists, who styled themselves the 'AA guerrillas', orchestrated a low-key protest against establishment figures Fry & Drew, whose recent clients included a British subsidiary of napalm manufacturer Dow Chemicals.[17] In a contribution to a general meeting of the association in November 1969, David Allford went so far as to liken the council's immobility in the matter of the ICST merger to the stubbornness of the US government in its handling of the situation in Vietnam:

> What the AA has stood for will crumble under the inevitable weight of the university statutes, rules, degrees, forms, structure, to say nothing of the UGC and, ultimately, the Treasury. The very weight of IC will sink the AA without trace. [. . .] I can see that the sincerely motivated but, I believe, misguided people on the platform and elsewhere have so committed themselves that

withdrawal is unthinkable. But bad positions are never unthinkable, especially among the lumpen proletariat – which is well represented here tonight, I see. I give you Vietnam. Johnson was committed to bad positions. Nixon is committed to bad positions, and meanwhile the positions get worse, more and more entrenched, dishonest and remote, and meanwhile unrest abounds and the texture of American society degenerates sadly and fast. This, I see, is the position. For heaven's sake let us re-think it.[18]

One month later, Allford and a small number of likeminded students and staff who had formed themselves into the so-called 'school community' took a last-ditch stand against the impending merger. At a meeting on 11 December 1969, the school community – a body without constitutional standing – passed resolutions asserting their 'right to determine their education, now and in future', rejecting the reinforcement of any 'power structure within the School [. . .] to the extent that it cannot be changed within a short period of time by the School Community', and demanding 'the responsibility of laying down the terms on which [the] negotiations [with the ICST] shall be conducted'.[19]

Linstead's successor William Penney and his governors watched these developments with growing unease – not least because the resolutions, which were in direct contravention to the heads of agreement for the merger, had been signed (and indeed seconded) by staff member Anthony Wade, an official representative of the AA on the negotiating panel.[20] Deeply distrustful of President Drew and her council, on 3 February 1970, Penney announced that in the eyes of the ICST 'the basis for a merger no longer existed and [. . .] the negotiations should therefore be terminated'.[21] Coming at a time when joint AA-ICST working parties were in the process of finalising the merger, the move startled a completely unsuspecting AA council and sent shockwaves through the architectural press. The *Architects' Journal* was bewildered by the governors' 'uncivilised behaviour',[22] and the *RIBA Journal* expressed its consternation in no uncertain terms:

69

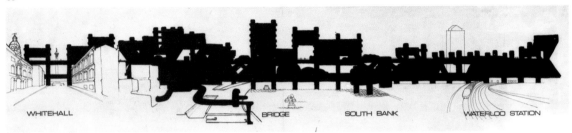

WHITEHALL · BRIDGE · SOUTH BANK · WATERLOO STATION

70

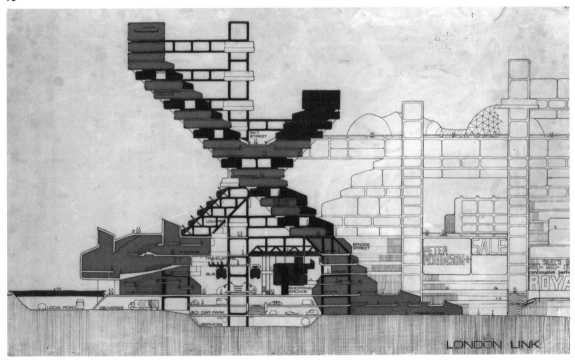

LONDON LINK

London Link (Sylvia Bartlett, thesis, 1965/66)

Sylvia Bartlett's thesis for a 'London Link' spanning the River Thames is another example of the pervasive influence of Peter Cook's Plug-In City (which was to reach across the Channel to France). As in Cook's scheme, the basic idea was that of a diagonal framework made of steel tubes, supporting and servicing a multitude of functions which could be slotted in and removed as required.

Tony Dugdale's fully serviced 'learning shed' – a university for 20,000 on a six-acre site next to Charing Cross Station – links Cedric Price's thinking into adaptable structures, as exemplified by the Fun Palace of 1961, with its first major real-life output, the Centre Pompidou of 1971 (which Dugdale co-designed as a member of Richard Rogers's team). Each unit sits on eight massive pylons crowned by an octagonal craneway and carrying 6 ft deep space frames with an interior span of 150 ft (roughly equivalent to the Centre Pompidou). The axonometric view shows the first unit operational and the second one under construction, and the idea was to expand the structure in any direction if and when additional land became available.

71   Advanced Educational Study (Tony Dugdale, fifth year, 1965/66)

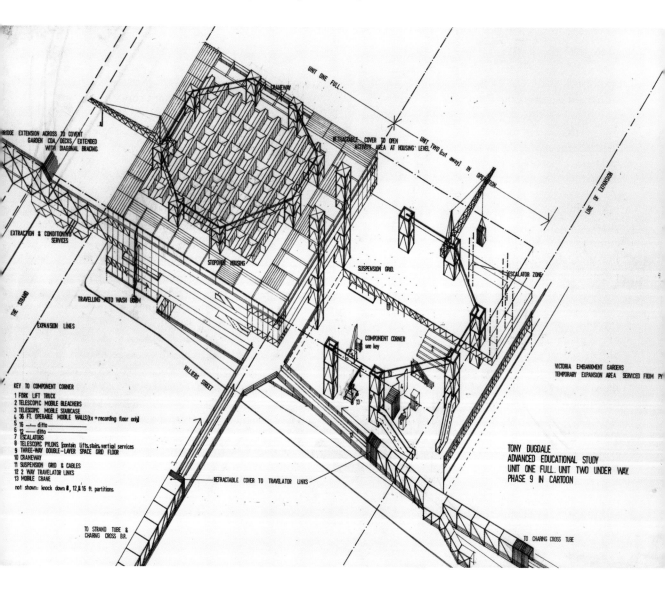

There really has not been anything since Pearl Harbor quite like Imperial College's letter breaking off negotiations with the Architectural Association. The Japanese kept up talks in Washington while they were preparing their attack. Imperial College kept up the talks with the AA while they were summoning an emergency meeting of the governors [and] struck at the moment when [. . .] time for the AA to produce an alternative scheme for survival had almost run out.[23]

Enter the Chairman

Having briefly tried to salvage the negotiations with the ICST, the council entered talks with half a dozen other institutions courting the AA school for possible amalgamation, among them the Central School of Art and Design, now headed by Michael Pattrick. Meanwhile, on 13 April 1970, the council following a four-year campaign by its guerrilla member John Smith agreed to restore full membership rights to students, and the elections in June 1970 swept a new governing body committed to 'maximum independence for the AA' into power.[24] Not surprisingly, negotiations with potential partnering schools ended in failure, and in September 1970 John Lloyd announced his intention not to seek renewal of his contract when it ended in the following summer.[25] Leslie Ginsburg, the head of the planning school, resigned at the same time, and two months later Otto Koenigsberger followed him out of the door, taking his entire tropical department with him to University College.

With no alternative funding in sight and the school literally disintegrating before his eyes, in December 1970, John Lloyd announced its closure within two years' time, and the *Architects' Journal* published its obituary:

All that is left for the AA now is a miracle – and they just don't happen anymore. It is time the council faced facts and the members and the school were told the truth: the last independent school is closing, the comedy is ended.[26]

The comedy, however, was not ended. Unwilling to share Lloyd's defeatism, the 'guerrillas', though unable to force Lloyd's immediate departure, coerced the council to transfer executive powers to a newly appointed 'special committee' composed of sympathetic councillors, staff and students and entrust it with formulating a survival strategy for the school.[27] Owing to inflation, rising staff wages and diminishing assets, the AA had accumulated an unsustainable deficit and without a cash injection from the public purse was facing imminent insolvency. The primary task of the special committee was therefore to persuade the local education authorities (LEAs) – and particularly the Inner London Education Authority (ILEA), which funded the largest contingent of grant-aided students – to continue their financial support at a substantially increased rate of £580 per student. To the council's surprise, the ILEA indicated its willingness to do so, which averted the threat of immediate closure and threw the school a much-needed lifeline.

The council's announcement to keep it open reinvigorated the school and triggered a burst of voluntary activity to help reduce expenditure. In the first half of 1971, the council launched an emergency appeal for funds and cut down the number of full-time staff, while students and teachers made savings by sharing cleaning and catering duties between them.[28] In July 1971, the LEAs adopted a recommendation from the Department of Education and Science and agreed to support the school for another year at the increased rate – on condition that the AA would produce a plan to lower its fees to the level of the polytechnics (£180) or alternatively use the money to run the school down in an orderly fashion.[29]

The special committee meanwhile drew up a proposal to unify the AA's administrative and educational activities (i.e. the association and its school) following the forthcoming departure of John Lloyd and Roger Cunliffe, who had succeeded Carter as director. It recommended that all executive powers should be delegated to a chairman, democratically elected by, and answerable to, the school community through a new management board called 'Forum'. The future role of the council was to be that of a senior body ratifying the decisions taken by Forum, which was to comprise representatives from all parts of the AA and assist the chairman in developing his educational policy.[30]

The chairman's appointment board under Elia Zenghelis vetted 15 applications and invited the two shortlisted candidates – Kenneth Frampton and Alvin Boyarsky – to make their bids to the school. Under the circumstances it was not altogether a fight of equals. Frampton, an associate professor at Princeton, was a product of Pattrick's AA and had taught under Allen – fairly or not, he appeared compromised by his ties with the *ancien régime* at the AA. Boyarsky, on the other hand, had impeccable anti-establishment credentials. He was seen as a member of the group which in the early 1960s had taken up the fight against the ICST merger and thus safeguarded the AA's survival as an independent school. Expelled by Allen and his allies, in 1965 he had joined the University of Illinois at Chicago as associate dean before making a spectacular reappearance in London five years later. As the founder-director of the International Institute of Design (IID) Boyarsky had, in July and August 1970, organised a six-week 'summer session' at the vacated premises of the nearby Bartlett – a widely publicised and highly successful series of workshops, lectures and seminars, for which he managed to gather a star-studded international faculty without any independent funding whatsoever. Boyarsky envisaged the IID as an 'antidote to the localised introspective boredom to be found in many architectural institutions' and considered it the task of architectural education to critique rather than to serve the profession.[31] Unlike Frampton, who set forth a schematic if nonetheless sophisticated curricular framework for the AA school, Boyarsky did not know, nor care, about the administrative or educational minutiae of its future academic structure. What he did have was an exhilarating vision of the AA as an 'ambience where [. . .] conversations can be elevated, amplified and counterpointed [. . .] on a world stage'[32] and evidence for his ability to conjure it up out of thin air. The electorate needed little convincing and delivered him a landslide victory.[33]

The AA under Alvin Boyarsky

Once Boyarsky had secured his appointment in June 1971, he was in fact reluctant to accept it. In part this was due to his concerns that continuing council oversight over policy and budget might limit his room for manoeuvre – not least, one must presume, because he had witnessed (and in Allen's case actively exploited) the inherent weakness of AA principals subjected to the whims of an ever-changing governing body. Conscious of his strong support among students and staff, Boyarsky drove a hard bargain in his contract negotiations; he eventually obtained a position which gave him complete financial and administrative control over both school and association.[34] While this afforded Boyarsky an unprecedented level of power, the council remained legally in charge of the AA, and tensions between the two parties would persist throughout his incumbency. Even so, in educational terms Boyarsky's authority was unrestricted as the system of checks and balances vested in Forum never carried any constitutional weight. When after three years he was confirmed in his post, Boyarsky reduced Forum from the originally intended executive to a purely advisory body and stopped attending its meetings. After a few years of adversarial co-existence, Forum slipped into apathy, and it eventually folded in May 1977.[35]

Boyarsky also hesitated to accept the position of chairman because of his misgivings about the successful integration of the AA with his IID network (which he, rather optimistically, intended to carry on alongside his new duties).[36] The IID summer sessions were drawing their particular strength from the fact that they had no permanent basis or faculty and were thus not restrained by a stifling institutional apparatus. The question was if and how these qualities could be translated into a conventional school setup. Seeking to transform the AA into a loosely structured 'ambience' akin to the IID, the idea of a fixed curriculum was anathema to Boyarsky – as indeed it had been to Lloyd, who had devised the vertical unit system to overcome it. Unsurprisingly, Boyarsky adopted this

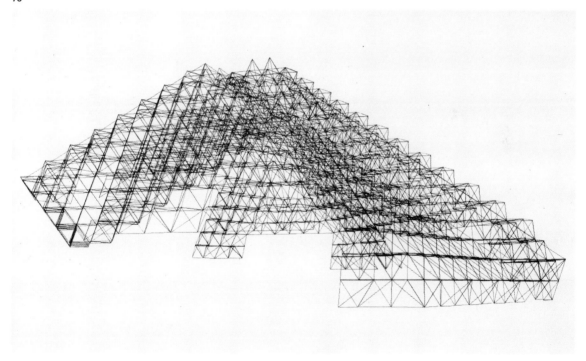

Enclosure System (John Frazer, fourth year, 1967/68)

With the continuing obsession with building systems, it was perhaps only a matter of time before students began to subject the components of these systems to further scrutiny. John Frazer's 'Enclosure System' relies on two types of folded and translucent fibre-glass chevrons, which were rigid enough to be self-supporting and could be bolted together in 18 different ways. It was a critique of traditional grid-based systems as well as the then fashionable Fulleresque geodesic domes – unlike the former, Frazer's method allowed for a vast range of crystalline shapes; unlike the latter, it was compatible with the orthogonal geometries on which architecture generally depends. Frazer demonstrated the feasibility of his system by attaching a gymnasium to an existing school, and he developed pioneering computer software to help designers overcome its complexity.

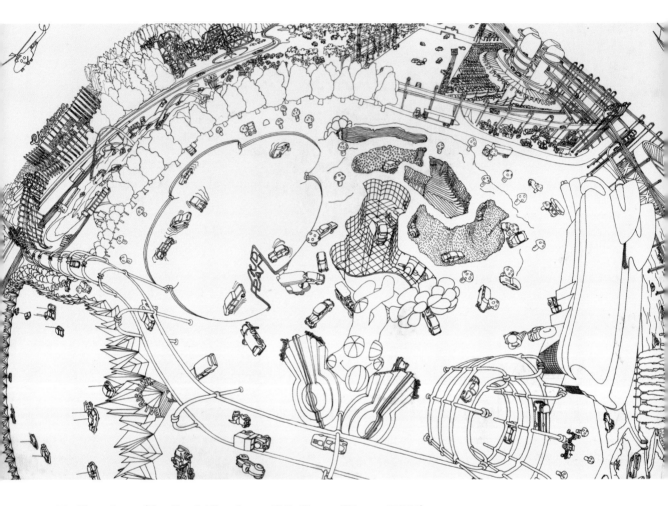

74 Motorolarama (Piers Gough, Diana Jowsey, Philip Wagner, fifth year, 1970/71)

*By the end of the decade, student work reflected growing concerns with ecological, social and cultural issues, enriched by a revived pleasure in the sheer act of designing. According to Peter Cook (*AR, *Oct 1983), the result of this was the emergence of a 'dreamy concept-architecture', most notably in the work of future CZWG partner Piers Gough. 'Motorolarama', his joint thesis with Diana Jowsey and Philip Wagner, was a funfair for sentient cars replete with pop gadgetry, including mechanically operated usherettes for drive-in cinemas and multi-purpose service poles in the shape of mushrooms.*

system and expanded it over the entire course.[37] In the first year, he replaced the Bauhaus-type foundation course with new 'briefing units', which gave incoming students the choice between an urban, technological or more traditionally architectural pathway.[38] However, the second and third years (now called 'intermediate school') remained largely unaltered, while the unit-based 'diploma school' (fourth and fifth years) and the new 'graduate school' (which replaced the previous department-based postgraduate courses) reflected the trend for more diversified courses manifest not just in Lloyd's school but in British architectural education more generally.

The novelty of Boyarsky's system lay not in its basic setup but in his handling of it. Under Lloyd, the teaching model had centred upon the individual student, who was encouraged to pursue his or her personal line of enquiry under the sympathetic guidance of the unit staff. In contrast, Boyarsky put the units themselves at the heart of his pedagogical concept.[39] By compelling his studio masters to adopt a distinct ideological position and advertise it to students at the beginning of the academic year, he fostered a highly competitive climate between the various units, which incidentally converged them with their spiritual precursor – the Beaux-Arts atelier.

The plethora of positions and methods investigated by the various units have been examined in detail elsewhere and ranged from Léon Krier's Neorationalism to Bernard Tschumi's urban politics and Brian Anson's community action (Fig.75; Plates 22–23).[40] The fact that all these positions were implicitly deemed of equal merit suggests, as Andrew Higgott observes, a lack of intellectual conviction pervading the architectural discourse in the school.[41] Of course, the same in principle applies to any type of unit system. Indeed, Boyarsky's variation found a close affinity not just with Lloyd's, but particularly with Michael Pattrick's parallel unit system of the mid-1950s, which in the absence of a dominant architectural philosophy had likewise promoted a decidedly eclectic design approach in the school.

According to Irene Sunwoo, Boyarsky's competitive framework of design studios constituted a radical break with the universally established 'postwar professionalized studio curriculum' as the embodiment of 'an institutionalized pedagogical practice of architectural modernism'.[42] While by the mid-1960s a modernist monoculture of sorts had undoubtedly become the norm at the leading British and American schools – at the former, systemically through the RIBA following the Oxford Conference, at the latter, incrementally through influential educators such as Gropius and Mies van der Rohe – the postwar AA never fully conformed with it. The pluralism of Boyarsky's AA may have reflected the postmodernist moment of its inception and distinguished it from the pedagogical mainstream at the time, but it did continue a major thread in the school's recent history. Indeed, one might argue that the reason why Boyarsky managed to nurture an open-ended and inclusive culture at the AA was precisely because it was in fact in the tradition of the place.

Also in the tradition of the place was its uneasy co-existence with the RIBA's Board of Education. Of all the postwar principals, only Allen had ever consciously tried to align the AA with RIBA policy (rather than the other way around), and it is not without irony that in doing so he lost the confidence of both. John Lloyd, despite continuing frictions, proved altogether more successful in reconciling the AA's idiosyncrasies with the RIBA's demands and even in the chaotic final weeks of his tenure managed to produce a display which fully satisfied its visiting board.[43] With his unconcealed disdain for the parochial outlook of British architectural education, and the RIBA as its custodian, a similarly positive response to Boyarsky's transformation of the school was perhaps not to be expected. Even so, the hostility of the visiting board which inspected the school in 1975 came as a considerable surprise not just to the council but to Boyarsky as well. The board criticised the pedagogical system for being 'weighted against coverage' and failing to convey to students even 'a basic and minimum understanding of the principles upon which a successful design depends'.[44] This concerned especially, but by no means exclusively, the technological side, and the board, which rejected much of the work as 'unacceptable', attached stringent conditions to the continued recognition of the course.[45]

Like Jordan in the early 1950s, Boyarsky regarded the RIBA's directives as little more than misguided interference with his educational vision – unlike then, however, the AA never seriously considered cutting itself loose from the RIBA's embrace. Though Boyarsky rejected the report of the visiting board as 'misinformed', its criticisms as 'invalid', and its 'diagnosis' and therefore its recommendations as 'unacceptable',[46] he nevertheless complied with them to retain RIBA validation for his course.[47] The breakaway from the nationally administered system of architectural education was thus never as complete as myth has it. Not only did the AA continue to operate within the parameters set by the RIBA, it also made sustained efforts to retain (and later regain) its inclusion in the government's mandatory list of grant-aided institutions and thus remain part of the framework of state-funded education. It was the failure of these efforts which eventually established the AA as the global enterprise it remains today.

Alvin's Autocracy

Boyarsky's educational and administrative changes had been implemented by the middle of 1974. The remarkable longevity of his system, and indeed of his reign (he died in office in 1990), raises the question as to how Boyarsky managed to secure a position of seemingly unassailable power over a school whose defining feature had hitherto been its conspicuous lack of continuity and long-term leadership. The answer to this question lies in two, on the face of it, unrelated but in fact inextricably linked developments in the 1970s: the waning influence of the council on the one hand, and the internationalisation of the school on the other. It is tempting to interpret this latter development as the logical continuation of the IID programme. Though it is questionable whether Boyarsky's outlook was ever truly global (certainly he did not share his predecessor's interest in the developing world), he was contemptuous of the current state

of architectural education and saw it as a problem which transcended national barriers.[48] Be that as it may, the records do not support the view that Boyarsky's drive to increase the presence of overseas students at the AA was a deliberate strategy to draw 'a wedge between the institution and its British context', as has been suggested.[49] It was forced upon him by circumstances.

To cast our minds back, by June 1971, when Boyarsky was appointed as chairman, the AA had accumulated a critical deficit in the region of £70,000 (more than a million pounds in today's money). The school was being kept afloat by local authorities committing to fund their grant-aided students for one more year, provided that this time would be used to either run the school down or reduce its fees to the level of the polytechnics. The first course of action was never seriously considered, and it emerged that owing to inflation the second would only be viable if the DES agreed to subsidise the school with an annual grant of £250,000.[50] Chairman and council launched a cross-party lobbying campaign to influence its decision – Boyarsky, for instance, met with both government officials and Labour backbenchers – but to no avail. In July 1972, Margaret Thatcher, then in charge of the department, announced that no direct grant would be given to the AA. Worse still, the school would be removed from its mandatory list, meaning that local authorities were relieved from their statutory duty to cover AA students' fees even if the school managed to drop them to an acceptable level after all.[51]

Boyarsky, whose aim it was to expand the offerings of the school, never contemplated cutting down on expenditure. Despite publicly accusing Thatcher of putting money 'into a series of other institutions where people don't want to go' and describing negotiations with her as 'akin to Kafka's *The Castle*',[52] he remained hopeful that it would eventually be possible to get the DES to reverse its decision and pursued this objective persistently over the following decade. For the time being, however, the school faced a dramatic shortfall in its revenue, and Boyarsky's proposition was to cover it by significantly increasing the intake of overseas students able to pay the school's exorbitant fees.[53]

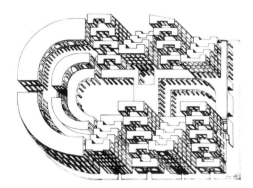

Axonometric
Housing scheme in Swiss Cottage
Zaha Hadir Units 1 Third Year

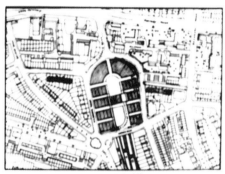

SITE PLAN
OLD & NEW BUILDINGS

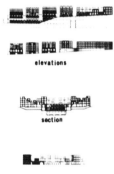

elevations

section

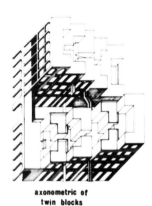

axonometric of
twin blocks

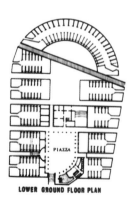

LOWER GROUND FLOOR PLAN

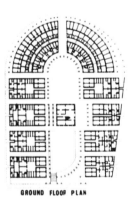

GROUND FLOOR PLAN

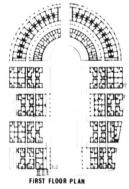

FIRST FLOOR PLAN

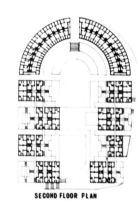

SECOND FLOOR PLAN

75   Urban Nucleus, Swiss Cottage (Zaha Hadid, Intermediate Unit 10, 1974/75)

Zaha Hadid developed her distinct formal language in the senior years of the course, when she came under the influence of OMA partners Rem Koolhaas and Elia Zenghelis. In her third year, she had joined Léon Krier's unit, whose interest in urban morphology and building types echoed the work of Aldo Rossi and the Italian Neorationalists. This ten-week project for a housing scheme over a railway cutting in north London was preceded by research into urban block types as well as a short project for an 'urban piazza' on the site of Trafalgar Square.

Fearful of turning the AA into an elitist school affordable only to the privately wealthy, Boyarsky suggested waiving the tuition fees for the first-year intake of local authority students, but the council dismissed this out of hand.[54]

Boyarsky's strategy proved successful as the number of full-fee-paying candidates applying for admission far exceeded expectations. The anticipated extra income prompted Boyarsky to guarantee a freeze in tuition fees for the forthcoming five years, which in turn persuaded the majority of LEAs, including the all-important ILEA, to give the school their continued support.[55] In fact, the number of grant-aided students rose slightly in the 1972/73 session, while the number of international students doubled. Overall, enrolment increased by a third, from 465 to 619 students, allowing the school for the first time in living memory to generate a substantive surplus.[56]

Boyarsky was aware that the situation remained precarious – first, because there was no guarantee that with rising inflation the AA would in fact be able to maintain its fee levels and thus retain the LEAs' goodwill; and second, because Thatcher, angered by the volte-face of the mostly Labour-run LEAs (and the ILEA in particular), agitated actively for the closure of the AA.[57] It was in this situation that Boyarsky, towards the end of the academic year 1972/73, fully committed to an expansionist policy. He drew on his IID contacts to pursue this policy; more importantly, he turned a travelling exhibition of predominantly postwar student work, planned in connection with the 125th anniversary of the AA, into the vehicle of a transatlantic promotion campaign for the school. Curated by its new director, former fifth-year master Peter Cook, the exhibition was first shown at the Institute of Contemporary Arts in April 1973; over the following five years, it toured more than 40 venues all over Europe and North America and was chiefly responsible for the sustained influx of foreign students into the AA.[58]

From a present-day perspective, it is worth highlighting that by the time Boyarsky's new system was fully operational in the autumn of 1974, the internationalisation of the school was already in progress – between 1971 and 1974 the proportion of overseas students had risen from 25 to 40 per cent, and three years later, when the AA125 travel show reached the end of its life, it stood at 50 per cent. In other words, while in recent decades it has arguably been Boyarsky's unique pedagogical model which attracted international students (who today make up 90 per cent of the student body), the campaign which had initially carried this development relied on the AA's postwar record and celebrated not the work done during his tenure but that done under his predecessors.

In this context, it seems also opportune to dispel the assumption that it was Boyarsky's powerful position as chairman which allowed him to advance a policy of internationalisation in the first place. The contrary was the case. At a time of great administrative ambiguity following Boyarsky's appointment, it was his immensely successful recruitment strategy which gave him leverage over the other stakeholders vying for influence within the AA, specifically the council and (to a lesser extent) the school community through Forum. In the first year of Boyarsky's tenure, the AA had been forced to write off a £37,000 deficit which the school had incurred in the previous session; its reserves were further drained by the continuing depreciation of its assets and a contractually guaranteed £20,000 chairman's fund.[59] While the association's finances were thus in dire straits, the school, as mentioned, was generating an unprecedented amount of revenue owing to high student numbers and high student fees. Boyarsky, who was responsible for the overall budget of the AA, studiously maintained an artificial division between school and association accounts to highlight the success of the former and the corresponding failure of the latter. Throughout the AA's history the association had subsidised the school – now the roles were reversed: the association was becoming a liability on the school, and Boyarsky missed no opportunity to drive this point home.[60]

Acutely aware that the balance of power had shifted, Boyarsky invested his new riches exclusively in the school (which after all had elected him) – at the expense of the association and its wider membership, in which he had not the slightest interest. In fact, over the course of the decade

Boyarsky's school gradually absorbed many of the traditionally association-led functions and merged them with its educational programme. These included the AA's unrivalled lectures and exhibitions programme, now curated by Robin Middleton's 'general studies unit', but also its vastly extended range of publications (though tellingly not the association's chronically loss-making in-house journal).[61] In so widening its purview, Boyarsky built himself an impregnable power base within the school community, while the members became a 'neglected constituency' and abandoned the AA in droves.[62] Between 1973 and 1983, the AA's membership halved from 5,000 to 2,500[63] and the concomitant loss of subscription income further weakened the association and tipped the scales in favour of the school. Boyarsky saw the association as an obsolete entity, and he left little doubt that the same ultimately applied to the council as its representative body.[64] The internationalisation of the school, it is worth reiterating, was not the consequence of Boyarsky's power over the AA – it was its precondition.

Showdown in the Late Seventies

For Boyarsky, the AA's success was tantamount to the school's success – the association was of no concern to him, and neither were its financial troubles. This attitude was tenable as long as the school was in fact sufficiently profitable to mitigate the association's shortfall. Yet an audit of the AA's accounts carried out during the 1974/75 session revealed that owing to inflation, heavy expenditures and a lack of financial control the school, too, was in fact operating on a deficit.[65] Unable to cover this deficit from its reserves, in the autumn of 1975 the AA was forced to raise its tuition fees from £580 to £825, thus breaking its commitment to the LEAs to keep them steady for five years. The response was instantaneous as the vast majority of them, including the ILEA, announced that they would no longer support new students entering the AA. In the absence of grant-aided applicants the intake dropped significantly, and the council, worried

about the prospect of seeing the AA's remaining capital completely wiped out by Boyarsky's operation, called on him to consolidate the position by making severe cutbacks.[66] Boyarsky, however, stayed his course and only a few months later announced another rise in tuition fees to an egregious £1,125, meaning that within two years the costs of studying at the AA would have all but doubled.[67]

It was at this point that the council rallied its strength to prevent Boyarsky from severing the school from its British roots by pricing out all except the most affluent of domestic students – an endeavour in which it was supported by the students' union. Indeed, while Boyarsky claimed for himself an 'electoral mandate [. . .] to represent the students against the repressions of a detached council', the students themselves became increasingly critical of his own autocratic demeanour.[68] In June 1976, the 'Student Representative Council', a short-lived action group whose stated aim it was to 're-democratize' the school and 'alter [its] present economic basis', canvassed for its anti-Boyarsky candidates and managed to win nine of ten vacant seats in the council election (including one for future Live Aid Trust director Kevin Jenden).[69] Dominated by its new student members, the council demanded that Boyarsky drastically downsize the school and in the process produce not just a balanced budget but a substantial surplus to enable it to drop its tuition fees to a level acceptable to the LEAs.[70] Unwilling to carry out what he considered to be 'virtually a dismantling operation',[71] Boyarsky ignored the council's instructions and instead announced yet another rise in student fees for the coming year.[72]

Discerning between itself and the chairman 'a fundamental conflict of philosophy in the way [the AA] was run',[73] in early February 1977 the council advised Boyarsky that it was not prepared to renew his contract for another term unless he engaged constructively in finding a compromise on the way forward.[74] Boyarsky immediately mobilised his supporters against, what he inaccurately portrayed as, his 'dismissal' by the council.[75] Over the following days, the council was flooded with

76   Political Building (Eric Parry, Diploma Unit 1, 1978/79)

Dalibor Vesely, who ran this diploma unit together with Mohsen Mostafavi, inspired a wave of atmospheric pencil drawings which affected the whole of the school in the late 1970s. There was a whiff of postmodernism and a superficial similarity with Aldo Rossi's Neorationalism in the projects which emerged from his unit. The historic frame of reference, however, was broad, and the subjects – cemeteries, monasteries, libraries, museums – were seen as precedents with rich and meaningful historical associations rather than as types to be reproduced in a modern context (AR, Oct 1983). The results were highly complex and resolutely non-modernist projects such as Eric Parry's 'Political Building' for a site in Kentish Town, which contains a public domain at ground level, complemented by a hostel and an 'academy of rhetoric' on the upper floors.

correspondence supporting the chairman, and at a contentious meeting on 18 February 1977 the school community passed a vote of no confidence in the council and issued an invitation to Boyarsky to continue in his post.[76] The meeting marked the culmination of a six-year power struggle between Boyarsky and the council, which had misjudged the grassroots feeling in the school. Maintaining that it was 'not in the best interest of the Architectural Association that Alvin Boyarsky should remain as Chairman', the council retreated and several of its student members resigned.[77] Boyarsky eventually secured a new contract on much-improved terms, relieving him from any responsibility for membership affairs and – with Forum finally disbanded – leaving any consultation with students and staff entirely to his own devices.[78]

'The AA Look' – The School in the Eighties

The financial situation, of course, remained unchanged. Fee increases in step with inflation became an annual occurrence, and with little local authority support remaining, the proportion of British students dropped from 50 per cent in 1977 to 20 per cent three years later. By the time Boyarsky finally succeeded in getting the school reinstated on the DES's mandatory list in 1982, it had become a meaningless gesture. The contributions of £480 that local authorities were liable to pay covered only a fraction of the roughly £3,000 students were now charged, and the AA itself had long embraced its role as an actor in a global rather than a merely national arena.

In educational terms, the late 1970s had been a period of consolidation. Boyarsky's often-challenged assurance that the increased intake of overseas students would have no adverse effect on the academic standards of the school was vindicated and relations with the RIBA improved.[79] In part this was due to the fact that it had also been a period of homogenisation. While in the early 1970s the school had accommodated a wide range of methods and

theoretical positions, towards the end of the decade units with a distinct social bent were gradually phased out – primarily, one would presume, because local housing issues and community action were of little concern to an increasingly international student body.[80] Having established the unit system to 'restructure' the course 'away from a central architectural axis to one of diversity', there nonetheless emerged a consensus within the school, and Boyarsky, who had his ears close to the ground, wondered if the time had not come to abolish this system.[81] The streams in which the remaining units immersed themselves were no less varied, but they fed into a single current. According to Higgott, the AA became preoccupied with a 'search for form',[82] and Robin Evans identified a 'revival of interest in architecture as such', relying on the medium of the drawing to an extent not seen since the Beaux-Arts period (Fig.76; Plates 24–25).[83]

Diverse yet profoundly hermetic and resistant to outside influence, the AA developed a reputation for paper architecture and a self-indulgent urge to exude an inexhaustible flow of fashionable 'isms'. It took the real-world success of one of these isms – Deconstructivism or, more prosaically, the 'AA Look'[84] – to turn disdain into timid admiration in more conservative quarters. In one fateful week in May 1983, current staff member Zaha Hadid won the international competition for the Peak Club in Hong Kong while her erstwhile tutors Rem Koolhaas and Elia Zenghelis narrowly missed out with their design for the Parc de Villette in Paris to their former colleague Bernard Tschumi.[85] As Higgott writes, by the mid-1980s, after a decade's worth of experimentation, the AA had reached 'the stage of *achieved* work'.[86] This, more than anything else, cemented the global renown the AA enjoys to the present day.

By the time Alvin Boyarsky passed away in August 1990, the school he had inherited had changed beyond recognition. Yet the break with its British context was never as complete as commonly assumed. Despite mutual aversion, the AA never relinquished RIBA accreditation, and it continually sought to reconcile its independence with the broader restrictions imposed by the state system of education – under Boyarsky as much as (or indeed even more than) under his predecessors. When in the early 1970s the need to attract wealthy overseas students became inescapable, council and chairman were equally worried that the AA might turn into an elitist school impenetrable for all but the most extraordinary of native talents. The fact that this eventually happened owed much to Boyarsky's expansionist policy, but it was decidedly not a situation he created on purpose. If archival scrutiny exposes some of the assumptions surrounding Boyarsky's tenure as myths with little basis in fact, it should nonetheless be emphasised that the most persistent of them – the notion of Boyarsky as the saviour who salvaged the school from its all-but-certain demise and restored its international reputation – survives largely unscathed. When asked to provide a reference in 1971, Boyarsky's then superior, UIC Dean Leonard Currie, had ventured the prediction that his appointment 'could well be the making of the AA'.[87] As indeed it was.

Conclusion

The AA was founded in 1847 as an independent school – today, 173 years later, it is still an independent school. Through much of the period discussed in this book, this seemed an improbable outcome. Unlike, for instance, the French Beaux-Arts system or the German system of technical universities, the British model of architectural education had historically been free of direct state involvement. In the United Kingdom, in the years and decades following the end of the war, the drive towards a more uniform educational framework – coming in part from the state and in part from the RIBA – darkened the outlook for 'one of the outstanding remaining vestiges of free enterprise in the field of technical education', as Howard Robertson put it in 1948.[1] What we have seen is how these competing forces – government, profession and independence – played out.

From the AA's point of view, it was a quixotic struggle to buttress its autonomy against the mounting tide of government interference in higher education. Successive AA councils and principals were virtually unanimous in their view that in its traditional form this autonomy would soon be a thing of the past. A. R. F. Anderson, who presided over the AA at its most crucial juncture in the early 1950s, was only half-joking when he called on potential donors to 'endow a lectureship or a chair or the whole place, if you like!'[2] Infused by a Victorian spirit of self-initiative and self-reliance, the AA school began to look like a relic of a bygone era – anachronistic and in the long run unaffordable.

The RIBA's intention to play a more active role in architectural education added to the AA's predicament though its impact was less immediate and less one-sided. In the immediate postwar years, the RIBA struggled to agree on a coherent policy and define universally binding pedagogical standards – standards which would in any way have been difficult to enforce at a time when the schools were struggling to cope with the inflow of hundreds of students returning from the war. With its flexible organisation, the AA proved ideally suited to take advantage of this unsettled state of affairs. Robert Furneaux Jordan, in particular, recognised that in doing so the school was detaching itself from the mainstream of thought in architectural education. Relations between the AA and the RIBA became acrimonious in the early 1950s as the RIBA tightened its grip on the schools and initiated the process leading to the Oxford Conference and the establishment of its 'Official System'. The fact that Jordan's successor, Michael Pattrick, was intimately involved in this process was ultimately of little benefit to the AA, which never embraced the system it had helped to create. William Allen, who took over as principal in 1961, failed in his attempt to align the AA with the RIBA's educational policy, and the following decades are best understood as a period of growing alienation between the two institutions.

The AA council was alive to the challenges facing the school from the increasingly interventionist policies of both the RIBA and the government. Yet due to its institutional setup, specifically the rapid turnover of its membership, it was ill-equipped to counter them through a long-term strategy of its own. The same volatility affected the governance of the school itself. Paradoxically, the principal – the only person who entered into a long-term contractual commitment with the school – answered to a short-term governing body deciding upon its broader policy. The annual changeover of the council undermined the position of the principal as within two or three years few of the members who had appointed him were still present to give him their backing. Those who replaced them often did not agree with the prevailing ideas and accepted nomination to the council precisely because it allowed them to influence the direction of the school. It was chiefly by lobbying such members of council that the students' committee, a body without constitutional standing, managed to exert its influence on the school.

The AA system was thus geared to continuous change and renewal. While this complicated the position of the principal, it also enabled him (and, until the appointment of Eva Franch i Gilabert in 2018, it was always a him) to effect modifications to the course and the respective staff changes almost instantly. Throughout the postwar period, the AA remained thus an inexhaustible source of educational novelty. Financial constraints prevented the implementation of several ambitious schemes, particularly under Pattrick. On the other hand, the AA's lack of money was a major reason for its continuing thirst for experimentation as it was felt, probably rightly, that only by offering a unique type of education would the school be able to attract a sufficient number of students willing to pay its higher fees. More important was the genuine desire, shared by all principals and councillors, to adapt the AA's school model to the changing demands of the profession. Lack of oversight by, and accountability to, a higher authority, be it a government agency or a university senate, meant that the AA was able to respond to such demands at once. As a result, the AA mirrored events in the architectural world more immediately and more directly than any other school did or could have done.

The somewhat incoherent nature of Gordon Brown's course, combining as it did a revival of drawing skills in the Beaux-Arts tradition with a Lethabite strengthening of technical expertise, reflected a certain lack of confidence within modernist circles immediately after the war. New buildings of true architectural merit such as Powell & Moya's Churchill Gardens or ACP's Brynmawr Rubber Factory were few and far between. The informal so-called 'New Empiricism' offered a suitable and briefly popular model for AA students at a time when material and labour shortages limited the scope of British architects. Frederick Gibberd's buildings at Harlow (and much of the architecture of the other first-generation New Towns) belong in this tradition, as does the work of AA graduates Herbert Tayler and David Green in Norfolk. Few of these buildings were easily accessible for London-based architects and students. More present in their collective consciousness were the dispiriting housing schemes produced by the valuer's department of the LCC in the second half of the 1940s, despised in equal measure by those who deplored the rise of official architecture and those who welcomed it provided the officials in charge were in fact architects. The LCC's housing programme eventually reverted back to the architect's department, but it was the school building programme at Hertfordshire which galvanised British modernists in the immediate postwar years. Recent AA graduates such as Bruce Martin, David Medd and his future wife, Mary Crowley, carried the school's pre-war ethos of collaboration and research into this programme. Yet its tremendous appeal to a postwar generation of AA students owed more to the fact that the direction of the school was entrusted to a man who had been instrumental in nurturing this ethos in the first place.

Robert Furneaux Jordan's short incumbency coincided happily with the heyday of the Hertfordshire programme, and he prepared his students specifically for their future practice in a public sector organised along similar lines. Never before or after did a course of study map out so clearly and coherently a career path for its students. This no doubt explains the great affection with which Jordan's term in office is remembered by those who studied under him. It also explains some of the hostility Michael Pattrick encountered when succeeding him in office. Pattrick's inauguration occurred against the colourful backdrop of the Festival of Britain. Yet rather than a hopeful sign of things to come, this showpiece of contemporary British architecture proved to be the swansong of an all-too-fleeting era. Having defeated Labour in the general election of October 1951, the new Conservative government immediately cleansed the South Bank of its Festival legacy, and the announcement of government cuts seemed to crush the dream of architecture as a public service to the nation.

It was not until the mid-1950s that building restrictions were lifted and the private sector recovered sufficiently to offer an alternative career path for AA graduates. In the meantime, the architectural landscape had changed profoundly. With modernism becoming the accepted mode of architectural expression, its source material enriched and factional struggles ensued. The 'Revived Picturesque' of the Festival of Britain offered one way forward, and so did the contextual modernism of architects such as Powell & Moya or Chamberlin, Powell and Bon, which found its inspiration in Frank Lloyd Wright's pre-war oeuvre as well as more recent work in Italy and elsewhere.[3] To a succeeding generation of AA students, both these approaches were inherently compromised by their sheer pleasantness and lack of rigour. Instead, the students drew their inspiration from the tough formalism of Mies van der Rohe's steel structures in the United States and Le Corbusier's concrete buildings in France, the former exemplified by the Smithsons' Hunstanton school and Yorke Rosenberg Mardall's Gatwick Airport, the latter by HKPA's version of the *Unité* at Roehampton and Stirling and Gowan's flats at Ham Common.

'The AA', wrote the *Builder* in 1951, 'is something of an enigma; its breadth of policy is so wide that the policy itself is frequently difficult to locate'.[4] The AA had always fostered a permissive studio environment, able to accommodate niche interests and singularly susceptible to changing trends. Never was this more the case than under Michael Pattrick, who has been unfairly dismissed as a capable administrator with little concern for the teaching process and the type of architect it might produce. Yet Pattrick was alert enough to recognise the fragmentation of the architectural scene and purposely accommodated the various factions in his school: 'Quite a number of Schools [. . .] believe in a very strict adherence to one method of approach and consequently nearly all the work looks as though it was done by one man. The AA is in complete disagreement with this attitude.'[5] More than anything else, it was this refusal to impose any aesthetic doctrine on its students which distinguished the AA from its competitors – and particularly so from the leading schools in the United States, many of which were under the spell of charismatic figures, including Gropius at Harvard and Mies van der Rohe at the Illinois Institute of Technology (not to mention Wright's fellowship at Taliesin).

Pattrick's parallel unit system, inaugurated in 1954, enshrined eclecticism in the AA's pedagogical model and ensured that for its students the choice of direction remained wide open. Festival designers and contextual modernists such as Leonard Manasseh and Elizabeth Chesterton were prominently represented on the AA staff and left a lasting legacy in the work of architects such as John Melvin and Ahrends, Burton and Koralek. Likewise, a Miesian influence, though never dominant, was a constant feature in student work throughout the postwar period, nurtured by John Winter, Roy Landau and other members of staff returning from the United States. Short-term tutor Eduardo Catalano, despite barely speaking any English, dazzled an entire cohort of fourth-year students with his Latin American disregard for social sentimentalities in favour of bold structural expression;[6] Quinlan Terry, Malcolm Higgs and

Andrew Anderson sought advice from John Brandon-Jones in their pursuit of a new vernacular rooted in the Arts and Crafts tradition;[7] and John Outram and Wilfred Marden developed their Bowellism without any obvious prototype at all.[8] Tellingly, when in the second half of the 1950s one tendency began to dominate all others, it was one with which neither Pattrick nor any of the other principals of the AA found themselves in sympathy.

Brutalism owed its rise to Smithson and Killick's advocacy of early modern precedents and to a generation of students eager to have these inform their own contribution to contemporary architecture. Yet it is worth emphasising that the Brutalist umbrella itself covered a variety of different approaches, many of them prefigured in AA student work – from the confluence of Corbusian and Wrightian influences in Bob Maguire and Edward Cullinan's 'Humanist Brutalism'[9] to the constructivism of Stirling and Gowan's Leicester Engineering Building, whose crystalline roof design derived from a fourth-year scheme by AA student Edward Reynolds; from the 'fashionable vernacular'[10] of Rodney Gordon's hard-edged shopping centres for the Owen Luder Partnership to Patrick Hodgkinson's and Neave Brown's comparatively restrained low-rise high-density experiments, which culminated in what is widely regarded as the best public housing this country has ever seen.[11]

While there may have been no discernible 'AA style', there was a certain ethos which permeated the school, manifest in a number of fundamental precepts common to all incarnations of the postwar curriculum. There was, first of all, a constant effort to infuse the work of the school with the utmost sense of 'realism'. In recent years, the schools of architecture have come under increased criticism for their alleged failure in preparing their students for professional practice. Such criticism is by no means a new phenomenon; indeed, it has been a running thread ever since school-based courses became an established form of training a century ago. Run by a professional association, the AA was particularly sensitive to such criticism. The various practical training

schemes reflected its desire to mitigate the artificiality of the school environment, as did the Lethabite ideal of integrating the training of architects and builders, which the AA pursued over much of the postwar period even if it failed to seize the opportunity when it actually presented itself. The same quest for realism characterised the curriculum itself, which comprised a succession of studio programmes taught, singularly at the time, by practising architects and set to resemble real-life practice – an approach encapsulated in the formula 'real problems, real sites, real clients'.

A second characteristic of the school course was its 'social perspective', the instillation of which the *Architects' Journal* in 1966 considered to be 'the AA's main contribution to architectural thinking and practice over the years'.[12] This was most evident under Jordan, whose vision of a nationalised building service catering to the greater good appealed to a generation of students eager to build a New Jerusalem. Yet even when in the mid-1950s the resurgence of private practice rendered the idea of an all-encompassing public sector obsolete, the underlying 'social perspective', shed of its overtly political connotations, persisted. Group working, introduced to approximate the collaborative working methods of public offices, remained a feature throughout the 1950s and 1960s, and it is worth pointing out that the most exuberant formal excesses of the late 1950s occurred in John Killick's fourth-year course, whose programmes were linked to current LCC projects. William Allen considered the AA's promotion of 'parity of esteem between the private and official sectors of the profession' to be its chief achievement since the war,[13] and his pedagogical vision with its distinct intellectual bias aimed to remove his students from the narrowness of private practice and equip them to play their part in policy decisions at government and industry level. It does not lack a certain irony that the only school which embraced the rise of the public sector in the postwar period and tried to adapt its curriculum to its demands was the one which operated outside its jurisdiction.

A third distinct feature of the postwar school was, what Bobby Carter called, its 'emphasis on the architect as the creator of total environment'.[14] The AA had pioneered the training of architect-planners in Rowse's postgraduate department in the late 1930s, and a concern for regional planning aspects remained a constant preoccupation of AA thesis students throughout the postwar period. In 1958, the school introduced a new curriculum which linked each studio programme to a progressive order of architectural scale – from the village in the second year to the town in the third and the city in the fourth. At a time when few other schools encouraged their students to consider the urban implications of their studio projects, the AA used these as the ideological framework for the entire course of study. As Peter Cook observes, 'By the mid-1960s, the tradition of treating architecture as essentially part of an urban process had become well-established. Few students of any significance passed through the system without leaving behind at least one pretension towards the city into which his or her architecture would sit.'[15]

The sum total of these features allowed the AA to take up a unique position in the formation and dissemination of modern architecture in Britain, providing as it did an intergenerational platform for pre-war pioneers serving on staff and council and the students, many of whom would become the leaders of the profession in the second half of the twentieth century. The AA's faith in the value of students' contributions and the corresponding lack of hierarchy and formality ensured that the exchange between these groups was not a one-way process. Given the perpetually rejuvenating mechanisms intrinsic to the AA, it was hardly surprising that dissatisfaction with modernist doctrines first manifested itself here. It seems noteworthy that Brown, Jordan, Pattrick and Allen were all born in a nine-year bracket prior to the outbreak of the First World War and belonged to an extended circle of pre-war British modernists captivated by the promise of a new architecture grounded in scientific methods and ambitious in scope and social purpose. After the end of the Second World War, they were among the first to consider the educational implications of this vision in postwar conditions, and it was

not until the Oxford Conference in 1958 that it became the basis for official RIBA policy. Two years later, Michael Pattrick was realistic about the consequences this would likely have on the position of the AA:

> Looking, say, five years ahead, we can see a time when the School might find itself in a position of rather greater competition. [. . .] The point is that for twenty years the AA was in the forefront of the battle, not only of modern architecture, but in the break-away from the educational tyranny left by the Beaux-Arts. This battle was a long one, and the new approach and new methods of teaching were still being contested less than ten years ago. But now the conflict is over, and many of the things which we once cherished as being our own progressive ideas have now become part of the accepted paraphernalia of many other schools of architecture. So in this respect our position must diminish.[16]

Indeed, in the early 1960s other schools rose to prominence, challenging the 'unique and rather lofty position'[17] which the AA had enjoyed in the past. Cambridge and the Bartlett became the two 'flagships of the Official System',[18] and by the middle of the decade all other schools in the country were following suit by aligning their curricula to the RIBA's modernist-technocratic vision. William Allen's failure as principal signalled that at the AA this vision had run its course – architecturally as much as pedagogically.

'How had the early sixties become so grey?' wondered Peter Cook ten years later, when, inspired by his Archigram group, students such as Nicholas Grimshaw had recaptured the daring, if not the style or social pretensions, of the Brutalists.[19] Prior to that, the school had witnessed the return of a dry 'neutrality of expression',[20] which came as a considerable shock after the excesses of the late 1950s. Alan Colquhoun's teaching inspired the cool and detached rationality of the Grunt Group around Christopher Cross, Michael Gold, Edward Jones, Jeremy Dixon and his future wife Fenella Clemens, whose early buildings would fit so seamlessly into the grid-patterned new town of Milton Keynes.[21] Cedric Price's ideas about adaptable and fully serviced structures meanwhile influenced an entire generation of AA students, most notably Tony Dugdale, who was to realise its earliest real-life output as a member of Richard Rogers's design team for the Centre Pompidou. The signature projects of the time, however, were the gargantuan urban housing schemes produced in the fourth year of the course. From a 21st-century perspective, one cannot help but be amazed by the sheer ambition and competence of the students who designed these schemes, and even more so by the happy readiness of developers and councils to hire them straight from the drawing boards to turn their adolescent visions into environments for people to live in. The perceived failure of many of these schemes challenged the hitherto unquestioned faith in master planning and modern technology as the appropriate means to restructure the urban landscape. Part of a broader wave of libertarianism which swept away the social and cultural certainties of the postwar period, this assault on the foundations of the modernist project triggered a crisis of identity in British architecture. In the second half of the 1960s, John Lloyd's liberal running of the AA school gave students free rein to explore and reset the parameters of their professional activities, encouraged by the Archigram group, which emerged as the dominant force on the teaching staff.

Lloyd's term in office must be seen as an interregnum – a transitional phase prefacing a school in which a continuous reassessment of the role of the architect became the central preoccupation. The epilogue has given an outline of the institutional entanglements out of which Alvin Boyarsky developed the AA in the 1970s and 1980s. The present-day situation is still conditioned by these events, and diligent historical scrutiny must therefore await its turn. If one were to speculate, it might be less Boyarsky's pedagogical model – the unit system in its peculiarly competitive manifestation – which will prove to be his lasting legacy. This system had its roots in previous pedagogical experiments, and although through fellow travellers such as Peter Cook, Bernard Tschumi and Nigel Coates it soon spread to other institutions, few other than the AA itself still use it today. Indeed, the exigencies of an increasingly international framework of architectural education dependent on student migration and the mutual recognition of degrees means that a more common model today is Michael Pattrick's modified unit system, that is, an arrangement of parallel units within a year-based framework.

Boyarsky's true legacy, I suggest, is indirectly linked to this globalisation of architectural education in so far as it was he who provided the ideological foundation for it. Boyarsky's bête noire, and the driver behind his pedagogical vision, was what he regarded as the parochial nature of architectural education across Europe: 'Provinciality reigned' – in Britain as much as anywhere else.[22] Parochial or not, so long as training models were dictated by the demands of the architectural profession, and therefore by the specific political and economic conditions within which it operated, the educational discourse was necessarily framed within a national dimension. In the two decades after the war only CIAM ever seriously considered the topic on a supranational level; tellingly, it never managed to formulate a universally applicable pedagogical charter. It was Alvin Boyarsky's understanding of architectural education as a critical discipline rather than a preparation for practice which allowed the debate to transcend national borders. The increasingly international makeup of the AA school was – and continues to be – the embodiment of this mindset.

Plate 1   Shops and Flats (James Cubitt, Unit 8, third year, 1937/38)

Like his fellow student Geoffrey Robson (see Fig. 9), James Cubitt made a name for himself through his distinctive sketch designs. The stone slabbing is a typical feature of the period, as is the horizontal emphasis of the facade, here particularly pronounced due to the projecting shop front and the clerestory windows.

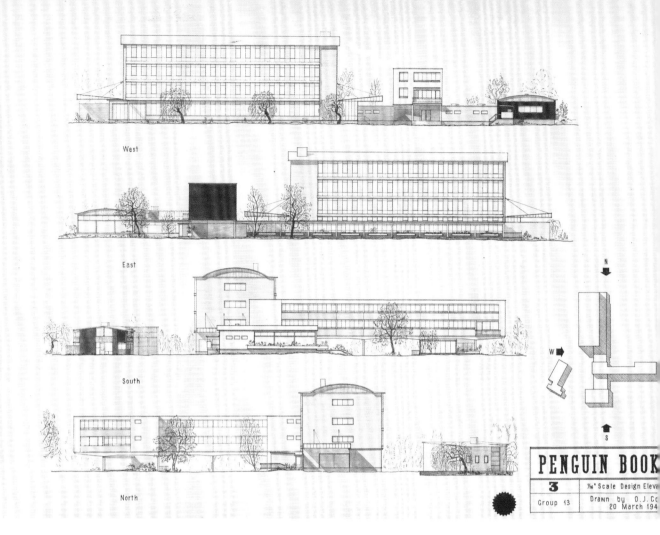

West

East

South

North

PENGUIN BOOK

3

%₆" Scale Design Eleva

Group 13 | Drawn by O.J.Co
20 March 194

Plate 2 Penguin Books (Oliver Cox, P. D. Dixon, Robert Forestier-Walker, Michael Nesbitt, Graeme Shankland, Lois Ventris, Michael Ventris, fourth year, 1946/47)

The informal detailing of this publishing company was inspired by Swedish examples. The functional planning, based on separate volumes for separate purposes, echoes Gropius's Bauhaus at Dessau, which also provided the motif of an administrative wing bridging the pond and connecting the main entrance with the production hall. Students were encouraged to work in groups, and the Architect and Building News *(4 April 1947) considered the result 'competent enough for the actual carrying out of the job'.*

The architects' department of the Miners Welfare Committee under John Forshaw had been a paragon of progressive public practice in the 1930s. When the war ended, there was a (vain) hope that it might soon resume its bustling activities. Alan Colquhoun, who drew the elevations of these pithead baths on behalf of his group, had previously studied at the Edinburgh College of Art. The change of style and content in his student work was striking – in his second year he had designed an orangerie in the classical style, complete with statue niches in the avant-corps.

Plate 3   Pithead Baths at Rawdon and Marquis Collieries (Alan Colquhoun et al., fourth year, 1947/48)

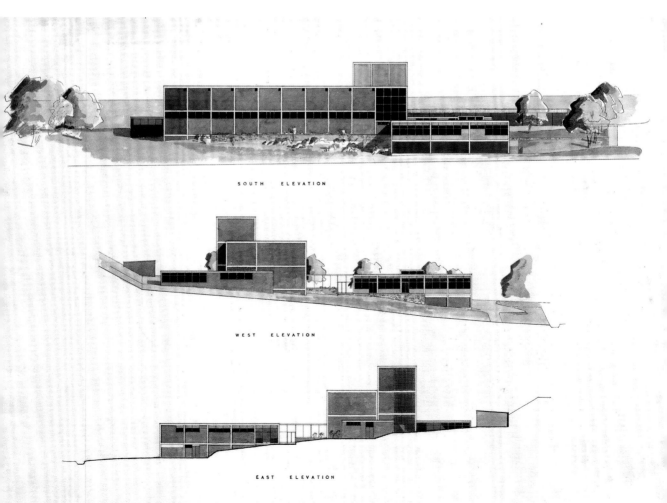

SOUTH   ELEVATION

WEST   ELEVATION

EAST   ELEVATION

P I T H E A D   B A T H S   *Marquis & Rawdon Collieries*

SCALE 1/16" = 1'	DRAWING NO
DATE 30/11/47	
DRAWN	**2**
GROUP No 5	
ELEVATIONS	

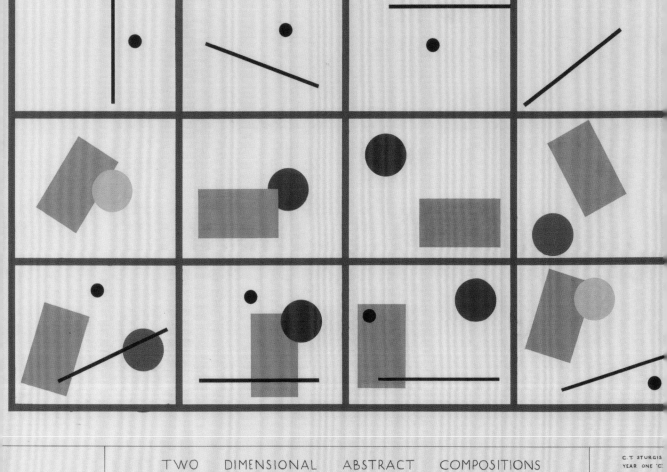

TWO DIMENSIONAL ABSTRACT COMPOSITIONS

C.T STURGIS
YEAR ONE 'C'
MAY 1949.

Plate 4   Abstract Composition (Tim Sturgis, first year, 1948/49)

*In the late 1940s, the AA abandoned traditional drawing instruction and
introduced a series of Bauhaus-derived exercises in colour, comparative
textures and three-dimensional composition. Reyner Banham (*Listener, 26
Sep 1968*) was critical of the 'neat and tidy' results of these exercises, which
in his view lacked the 'roughness of the newly-found' that had marked the
Bauhaus originals.*

Plate 5 1951 Festival Café (Nigel Grimwade, first year, 1949/50)

*With its colour accents and picturesque setting, Nigel Grimwade's design
singularly captures the mood of the forthcoming Festival of Britain. Grimwade
continued to produce unusually refined projects and remained largely
unaffected by the Brutalist tendencies which soon pervaded the AA – all the
more surprising that he adopted a particularly clunky version of the style when
he later designed Basil Spence's Falmer House at the University of Sussex.*

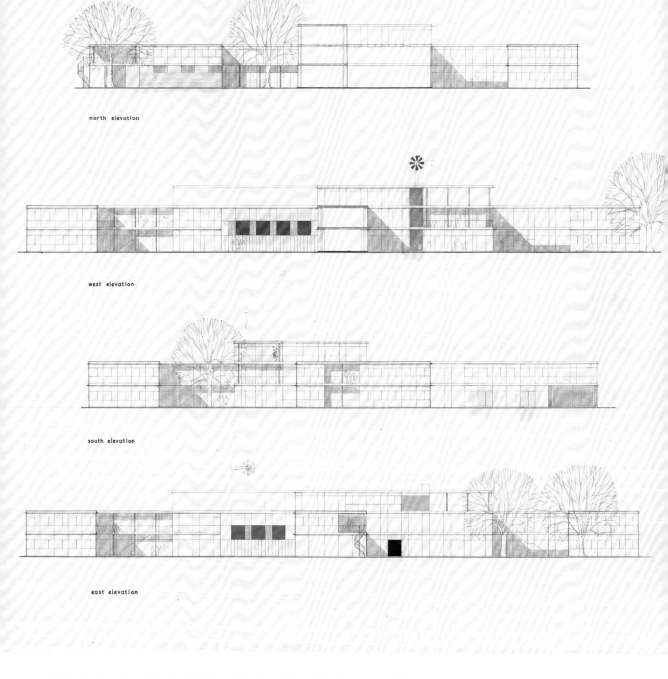

north elevation

west elevation

south elevation

east elevation

Plate 6   Secondary School at St Albans (Geoffrey Salmon, fourth year, 1950/51)

Geoffrey Salmon struggled with the merciless discipline imposed by the building system and enlisted the help of sculptors, painters and interior designers from the neighbouring art schools to add an 'element of creative impression' with which the school children could associate ('Memoirs', March 2003, AAA). Following his graduation, Salmon joined Michael Austin-Smith and soon after became a named partner of his firm.

This development plan for a new town in Kenya was conceived against the background of the Mau Mau Uprising and set out to propose a way in which the country's racial groups could live together harmoniously in integrated town and rural settlements. Richard Hughes had grown up in Kenya and returned there in the mid-1950s to set up in private practice. His collaborator Terence Powell was an engineering student at Imperial College and submitted the plan as his thesis on hydropower and irrigation.

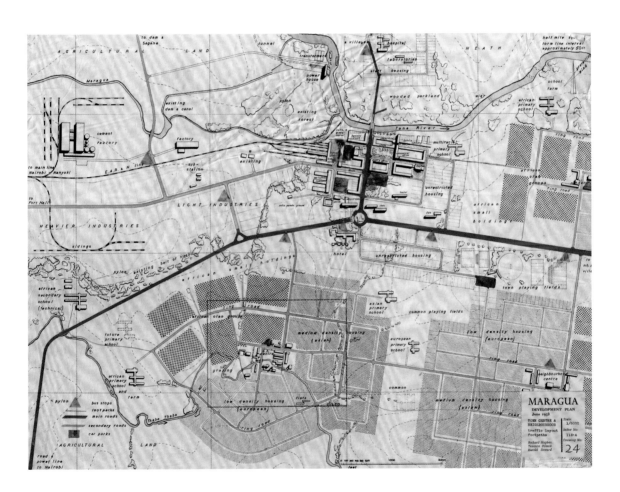

Plate 7   Maragua (Richard Hughes, Terence Powell, Harold Seward, thesis, 1952/53)

Cedric Price's design for a pub was not to everyone's taste. The Architects' Journal *(1 Aug 1957) was intrigued by this 'most unlikely marriage of Osbert Lancaster and Peter Smithson [. . .]'. Others were less generous in their judgement, and Price (*AA Quarterly, *vol.9, no.1) remembered one juror leaving the room mumbling 'I thought this was a school of architecture, not an advertising agency.'*

Plate 8   Pub (Cedric Price, fifth year, 1956/57)

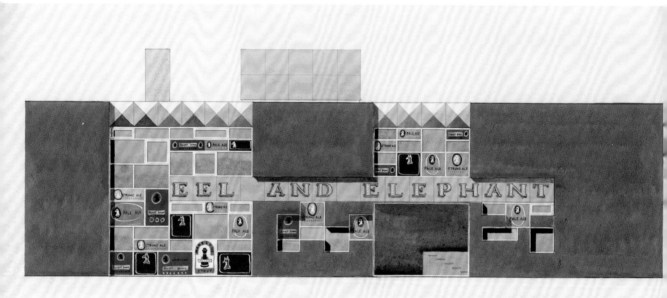

(*right*) Plate 9   Onitsha Market, Nigeria (Denise Lakofski and Robert Scott Brown, DTA, 1954/55)

After completing her thesis, Denise Scott Brown (née Lakofski) returned to the AA to attend the first instalment of the Department of Tropical Architecture, now joined by her future husband Robert Scott Brown. Like other 'colonial' students, they were scornful of how the English built in Africa and felt they knew rather more about tropical architecture than those who taught them (Scott Brown, interview, 1990/91). Their market was divided into four sections grouped around a central administrative building and featured a Festival-inspired 'pleasure gardens' along the banks of the Niger River. The structure was based on a grid of precast concrete columns covered by aluminium roofing on timber rafters and purlins; stalls were created through movable perforated partitions and fitted with timber pivot-shutters.

view of a courtyard

view of a shopping street

ARCHITECTURAL ASSOCIATION
SCHOOL OF ARCHITECTURE
STORE
148   YEAR 1954-55

onitsha market   nigeria
d. lakofski   r. scott brown.

OM 3

The text within the drawing reads:

THE GREAT METROPOLIS OUTSIDE
WOE TO THE BLOODY CITY. IT IS
ALL FULL OF LIES & ROBBERY —
THE PREY DEPARTETH NOT —
THE NOISE OF A WHIP AND THE
NOISE OF THE RATTLING OF
WHEELS AND OF THE PRANCING
HORSES AND OF THE JUMPING
CHARIOTS,
YE THAT PUT FAR AWAY THE
EVIL DAY AND CAUSE THE
SEAT OF VIOLENCE TO COME
NEAR — THAT LIE UPON
BEDS OF IVORY & STRETCH
THEMSELVES UPON THEIR
COUCHES & EAT THE
LAMBS OUT OF THE
FLOCK & THE CALVES
OUT OF THE MIDST
OF THE STALL — THAT
CHANT TO THE
SOUND OF THE
VIOL & INVENT

TO THEMSELVES
INSTRUMENTS
OF MUSIC LIKE
DAVID — THAT
DRINK WINE IN
BOWLS AND
ANOINT
THEMSELVES
WITH THE
CHIEF OINT-
MENTS
BUT THEY
ARE NOT
GRIEVED
FOR
THE
AFFLICTION
OF JOSEPH

THE STILL SAD MUSIC OF HUMANITY —

MOREOVER I WILL
TAKE FROM THEM
THE VOICE OF MIRTH
AND THE VOICE OF
GLADNESS — THE
VOICE OF THE BRIDE —
GROOM & THE VOICE
OF THE BRIDE — THE
SOUND OF THE MILL
STONES & THE LIGHT
OF THE CANDLE

THE WALL

THE GATE

SHALL NOT SLEEP PRO[...]MENTAL FIGHT NOR

SHALL NOT SLEEP PRO[...]

[...] SWORD SLEEP IN MY HAND TILL WE HAVE BUILT JERUSALEM IN ENGLAND[...]
GREEN & PLEASANT LAND.

THE REGENTS PARK INSIDE
CONSIDER THE LILIES OF THE FIELD HOW THEY
GROW — THEY TOIL NOT NEITHER DO THEY
SPIN AND YET I SAY UNTO YOU THAT EVEN
SOLOMON IN ALL HIS GLORY WAS NOT ARRAYED
LIKE ONE OF THESE.

ARCHITECTURAL ASSOCIATION
SCHOOL STORE
FOURTH YEAR 1959/[...]

Plate 10   Luxury Housing, Regent's Park (Quinlan Terry, fourth year, 1959/60)

Banham's expansion of the source material offered rich pickings for students in search of modernist precedents. The so-called 'Christian Weirdies' around Quinlan Terry, Andrew Anderson and Malcolm Higgs stood out by rejecting any kind of modernism. Terry's vaguely historicist luxury housing scheme – a similar programme to the Castle Complex of the previous year (Fig.53) – seems almost Rossi-esque in its reductive use of type-forms. According to Colin Rowe (AAJ, Sep/Oct 1959), it was an example of the 'quasi-Mackintoshian, quasi-Gothic Revival exercises', through which the group expressed its 'position of extreme dissent'.

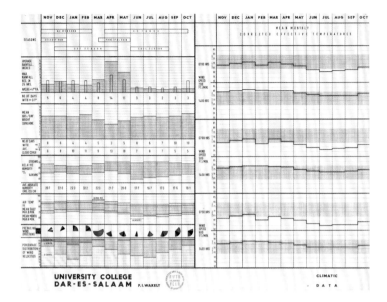

Plate 11

University College, Dar es Salaam
(Patrick Wakely, DTA, 1963)

Under Otto Koenigsberger, the Department of Tropical Architecture developed a strong research emphasis in its work and pioneered what is known today as climatic design. Patrick Wakely, later a professor of urban development at the University of London, compiled a wide range of climatic data as the basis of his design for a university college in Tanzania.

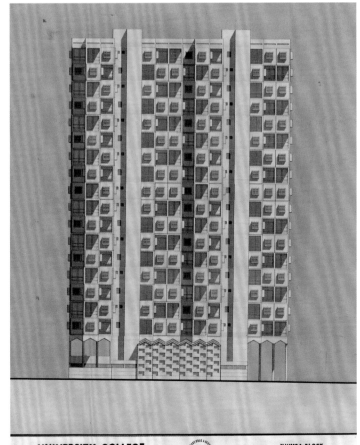

Plate 12

Existing roads

New roads

ARCHITECTURAL ASSO___ ___
SCHOOL OF ARCHITECTURE
SECOND YEAR 1961-62

**Plate 13   Aylesham Redevelopment
(Mehmet Konuralp, second year, 1961/62)**

*In the early 1960s, all major studio programmes were
linked to a specific gradation of architectural scale.
In the second year, students prepared a development
plan for an existing village, which formed the basis
of their subsequent design projects. It is interesting
to compare this plan for Aylesham with one for Vigo,
designed a decade earlier (Fig.26). Back then, there
had been an obvious attempt to extend rather than
replace the village by working with the existing street
pattern. Ten years later, 'development' was interpreted
as comprehensive renewal. Konuralp proposed a
reorganisation of Aylesham along Beaux-Arts lines,
with new axes cut through the existing building stock
in a ruthless Haussmannesque manner.*

Plate 14

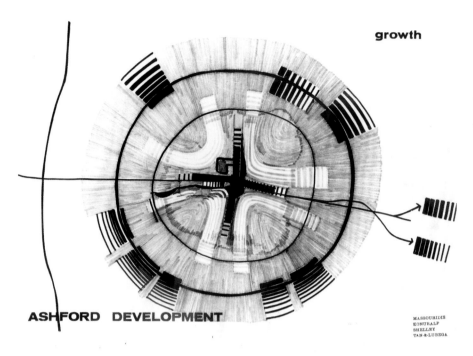

growth

ASHFORD DEVELOPMENT

MASSOURIDIS
KONURALP
SHELLEY
TAN-&-LUBEGA

In their third year, students were asked to consider the development of an existing town. This scheme for Ashford illustrates the current preoccupation with exponential growth facilitated by a series of ring roads. Inspired by the Smithsons' Berlin Hauptstadt proposal, the town centre itself is dotted by towers and layered into different modes of transport. A typical period feature is the new 'rapid transport system' in the form of a suspended monorail, then promoted in France and Japan as the solution to public transport problems in congested urban areas.

Plate 15

ASHFORD DEVELOPMENT

MASSOURIDIS
KONURALP
SHELLEY
TAN-&-LUBEGA

Ashford (Mehmet Konuralp, Anthony Lubega, Pandelis Massouridis,
A. W. Shelley, Andrew Tan, third year, 1962/63)

Plate 16

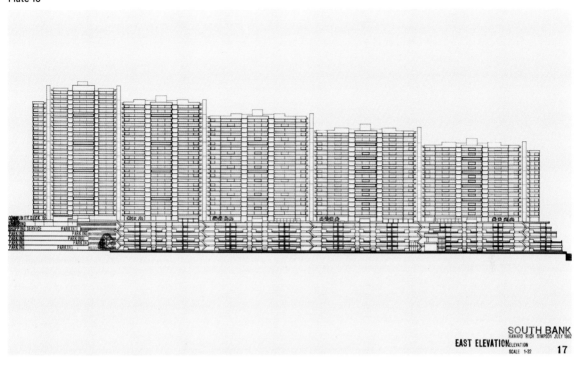

SOUTH BANK
HAWARD RICH SIMPSON JULY 1962
EAST ELEVATION ELEVATION
SCALE 1-32 **17**

Plate 17

Waterloo Road Area Redevelopment, South Bank (Birkin Haward, Peter Rich, Paul Simpson, fourth year, 1961/62)

In October 1960, John Winter succeeded John Killick as fourth-year master. The year continued to produce 'full-blooded injections into the Metropolis' (Ahrends, AAJ, Oct 1962), invariably set in central London. For their redevelopment of the Waterloo Road area on the South Bank, Haward, Rich and Simpson proposed a fan-shaped arrangement of housing slabs, each sitting on a ziggurat containing a multi-level car park. The assumption was that the site would be cleared for comprehensive redevelopment and connected to a new urban motorway system consisting of six-lane elevated roads. Louis Kahn, who inspected the scheme on his visit to London in mid-1962, disapproved of the finger blocks but liked the idea of transforming Waterloo Station into a circular 'multi-transport interchange'. (The image on the cover shows other proposals for the same brief).

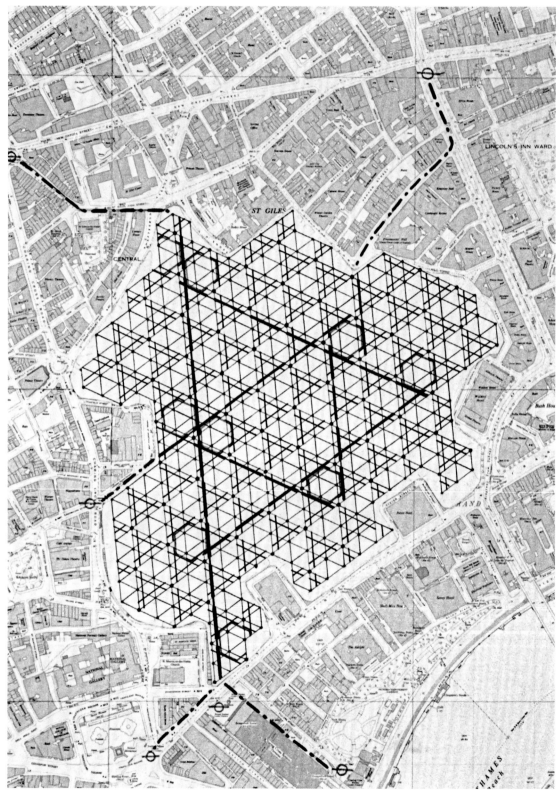

Plate 18

Urban University, Covent Garden
(Nicholas Grimshaw, thesis, 1964/65)

Plate 19

Nicholas Grimshaw's university network was to cover the whole (and wholly razed) Covent Garden area. The site was overlaid by a grid for travelators, with structural service and circulation towers placed at the nodal points. The objective was to coordinate the 60° movement grid (shown in Plate 18) with a more conventional yet highly flexible 90° spatial grid on the levels above and below. Grimshaw briefed the thesis jury ahead of his presentation about his objectives; he built a cardboard model to illustrate how the system could be built from a small number of components (Plate 19); and he prepared a film to show how faculties could expand and perish over time. With its emphasis on impermanence and motion patterns, Grimshaw's scheme recalls Peter Cook's Plug-In City and Dennis Crompton's Computer City, both of 1964; it also has obvious affinities with both Yona Friedman's Ville Spatial *and Candilis-Josić-Woods's Free University in Berlin, then in an early design stage. According to Cook ('Electric Decade', p.141), 'Grimshaw's University was a first staging-post in the process of disintegrating a tradition: that of designing a building as the pre-requisite of making architecture.'*

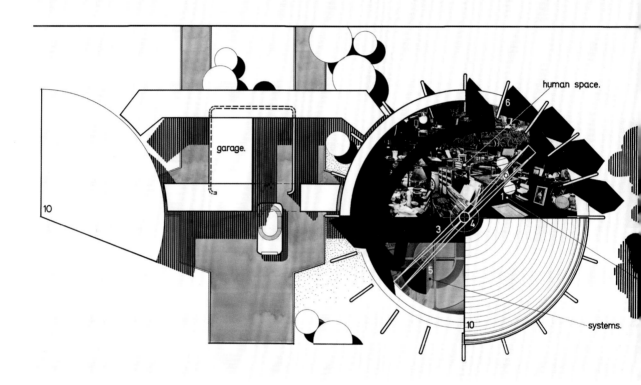

Plate 20   The Time House (Martin Pawley, thesis, 1966/67)

Pawley's dystopian house envisioned the apotheosis of privatisation and the corresponding extinction of the public ream. Consequently, he designed it as a defensive and – both metaphorically and literally – introspective concrete bunker. Anticipating 21st-century notions of 'smart technology', Pawley's house is equipped with a cybernetically controlled multi-sensory 'recall system' supplying residents with a complete record of their own behaviour. In 1962, Pawley's a-formal fourth-year scheme for a Film Institute (Fig.58) had been completely out of sync with the rationalist mood in the school. When four years later he returned to the AA to complete his course, he may have expected it to be more favourably disposed towards his idiosyncratic design ideas. Pawley's project, however, was failed; it only passed after he managed to get it published in Architectural Design *in the following year.*

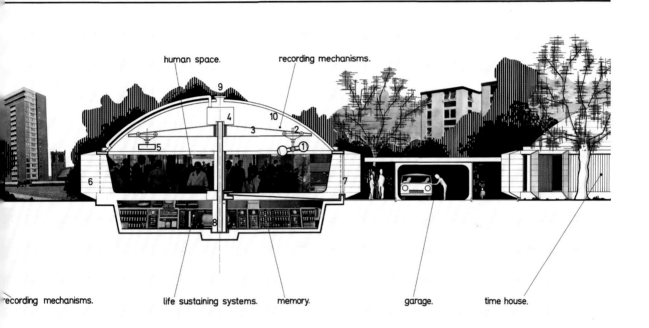

human space.

recording mechanisms.

9

4

10

3

2

5

1

6

7

8

recording mechanisms.   life sustaining systems.   memory.   garage.   time house.

Plate 21
Piezoelectrics
(Robin Evans,
thesis, 1968/69)

In July 1969, the world witnessed a live broadcast of Apollo 11 landing a man on the moon. The potential of modern technology seemed boundless and inspired a number of science-fiction schemes at the AA. Of these, Robin Evans's thesis was perhaps the most remarkable, and certainly the most persuasively argued. It drew on recent research into the so-called piezoelectric effect, that is, the ability of certain materials to transform mechanical energy into electrical energy (and vice versa). Evans suggested that the extreme speed of response that had been observed in piezoelectric systems might be exploited in the form of a new synthetic material enabling the construction of infinitely stiff piezoelectric compression structures. Such structures could operate as isolated 'peripatetic anthropods' or combine into a larger settlement, aptly named 'PiezoelectriCity'.

Plate 22   Prison Park (Nigel Coates, Diploma Unit 2, 1973/74)

*According to Higgott (*Mediating Modernism, *pp 163–5), Bernard Tschumi developed the position of his diploma unit in response to recent political upheavals, fusing contemporary art practices with the spatial-political analysis of Lefebvre. With its emphasis on process, the unit took a counter-position to the emerging postmodern mainstream and its obsession with form and style. Students were asked to explore the scope and parameters of architectural activity by engaging with questions of programme and representation. This process was itself the objective and did not necessarily lead to an architectural proposition. Nigel Coates, who later succeeded Tschumi as unit master, investigated the nature of spatial control by documenting a linear walk through Hyde Park in the form of 12 image boards. The pictured board includes Coates's entry for the Royal Mint Square Estate competition of 1974.*

Plate 23   ARC – Architects' Revolutionary Council (Diploma Unit 8, 1975/76)

Brian Anson joined the AA teaching staff in 1971 following his successful campaign for the preservation of Covent Garden. He saw his intermediate (from 1975 diploma) unit as a breeding ground for idealists engaging in grassroots political action in support of – and collaboration with – disadvantaged communities. Formal proposals were rarely an outcome of its work as students examined the social effects of post-disaster regeneration in Skopje, investigated the implications of North Sea oil extraction on coastal communities in Scotland and helped to set up residents' associations to fight the planning ambitions of local councils in Liverpool and elsewhere. In early 1974, Anson's unit gave birth to the Architects' Revolutionary Council, which set itself in opposition to the RIBA, seen as a hopelessly compromised agency of the privileged few acting against the interests of ordinary people.

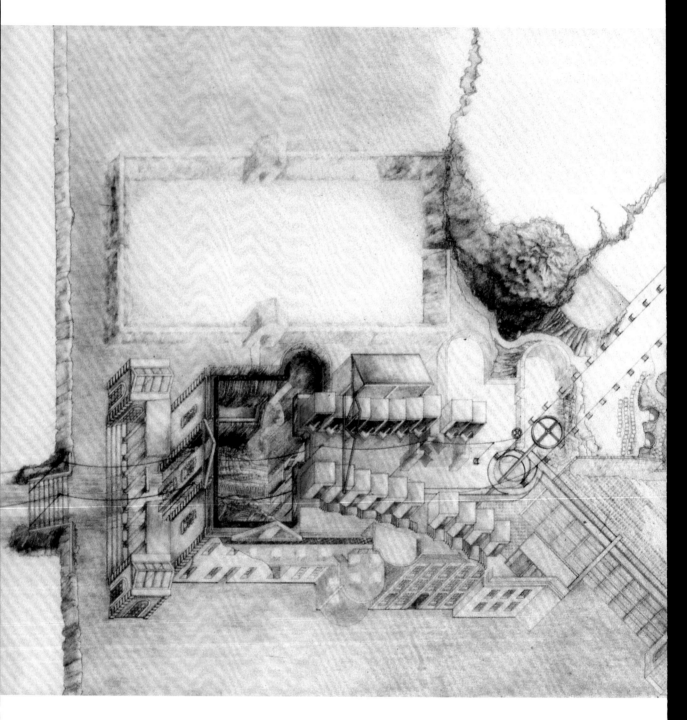

*Students were asked to design new facilities for Gunton Park, a vast country estate in Norfolk comprising an array of lakes, tunnels and follies as well as houses by James Wyatt and Robert Adam. Kathryn Findlay devised a cable car system which cuts through the south facade of Wyatt's Gunton Hall and links it to a series of theatrical venues spread across the sprawling grounds. Unlike many of their colleagues, Peter Cook, Christine Hawley and Ron Herron did not promote a uniform style in their unit. Modes of expression were as varied as they were skilful, and Cook (*Spirit and Invention, *London, 1982, p.5) noted with glee: 'Art has returned. That is the best thing of all.'*

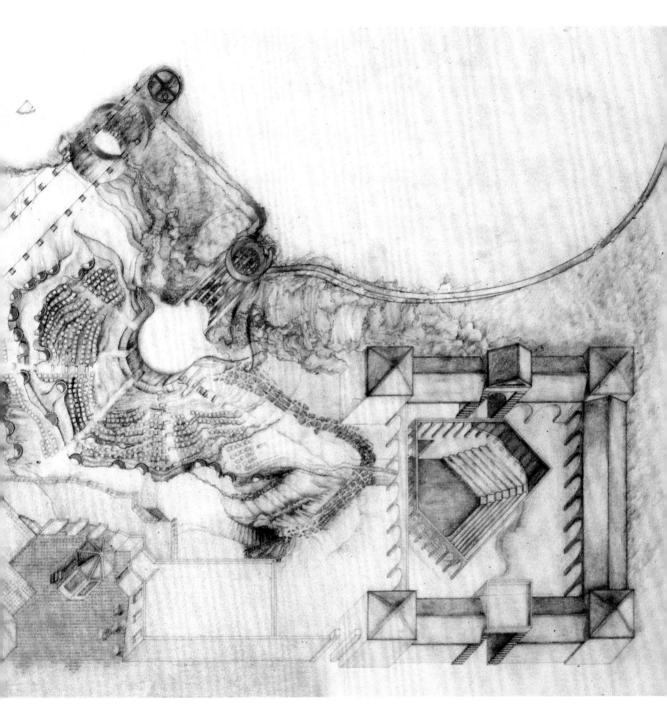

Plate 24   Gunton Hall Redevelopment (Kathryn Findlay, Diploma Unit 6, 1977/78)

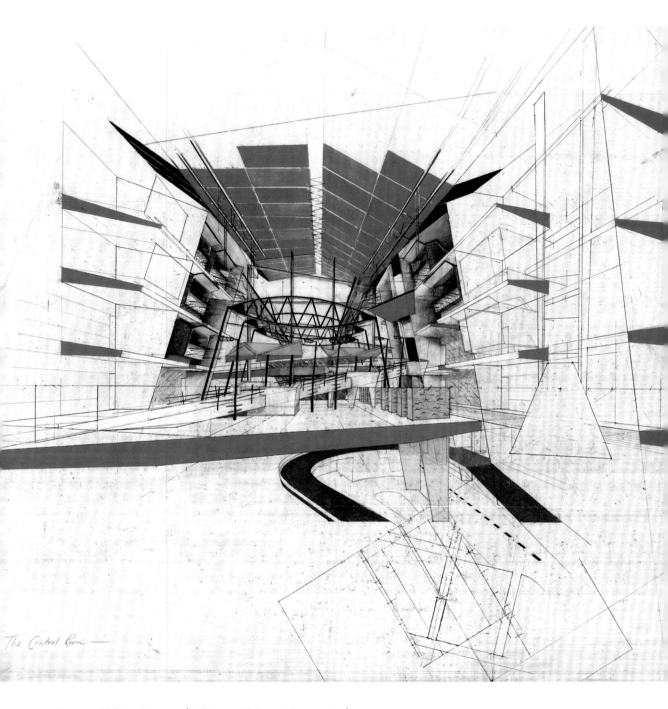

The Control Room —

Plate 25   BBC Headquarters (Neil Porter, Diploma Unit 1, 1982/83)

*Peter Wilson's Diploma Unit 1 concerned itself with annual 'themes', loosely interpreted and with little regard for context or indeed programme. In 1982/83, the theme was 'travel', and Wilson (*AA Projects Review 1982–83*) set the brief for an extension to the BBC headquarters because it needed to be 'an exceptional building worth travelling to see'. Neil Porter arranged the control room of his Radio 4 pavilion around a central canyon, diagonally transected by an access ramp and overlooked by the various recording studios.*

Abbreviations

Note: Factual information, unless otherwise cited, is drawn from the minutes of the AA council and its subcommittees.

AAA	AA Archives, London	BOE	Board of Education (succeeded by the MOE)
AAA/CM	Minutes of the AA Council, AA Archives, London	ETH/GTA/CIAM	CIAM Archive, GTA Archives, Swiss Federal Institute of Technology, Zurich
AAA/CSSCM	Minutes of the AA Council/Staff/Students' Committee, AA Archives, London	ICSTM	Imperial College of Science, Technology and Medicine Records, University of London
AAA/EC	Minutes of the AA Executive Committee, AA Archives, London	LMA	London Metropolitan Archives
AAA/OK	Otto Koenigsberger Archive, AA Archives, London	MOE	Ministry of Education (preceded by the BOE)
AAA/SCM	Minutes of the AA School Committee, AA Archives, London	MRC/ABT	Records of the Association of Building Technicians, Modern Records Centre, University of Warwick, Coventry
AAJ	*AA Journal*	RIBA/ED	Minutes of the RIBA Board of Architectural Education, its committees and subcommittees, RIBA Archive, London
AAL	AA Library, London		
ABA	Alvin Boyarsky Archive, private collection, London		
ABN	*Architect and Building News*		
AD	*Architectural Design*	*RIBAJ*	*RIBA Journal*
AJ	*Architects' Journal*	SRC	Students' Representative Council, AA School
AR	*Architectural Review*		
BAE	RIBA Board of Architectural Education	TNA: ED	Records created or inherited by the Department of Education and Science, and of related bodies, The National Archives, Kew
BLSA/NLSC:AL	National Life Stories Collection: Architects' Lives, British Library Sound Archive, London		

Notes

Introduction

1   Fred Scott, 'Myth, Misses, and Mr Architecture', in James Gowan (ed.), *A Continuing Experiment*, London, 1975, pp 167–8.

2   Edward Carter, 'The Architectural Association – Imperial College Project', 21 Nov 1966, AAA, 2006:S16b.

3   Restaurant: Leonard Manasseh (winner), Percy Davison (third prize); 'Vertical Feature': Powell & Moya (winners), Peter Dickinson (third prize).

4   As quoted by Denise Scott Brown in *Web of Stories*, www.webofstories.com/play/robert.venturi.and.denise.scott.brown/29.

5   See, e.g. Colin St John Wilson, interviewed by Jill Lever, 24 Sep 1996, BLSA/NLSC:AL.

6   Sarah Williams Goldhagen and Réjean Legault (eds), *Anxious Modernisms*, Cambridge MA, 2000, p.11.

7   Elizabeth Darling, *Re-forming Britain*, New York, 2007, p.179; see also, e.g. John Summerson, *The Architectural Association 1847–1947*, London, 1947; Andrew Saint, *Towards a Social Architecture*, New Haven, 1987.

8   Peter Cook, 'The Electric Decade: An Atmosphere at the AA School 1963–73', in Gowan, *A Continuing Experiment*, pp 137–46.

9   Irene Sunwoo, 'From the "Well-Laid Table" to the "Market Place": The Architectural Association Unit System', *Journal of Architectural Education*, March 2012, p.35; see also, e.g. Andrew Higgott, *Mediating Modernism*, London, 2007, pp 153–87; Igor Marjanović, 'Alvin Boyarsky's Delicatessen', in Jane Rendell, Jonathan Hill, Murray Fraser and Mark Dorrian (eds), *Critical Architecture*, London, 2007, pp 190–99; Irene Sunwoo, 'Between the "Well-Laid Table" and the "Marketplace": Alvin Boyarsky's Experiments in Architectural Pedagogy', doctoral dissertation, Princeton University, Nov 2013; Igor Marjanović, 'Drawing Ambience', in Igor Marjanović and Jan Howard (eds), *Drawing Ambience: Alvin Boyarsky and*

the Architectural Association, St. Louis MO/Providence RI, 2014, pp 23–57.

10   Barrington Kaye, *The Development of the Architectural Profession in Britain*, London, 1960, p.88.

11   Andrew Saint, *The Image of the Architect*, New Haven, 1983, p.x.

12   Mark Crinson and Jules Lubbock, *Architecture – Art or Profession? Three Hundred Years of Architectural Education in Britain*, Manchester, 1994, p.1.

13   [Edward Carter], 'The Future of the AA', memorandum att. to AA Council, 17 July 1961, AAA/CM.

1   Prologue

1   For a history of architectural education in Britain, see Mark Crinson and Jules Lubbock, *Architecture – Art or Profession? Three Hundred Years of Architectural Education in Britain*, Manchester, 1994.

2   For the origins of the AA, see John Summerson, *The Architectural Association 1847–1947*, London, 1947.

3   Summerson, *The Architectural Association 1847–1947*, p.12.

4   Summerson, *The Architectural Association 1847–1947*, p.19.

5   Nikolaus Pevsner, 'The AA', *AR*, March 1948, p.121.

6   Alan Powers, 'Edwardian Architectural Education: A Study of Three Schools of Architecture', *AA Files*, no.5 (1984), pp 48–59.

7   Powers, 'Edwardian Architectural Education', p.59.

8   Andrew Higgott, *Mediating Modernism*, London, 2007, pp 20–30.

9   Summerson, *The Architectural Association 1847–1947*, p.47.

10   Quoted in 'Annual General Meeting', *AAJ*, Dec 1962, p.198.

11   This, of course, was only the case for male students. Between 1917 (when they first joined) and 1920 (when the AA was incorporated) female students were, as mentioned, *not* members of the association.

12   AA Council, 1 May 1933, AAA/CM.

13   AA Council, 18 July 1935, AAA/CM; Susan Cox, 'Student Vote', 1948, AAA, 1991:7.

14   'The AA Story, 1936–1939', *Focus*, no.3 (Spring 1939), p.82.

15   Existing literature suggests that his position as director gave Goodhart-Rendel superiority over Rowse. While this may have been the council's intention, in reality the running of the school was in Rowse's hands. The fact that his was a full-time position, whereas Goodhart-Rendel was expected to give half a day once a fortnight, may put things into perspective.

16   AA School Committee, 14 Jan 1936, AAA/SCM; for the proposal itself, see AA Council, 22 Jan 1936, AAA/CM.

17   AA School Committee, 14 Jan 1936, AAA/SCM; AA Council, 22 Jan 1936, AAA/CM.

18   'The AA Story', p.84.

19   H. S. Goodhart-Rendel, 'Architectural Education', *AAJ*, March 1937, pp 381–4.

20   'Report of Students' Sub-committee on the School System', [May] 1937, rpt in *Focus*, no.3 (1939), pp 87–96; quotes, p.95.

21   'The AA Story', p.86.

22   H. S. Goodhart-Rendel, 'The Training of an Architect', *AAJ*, March 1938, pp 403–16.

23   Goodhart-Rendel, 'Training of an Architect', p.404. Some historians have rather willingly adopted the students' somewhat biased chronicle of these events. The most accurate account remains Alan Powers, 'Goodhart-Rendel: The Appropriateness of Style', *AD*, Oct/Nov 1979, pp 50–51.

24   AA Council, 3 May 1938, 4 July 1938, AAA/CM.

25   AA Council, 13 July 1938, AAA/CM.

26   For a discussion, see Elizabeth Darling, *Re-forming Britain*, New York, 2007, pp 191–8.

27   John Summerson, 'AA School of Architecture: Exhibition of Students' Work, Session 1937–38', *AAJ*, Aug 1938, p.68.

28   Anthony Cox, 'The Training of an Architect. An Open Letter to H. S. Goodhart-Rendel', *Focus*, no.1 (1938), pp 24–32; 'Editorial', *Focus*, no.2 (1938), pp 9–10.

29   AA Council, 13 July 1938, AAA/CM.

30   AA Council, 18 July 1938, 20 July 1938, AAA/CM.

31   AA Council, 8 Aug 1938, AAA/CM.

32   BOE, 'Report of H. M. Inspectors on The Architectural Association's School of Architecture and School of Planning', May 1937, TNA: ED 90/422, p.3.

33   Quoted in Cox, 'Student Vote'. There has been speculation that Rowse's dismissal may have been a result of the BOE's inspection. However, the report, while critical of certain aspects of the course, questioned neither Rowse's direction of the school nor indeed the unit system itself, which 'must be given a fair trial before judgment is passed on its efficacy'. (BOE, Report, May 1937, p.10.)

34   BOE, Report, May 1937, p.23.

35   BOE, Report, May 1937, p.4.

36   AA Council, 22 March 1938, AAA/CM; see also, Cox, 'Student Vote'.

37   *AJ*, 2 June 1938, p.930.

38   *AJ*, 9 June 1938, p.972.

39   AA Council, 14 June 1938, AAA/CM.

40   AA Council, 29 Nov 1938, AAA/CM.

41   'The Centenary of the AA', *AR*, Dec 1947, p.184.

42   BOE, Report, May 1937, p.5.

43   AA Council, 6 Oct 1938, AAA/CM.

44   Geoffrey Jellicoe, 'The Principal's Address to the School', *AAJ*, March 1939, pp 209–11.

45   AA Council, 28 March 1939, AAA/CM.

46   Summerson, *The Architectural Association 1847–1947*, p.49.

47   Geoffrey Jellicoe, 'Principal's Report to the Council of the Association', July 1940, AAA, 2006:S34.

48   Jellicoe, 'Principal's Report'.

49   Geoffrey Jellicoe, letter to Arthur Kenyon, [Sep 1941], att. to AA Council, 1 Oct 1941, AAA/CM.

50   Frederick Gibberd and F. R. S. Yorke, *The Modern Flat*, London, 1937; see also, Christine Hui Lan Manley, *Frederick Gibberd*, London, 2017.

51   'Report of the RIBA Visiting Board', [March 1943], AAA, 2006:S34.

52   'Report of the RIBA Visiting Board'.

53   Neville Conder, interviewed by Alan Powers, 1999, BLSA/NLSC:AL.

54   'Report of the RIBA Visiting Board'.

55   'Principal's Report to the Council', att. to AA Council, 23 Feb 1943, AAA/CM.

2   After the War (1945–1949)

1   Frederick Gibberd, 'A Plan for the Architectural Association School of Architecture', March 1944, AAA, 1991:7.

2   AA Council, 24 July 1944, AAA/CM.

3   AA Council, 13 Nov 1944, AAA/CM. The other two candidates were John Brandon-Jones, an AA graduate who currently taught at Liverpool, and Joseph Stanley Allen, at the time the head of the Leeds School of Architecture.

4   AA Council, 13 Nov 1944, AAA/CM.

5   Cecil St Clair Oakes, 'Obituary: Mr. Gordon Brown', *AAJ*, May 1962, p.279.

6   AA Council, 13 Nov 1944, AAA/CM.

7   Brown's battalion lost 65 killed, wounded or missing from the assaulting 150, and captured 22 enemy

prisoners; he himself was wounded and reported missing but managed to fight his way back to his own lines. (*AAJ*, Sep/Oct 1944, p.102; T. B. H. Otway, *The Second World War 1939–1945. Army: Airborne Forces*, London, 1990, p.180.)

8   AA Council, 6 July 1948, AAA/CM.

9   Michael Shattock, *Making Policy in British Higher Education 1945–2011*, Maidenhead, 2012, p.9.

10   Frederick Bray, Under-Secretary for Further Education, quoted in Ministry of Education, 'Interview Memorandum', 21 March 1946, TNA: ED 90/422.

11   AA Council, 25 March 1946, AAA/CM 1940–49.

12   By comparison, in the late 1940s, nearly two thirds of the average university income came from recurring UGC grants, with fees accounting for less than a fifth. (Shattock, *Making Policy*, p.12.)

13   AA School Committee, 4 Oct 1948, AAA/SCM.

14   Gibberd, 'A Plan'.

15   Gibberd, 'A Plan'.

16   AA Council, 26 March 1945, 11 June 1945, AAA/CM.

17   AA Council, 26 Feb 1946, AAA/CM.

18   For instance, both Harry Goodhart-Rendel and Ove Arup offered their services for free when, in January 1948, the AA faced an acute (and unbudgeted) shortage of staff.

19   AA School Committee, 27 April 1948, AAA/SCM. The other members of the practice, later renamed the Architects' Co-Partnership, were Kenneth Capon, Peter Cocke, Michael Cooke-Yarborough, Michael Grice and Michael Powers. Brown proposed a similar arrangement with the partners at Yorke Rosenberg Mardall, which failed to materialise. (AA School Committee, 13 Dec 1948, AAA/SCM.)

20   AA Council, 13 March 1944, AAA/CM; see also, AA Council, 19 Jan 1942, AAA/CM.

21   For instance, when Oakes was offered the post of principal architect to the Imperial War Graves Commission for South-East Asia, Brown, despite considerable objections, coerced the council to alter his contract, allowing him two months' leave of absence for each of the following five years. (AA Council, 14 April 1947, 27 May 1947, AAA/CM)

22   AA Council, 29 Jan 1945, AAA/CM.

23   AA School Committee, 2 Nov 1945, AAA/SCM.

24   AA School Committee, 3 March 1947, AAA/SCM.

25   AA, *School of Architecture War-Time Prospectus*, London, 1942, AAA, p.14.

26   Gibberd, 'A Plan'.

27   AA Council, 27 Nov 1944, 18 Dec 1944, AAA/CM.

28   'Technical Training and New Scholarships at the AA School of Architecture', *AAJ*, May 1945, p.156.

29   Incidentally, Douglas Jones's collaborator and successor at Birmingham was Denys Hinton, who had studied under Brown.

30   AA School Committee, 3 March 1947, AAA/SCM.

31   Quoted in Sarah Menin and Stephen Kite, *An Architecture of Invitation: Colin St John Wilson*, Aldershot, 2005, p.23.

32   Michael Ventris (ed.), 'Group Working', *PLAN*, no.2 (1948), pp 6–22.

33   AA School Committee, 3 March 1947, AAA/SCM.

34   AA School Committee, 28 March 1947, AAA/SCM.

35   Quoted in 'Opening of the Centenary Exhibition', *AAJ*, Jan 1948, p.102.

36   *ABN*, 4 April 1947, p.3; *Builder*, 25 July 1947, p.87.

37   'The AA Centenary', *AJ*, 11 Dec 1947, p.512.

38   Eric Mumford, *The CIAM Discourse on Urbanism, 1928–1960*, London/Cambridge MA, 2002, pp 168–73; John R. Gold, '"A Very Serious Responsibility"? The MARS Group, Internationality and Relations with CIAM, 1933–39', *Architectural History*, no.56 (2013), p.268.

39   Quoted in Howard Robertson, 'Quality in Architecture', presidential address, *AAJ*, Nov 1947, p.54.

40   AA Council, 16 Oct 1947, AAA/CM.

41   Alfred Roth, letter to M. Hartland Thomas, 9 Dec 1947, ETH/GTA/CIAM, 42-SG-23-218/219.

42   Sigfried Giedion, telegraph to Howard Robertson [Dec 1947], ETH/GTA/CIAM, 42-SG-19-53. Alfred Roth used the same phrase in *Das Werk*, Switzerland's leading architecture magazine (A. R., '100 Jahre AA-School in London', *Das Werk*, Feb 1948, p.23).

43   Howard Robertson, letter to Sigfried Giedion, 10 Dec 1947, ETH/GTA/CIAM, 42-SG-23-217.

44   [Gordon Brown], 'CIAM International School', [April or May 1947], ETH/GTA/CIAM, 42-SG-19-77/78/79.

45   [Brown], 'CIAM International School'.

46   Sigfried Giedion, letter to Gordon Brown, 7 June 1947, ETH/GTA/CIAM, 42-SG-19-80. Brown had joined MARS in 1945 but appears to have been a marginal figure within the group.

47   The commission had 15 members and was chaired by Gropius. Jaromír Krejcar, who represented the Czechoslovak branch on the commission, joined the AA staff in 1948, Robert Townsend of the MARS Group the year after.

48   'Commission IV. Architectural Education: Summary of Proceedings', ETH/GTA/CIAM, 42-AR-1.

49   Gordon Brown, letter to Sigfried Giedion, 14 Oct 1947, ETH/GTA/CIAM, 42-SG-19-65; also, Julian Huxley, 'UNESCO, General Conference, Second Session', 5 Oct 1947, ETH/GTA/CIAM, 42-SG-19-115.

50   Brown, letter to Giedion, 14 Oct 1947.

51   Brown, letter to Giedion, 14 Oct 1947.

52   Gordon Brown to Sigfried Giedion, 26 Nov 1947, ETH/GTA/CIAM, 42-SG-19-63.

53   M. Hartland Thomas, letter to Sigfried Giedion, 17 March 1948, ETH/GTA/CIAM, 42-SG-19-113; 'MARS Group: 1947–8 Session – Report of the Executive Committee to the AGM', 21 May 1948, AAL, 72.036(42) MARS.

54   AA School Committee, 13 Dec 1948, AAA/SCM.

55   R. Gordon Brown, 'A New Form of Architectural Education', *AAJ*, Dec 1948, pp 94–107.

56   Brown, 'A New Form', p.96.

57 Brown, 'A New Form', p.96.

58 Brown, 'A New Form', p.98. The idea of an AA country school was popular in the immediate postwar years, partly as a result of the experience of Mount House. The AA's woodland site at Hooke Park, acquired in 2002, is a modern-day incarnation of Brown's idea.

59 *AJ*, 2 Dec 1948, p.504.

60 Brown had indicated his interest in the position to James Macgregor, the current head of the Cambridge University School of Architecture and former head of the Edinburgh College of Art School of Architecture, who recommended him to the appointing committee. (Assistant Secretary, University of Edinburgh, letter to Gordon Brown, 29 Nov 1948, in *Records of the University of Edinburgh*, Centre for Research Collections, University of Edinburgh, EUA IN1/ADS/SEC/1/7.)

61 AA Council, 29 Dec 1948, AAA/CM.

62 AA Council, 29 Dec 1948, AAA/CM.

63 AA Council, 31 Dec 1948, AAA/CM.

64 AA Council, 3 Jan 1949, AAA/CM.

65 Brown, 'A New Form', p.98.

66 *AAJ*, Jan 1949, p.115.

67 John Brandon-Jones, interviewed by Jill Lever, May/June 1999, BLSA/NLSC:AL.

68 AA Council, 25 Nov 1946, 6 Jan 1947, AAA/CM. It appears that Brown used the grant, which was meant to cover the students' meals, for other student expenses.

69 James Richards, *Memoirs of an Unjust Fella*, London, 1980, p.225.

70 Grant Buttars (deputy university archivist, University of Edinburgh), email to the author, 17 Jan 2014.

71 Quoted in Christian Caryl, *Building the Dragon City*, Hong Kong, 2012, pp 27–8.

72 Caryl, *Building the Dragon City*, pp 28, 30.

73 Miguel Ydígoras, the president's son, had studied at the AA under Brown.

74 Richards, *Memoirs*, p.225.

3 Architecture as Collaborative Practice (1949–1951)

1 Lionel B. Budden, 'The Future of Architectural Education', *RIBAJ*, July 1945, p.255.

2 BOE, Report, May 1937, p.14.

3 Nikolaus Pevsner, *Pioneers of the Modern Movement*, London, 1936.

4 The RIBA intermediate examination included test papers on Greek and Roman, Byzantine and Medieval, and Renaissance; papers on 19th-century architecture were introduced in 1950/51.

5 For the American context see, e.g. Stanford Anderson, 'Architectural History in Schools of Architecture', *Journal of the Society of Architectural Historians*, Sep 1999, vol.58, no.3, pp 282–90.

6 Andrew Saint, *Towards a Social Architecture*, New Haven, 1987, p.30.

7 R. Furneaux Jordan, 'General History', lecture synopses, AAA, 2008:60.

8 'His famous phrase – and we almost used to chant it when we saw it coming up, you know, chant it with him – was: "But this contains . . . the seeds of its own decay!"' (Robert Maguire, interviewed by Linda Sandino, 2004, BLSA/NLSC:AL.)

9 R. Furneaux Jordan, 'The Architectural Significance of 1851', *RIBAJ*, July 1951, p.340.

10 R. Furneaux Jordan, paper read to the CID Furniture Design Conference at the RIBA, July 1949, in *AJ*, 4 Aug 1949, p.129; see also, [R. Furneaux Jordan], 'AA Students Exhibition', *ABN*, 29 July 1949, p.100.

11 R. Furneaux Jordan, 'The Teaching of Architectural History', *PLAN*, no.4 (1949), pp 5–6.

12 'AA School Appointment', *AAJ*, Jan 1949, p.129.

13 R. Furneaux Jordan, 'An Inaugural Address', *AAJ*, Feb 1949, pp 136–46.

14 Jordan, 'An Inaugural Address', p.141.

15 Jordan, 'An Inaugural Address', p.137.

16 AA School Committee, 27 June 1949, AAA/SCM.

17 John Brandon-Jones, interviewed by Jill Lever, May/June 1999, BLSA/NLSC:AL.

18 AA School Committee, 3 Oct 1949, AAA/SCM; see also, e.g. Hugh Crallan, letter to S. E. T. Cusdin, 5 March 1951, AAA, 2006:S30.

19 Programme excerpt quoted in *Builder*, 4 Nov 1949, p.575.

20 *ABN*, 11 Nov 1949, p.466.

21 Denise Scott Brown, interviewed by Peter Reed, 25 Oct 1990 – 9 Nov 1991, Archives of American Art, Smithsonian Institution, www.aaa.si.edu/collections/interviews/oral-history-interview-denise-scott-brown-13059.

22 True to form, the idiosyncratic 83-year-old alternately shocked and delighted his audiences with his hard-hitting one-liners. Asked by a student whether he admired the work of contemporary architects, he reportedly replied: 'They have my sympathy.' (*AJ*, 20 July 1950, p.51.)

23 Quoted in Ad-hoc Committee on Architectural Education, 9 Jan 1951, RIBA/ED 7.1.2.

24 Quoted in 'Annual Prize Giving', *AAJ*, July/Aug 1951, p.56.

25 Alan Powers, 'Casson, Sir Hugh Maxwell', *Oxford Dictionary of National Biography*, Oxford, 2007, https://doi.org/10.1093/ref:odnb/72656.

26 *Guardian*, 13 July 1951, p.6.

27 Jordan, 'An Inaugural Address', p.140.

28 Jordan, paper read to the CID Furniture Design Conference at the RIBA, July 1949, p.128.

29 Quoted in 'Research and Development in Public Offices', *AAJ*, March 1951, p.167.

30   John Summerson, *The Architectural Association 1847–1947*, London, 1947, p.50.

31   Roderick Enthoven, 'Presidential Address', *AAJ*, Nov 1948, p.77.

32   Anthony Cox, 'Public and Private Architecture', *AAJ*, April 1948, pp 205–13.

33   R. Furneaux Jordan, 'The Situation in Architecture', *Keystone*, MRC/ABT, MSS.78/BT/4/6/10, Oct 1950, p.37.

34   'School Notes', *AAJ*, Nov 1949, p.86.

35   'Principal's Report', AA School Committee, 6 Oct 1950, AAA/SCM.

36   For a discussion, see Saint, *Towards a Social Architecture*.

37   Saint, *Towards a Social Architecture*, p.63.

38   R. Gordon Brown, 'A New Form of Architectural Education', *AAJ*, Dec 1948, p.97.

39   'AA Information and Curriculum Notes 1949–50', AAA, 1991:31.

40   Of course, Brown himself had co-authored a rare group thesis in the early 1930s (Fig.5).

41   'At no point in the AA training is group work *yet* compulsory.' ('AA Information and Curriculum Notes 1949–50' – author's italics.)

42   'AA Information and Curriculum Notes 1949–50'.

43   'AA Information and Curriculum Notes 1949–50'.

44   AA School Committee, 2 March 1951, AAA/SCM.

45   Quoted in Dennis Sharp (ed.), 'Arthur Korn (1891–1978) in memoriam', *AA Quarterly*, vol.11, no.3 (1979), p.49.

46   Chris Whittaker, interview with the author, 11 Jan 2014; see also, Stephen R. Parsons, 'Communism in the Professions: The Organisation of the British Communist Party among Professional Workers, 1933–1956', doctoral dissertation, University of Warwick, 1990, p.446.

47   Gabriel Epstein, interviewed by Niamh Dillon, 24 Sep 2009, BLSA/NLSC:AL.

48   AA Council, 12 April 1948, AAA/CM.

49   Though not a communist organisation per se, between 1945 and 1948 the SCR was – along with the party branch at the AA – the main meeting place for communist architects (Parsons, 'Communism in the Professions', p.450).

50   'Principal's Report to the Officers', 30 July 1950, att. to AA Council, 1 Aug 1950, AAA/CM.

51   'Note of a meeting with David Goddard', 24 July 1950, att. to AA Council, 1 Aug 1950, AAA/CM.

52   AA Council, 14 Aug 1950, AAA/CM.

53   S. E. T. Cusdin, 'Fumbling in the Quiver', *AAJ*, Nov 1950, pp 70–75.

54   AA Council, 13 Nov 1950, AAA/CM. Walker's actual statement was not included in the published version of the speech, but apparently he had asked Cusdin to 'clean out the Reds'. ([John Kay], 'Archts Grp: WW/AA', 29 Nov 1950, private collection.) Walker, an AA graduate and member of the Labour Party, headed the architectural department at the Hammersmith School

of Building. He was the younger brother of Raymond Myersclough-Walker.

55   'Architecture and Politics', *Builder*, 24 Nov 1950, pp 521–2; Walker's letter, ibid., p.537.

56   James Richards, 'Architecture and the Common Man', *AAJ*, Feb 1948, pp 153–61.

57   'Architects and Communism – A London Meeting', *Builder*, 26 March 1948, p.368.

58   'Architects and Politics', *Builder*, 26 March 1948, p.356.

59   F. E. Shrosbree (national organiser, ABT), letter to the editor, *Builder*, 9 April 1948, p.431.

60   AA Council, 8 Dec 1950, AAA/CM.

61   AA Council, 18 Dec 1950, AAA/CM.

62   Cusdin, letter to the editor, *Builder*, 1 Dec 1950, p.571.

63   *AJ*, 7 Dec 1950, p.469. Amusingly, James Richards, who was the author of the note, sang his own praises as it was he who had drafted Cusdin's letter to *Builder*.

64   [John Turner], 'Military Service', *PLAN*, no.8 (1950), p.32.

65   *Builder*, 29 Dec 1950, p.685.

66   'M.P.'s Question on Tips to "Conchies"', *Empire News*, 11 March 1951, p.1; *HC Deb*, 12 March 1951, vol.485, col.114W; AA Council, 19 March 1951, AAA/CM.

67   AA Council, 26 Feb 1951, AAA/CM.

68   AA Council, 1 Jan 1951, AAA/CM.

69   AA Council, 28 May 1951, AAA/CM.

70   AA Council, 9 July 1951, AAA/CM.

71   'Report of the Development Sub-Committee', att. to AA Council, 11 July 1949, AAA/CM.

72   AA Council, 20 Oct 1949, AAA/CM. £6,000 amounts to approximately £200,000 in today's money.

73   AA Council, 28 Nov 1949, AAA/CM.

74   AA School Committee, 16 May 1950, AAA/SCM.

75   'Report of the RIBA Visiting Board on the School of Architecture, The Architectural Association', 17 Nov 1950, att. to AA School Committee, 8 Dec 1950, AAA/SCM; Jordan's comments, dated 24 Nov 1950, att. to AA School Committee, 6 Dec 1951, AAA/SCM.

76   'Report of the RIBA Visiting Board', Nov 1950.

4   Chuzzlewit's Heirs (1945–1951)

1   John Greenwood (fifth-year student), quoted in 'AA School Annual Prize-Giving', *AAJ*, Aug/Sep 1948, p.34.

2   Andrew Saint, *Towards a Social Architecture*, New Haven, 1987, p.31.

3   Herbert Morel, letter to Edward Bottoms, 4 Feb 2008, AAA. Fellow student Ralph Smorczewski joined the AA in 1946, having been rejected by all the other London schools: 'The deciding factor, I believe, was my sharing war experiences with the Principal [. . .], something we discovered over several glasses of sherry during my

extended interview with him.' (Ralph Smorczewski, *Bridging the Gap*, Leicester, 2007, p.213.)

4   Quoted in 'Modern Trends in Education', *AAJ*, Jan 1947, p.84.

5   Archie McNab, 'The Architectural Association since the War', *Building*, 29 Oct 1972, p.72.

6   R. Gordon Brown, 'A New Form of Architectural Education', *AAJ*, Dec 1948, p.98.

7   AA School Committee, 9 Dec 1946, AAA/SCM.

8   Rykwert, email to the author, 5 Feb 2014.

9   Rykwert, email to the author, 5 Feb 2014.

10   AA Council, 15 July 1946, AAA/CM.

11   Smorczewski, *Bridging the Gap*, pp 163, 164–5.

12   John Cordwell, interviewed by Betty J. Blum, 1993 (rev. 2004), Chicago Architects Oral History Project, Ryerson and Burnham Libraries, Art Institute of Chicago, http://digital-libraries.saic.edu/cdm/ref/collection/caohp/id/2502. After qualifying, Cordwell worked for Fry + Drew before emigrating to the USA, where he became the director of the Chicago Plan Commission. Frank Knight, who took over his vacant position, had been imprisoned with Cordwell and subsequently studied with him at the AA.

13   John Brandon-Jones, interviewed by Jill Lever, May/June 1999, BLSA/NLSC:AL.

14   Both Brown and the council used the expression '50 per cent intake of women' (or '20 per cent intake of women' when referring to the pre-war numbers) in a misleading fashion. What was meant was a ratio of 1:2 (one woman to two men), which amounts to a 33 per cent intake. Likewise, a '20 per cent intake' meant a ratio of 1:5, i.e. an intake of 17 per cent.

15   AA School Committee, 2 Nov 1945, AAA/SCM.

16   AA School Committee, 3 Dec 1945, AAA/SCM; see also n.14 above.

17   Roy Lowe, *Education in the Post-War Years: A Social History*, London, 1988, p.i.

18   On the other hand, Elizabeth King, the only female tutor at the time, received the same salary as her male colleagues even though she was not legally entitled to it. (AA Council, 26 Feb 1946, AAA/CM.)

19   C. K. [Christopher Knight], 'The Foundation Society', *AAJ*, March 1948, p.190.

20   'School Notes', *AAJ*, Jan 1947, p.89; AA Students' Committee, 26 Sep 1947, private collection.

21   J. C. C., 'Students in World Politics: The Role of the IUS', *The World Today*, vol.7, no.8 (Aug 1951), pp 346–56; also, 'Constitution of the International Union of Students', 1946, private collection.

22   Giuseppe Campos, 'The Architectural Faculty Bureau of the I.U.S.', Feb 1948, private collection.

23   AA Council, 13 March 1944, AAA/CM.

24   ArchSA Council, 9/10 April 1946, private collection.

25   Oliver Cox, interviewed by Neil Bingham, 23 Nov 1999, BLSA/NLSC:AL.

26   Giuseppe Campos, 'Report on the International Meeting of Architecture Students on the Occasion of the Centenary of the School of Architecture of the Architectural Association', Dec 1947, private collection.

27   Le Corbusier's talk was published in *AJ*, 8 Jan 1948, pp 35–6.

28   Students' Discussion on Architectural Education', 19 Dec 1947, private collection; Campos, 'Report', Dec 1947.

29   'IIIème Commission – Réform de l'enseignement de l'architecture et de l'urbanisme', ETH/GTA/CIAM, 42-X-116.

30   'International Students' Congress', *AJ*, 21 April 1949, pp 357–8.

31   *AJ*, 26 May 1949, p.472.

32   *RIBAJ*, May 1949, p.298.

33   *ABN*, 20 May 1949, p.441.

34   Margaret Swann (secretary, AA students' committee), letter to the editor, *ABN*, 20 May 1949, p.440.

35   C. J. Briggs (chairman, AA students' committee), letter to the editor, *ABN*, 2 Dec 1949, p.573.

36   *PLAN*, no.7 (1950), p.28.

37   Oliver Cox, interviewed by Neil Bingham, 23 Nov 1999, BLSA/NLSC:AL.

38   'MARS/ArchSA Committee on Architectural Education – Interim Report', June 1948, AAL, 72.036(42) MARS (published in an abridged version in *PLAN*, no.3 (1948), pp 19–22).

39   A. Douglas Jones, 'Mars / Arch. S.A. Interim Report on Architectural Education', *ABN*, 24 Dec 1948, p.533.

40   'Architectural Education: Numbers under Training', *RIBAJ*, Jan 1949, pp 131–2.

41   Oliver Cox, interviewed by Neil Bingham, 23 Nov 1999, BLSA/NLSC:AL.

42   Cox, interviewed by Bingham, 23 Nov 1999.

43   AA Council, 27 Oct 1947, AAA/CM.

44   John Killick, letter to Sigfried Giedion, 1 Jan 1948, ETH/GTA/CIAM, 42-SG-23-211.

45   'Annual General Meeting of the ArchSA, Brighton, 3/4 April 1950', private collection; see also, Michael Ventris, 'Function and Arabesque', *PLAN*, no.1 (1948), pp 6–12; Stephen Macfarlane, 'Unité d'Habitation', *PLAN*, no.4 (1949), pp 23–7.

46   [Stephen Macfarlane], 'RT3', *PLAN*, no.5 (1949), pp 5–16; [Andrew Derbyshire], 'New Feelings, New Techniques', *PLAN*, no.8 (1950) pp 12–23.

47   *PLAN*, no.6 (1949), p.2.

48   Robert Furneaux Jordan, letter to Anita Flateau, 30 Jan 1950, private collection.

49   Saint, *Towards a Social Architecture*, p.30.

50   'Editorial', *PLAN*, no.8 (1950), p.1; Bertram Carter et al., letter to the editor, ibid., p.34; [John Turner], 'Military Service', ibid., p.32.

51   Chris Whittaker, interview with the author, 11 Jan 2014. Whittaker was the national secretary of the ArchSA at the time of its dissolution.

5   The Battle of the Principal (1951–1956)

1   Peter Ahrends, interview with the author, 4 July 2013.

2   AA Council, 30 Oct 1951, AAA/CM.

3   AA Council, 30 Oct 1951, AAA/CM.

4   AA Council, 30 Oct 1951, AAA/CM.

5   AA Council, 30 Oct 1951, AAA/CM; see also, 'Report on Recent Events in the School, and Suggestions Toward a New Policy', June 1953, AAA, 1991:26.

6   Geoffrey Spyer, interview with the author, 24 July 2014. Spyer asserted that Casson 'fought tooth and nail to get rid of Jordan', whom he disliked both politically and personally. Jordan's 'resignation' came at just the moment when, according to Spyer, he intended to sack Michael Pattrick, a close friend of Casson's.

7   John Brandon-Jones, interviewed by Jill Lever, May/June 1999, BLSA/NLSC:AL.

8   AA Council, 30 Oct 1951, AAA/CM.

9   AA Council, 30 Oct 1951, AAA/CM.

10   AA Council, 7 Nov 1951, AAA/CM.

11   AA School Committee, 29 June 1951, AAA/SCM.

12   AA Council, 30 Oct 1951, AAA/CM.

13   'Principal's Report', att. to AA School Committee, 6 Dec 1951, AAA/SCM; Jordan's comments, dated 24 Nov 1950, att. ibid. Pattrick's reply to the visiting board was more diplomatically worded than Jordan's original draft but similar in content. (Michael Pattrick, letter to Everard Haynes, 30 Jan 1952, att. to RIBA Visiting Board, 27 Feb 1952, RIBA/ED 7.1.2.)

14   Andrew Derbyshire, interview with the author, 17 Oct 2013.

15   AA School Committee, 3 Dec 1953, AAA/SCM.

16   Tony Moore, letter to the editor, AJ, 6 March 1952, p.296.

17   AA Council, AAA/CM, 7 July 1952.

18   Tony Shepherd, quoted in Council/Staff/Students' Committee, 8 Oct 1952, AAA/CSSCM. Shepherd had succeeded Spyer as chairman of the students' committee for the 1952/53 session.

19   AA Council, 30 March 1953, AAA/CM.

20   Michael Pattrick, letter to A. R. F. Anderson, 13 March 1953, AAA, 1991:26.

21   AA Council and Advisory Council, joint meeting, 21 May 1953, AAA/CM.

22   'Report on Recent Events', June 1953.

23   'Report on Recent Events', June 1953.

24   'Report on Recent Events', June 1953.

25   AA Council, 9 June 1953, AAA/CM.

26   Michael Pattrick, letter to Colin Glennie, 12 June 1953, AAA, 1991:26. Glennie had succeeded Shepherd as chairman of the students' committee for the 1953/54 session.

27   Pattrick, letter to Colin Glennie, 12 June 1953, AAA, 1991:26.

28   Pattrick, quoted in AA School Committee, 15 April 1953, AAA/SCM.

29   'Principal's Report', 18 June 1953, att. to AA School Committee, 22 June 1953, AAA/SCM.

30   Council/Staff/Students' Committee, 18 June 1953, AAA/CSSCM.

31   Council/Staff/Students' Committee, 18 June 1953, AAA/CSSCM.

32   AA Council, 25 June 1953, AAA/CM.

33   AA Council, 25 June 1953, AAA/CM.

34   Richard Arthur de Yarburgh-Bateson, letter to Hugh Casson, 23 June 1953, AAA, Box 1991:26.

35   Council/Staff/Students' Committee, 8 July 1953, AAA/CSSCM.

36   Hugh Casson, letter to Ronald Sims, 17 July 1953, AAA, 1991:26.

37   AA Council, 13 July 1953, AAA/CM.

38   Quoted in Council/Staff/Students' Committee, 12 Nov 1953, AAA/CSSCM 1952–53.

39   Quoted in Council/Staff/Students' Committee, 12 Nov 1953, AAA/CSSCM 1952–53.

40   AA Council, 26 May 1952, AAA/CM.

41   Pattrick, quoted in Council/Staff/Students' Committee, 2 July 1953, AAA/CSSCM.

42   Pattrick, quoted in Council/Staff/Students' Committee, 2 July 1953, AAA/CSSCM.

43   AA Council, 28 July 1953, AAA/CM.

44   AA Council, 9 Nov 1953, AAA/CM.

45   AA Council, 23 Nov 1953, AAA/CM; R. G. Medley (Field Roscoe & Co.), letter to the BOT, 26 Nov 1953, AAA, 2006:S57.

46   R. J. Crabb (BOT), letter to Field Roscoe & Co., 21 Jan 1954, AAA, 2006:S57.

47   Hugh Casson, letter to Brian Smith, 1 March 1954, AAA, 2006:S57. Smith chaired the students' committee when it was reinstated towards the end of February 1954.

48   MOE, 'Interview Memorandum', 23 April 1954, TNA: ED 74/72.

49   AA Council and Advisory Council, joint meeting, 27 April 1954, AAA/CM.

50   Minute of Meeting, 13 Dec 1954, AAA, 2006:S57.

51   AA Council, 25 April 1955, AAA/CM.

52   Gordon Michell, quoted in 'Alteration of By-laws – Report of the Discussion at the Special General Meeting Held on 7th December 1955', AAA, 1991:7.

53   John Miller, interview with the author, 17 June 2013.

54   Quoted in 'Annual Prize-Giving', AAJ, Sep/Oct 1954, p.70.

55   Quoted in AA Council and Advisory Council, joint meeting, 23 June 1955, AAA/CM.

6   The AA School under Michael Pattrick (1951–1961)

1   Robert Furneaux Jordan, comments, 24 Nov 1950.

2   Michael Pattrick, letter to Everard Haynes, 30 Jan 1952.

3   AA, *School of Architecture*, prospectus, London, 1953, AAA, p.23.

4   'Report on Recent Events in the School, and Suggestions Toward a New Policy', June 1953.

5   Quoted in AA School Committee, 15 April 1953, AAA/SCM.

6   Quoted in Council/Staff/Students' Committee, 8 July 1953, AAA/CSSCM.

7   Quoted in Council/Staff/Students' Committee, 18 June 1953, AAA/CSSCM.

8   Council/Staff/Students' Committee, 8 July 1953, AAA/CSSCM.

9   AA Council, 4 Jan 1954, AAA/CM; AA School Committee, 4 March 1954, AAA/SCM.

10   AA Council, 22 March 1954, AAA/CM.

11   'Report on Recent Events', June 1953.

12   AA School Committee, 7 March 1952, AAA/SCM.

13   Quoted in AA Council, 31 March 1952, AAA/CM.

14   Peter Smithson would later stress this point in his resignation letter to Pattrick (18 Aug 1960, AAA, 2012:13), in which he expressed his 'thanks for the opportunities I have been given in the School, to teach without any compromise of my deepest beliefs [. . .]'.

15   AA School Committee, 9 Feb 1954, AAA/SCM.

16   'The Decaying Neighbourhood', *AD*, Oct 1956, pp 318–26.

17   Quoted in 'The Decaying Neighbourhood', *AD*, Oct 1956, p.321.

18   Quoted in 'Annual Prize-Giving', *AAJ*, Sep/Oct 1952, p.45.

19   A. R. F. Anderson, letter to the chairman of the RIBA Joint Committee on Education, 27 Jan 1953, AAA, 1991:8. The letter was signed by AA President Anderson but written by Pattrick (AA School Committee, 16 Jan 1953, AAA/SCM).

20   Pattrick, memorandum att. to AA School Committee, 14 Nov 1955, AAA/SCM.

21   Pattrick, quoted in Council/Staff/Students' Committee, 8 Oct 1952, AAA/CSSCM.

22   Smithson felt that 'the existing course was already too short and that no time should be given to office training at the expense of design projects', and Killick warned that 'the present fourth-year programme would be ruined if part of it were removed' (AA School Committee, 22 Sep 1958, AAA/SCM).

23   *ABN*, 4 May 1951, p.508.

24   Arthur Foyle (ed.), *Conference on Tropical Architecture 1953*, London, 1954, p.125.

25   G. Anthony Atkinson, 'British Architects in the Tropics', *AAJ*, June 1953, p.14. George Atkinson, a member of the AA council, was the older brother of fourth-year master Fello Atkinson.

26   *AJ*, 17 April 1947, p.313.

27   Otto Koenigsberger, 'Early Days Abroad', *AJ*, 7 July 1982, p.36.

28   AA Council, 4 Jan 1954, AAA/CM.

29   AA School Committee, 5 May 1955, AAA/SCM. Fellow AA students attending the inaugural course included George Finch, Kenneth Frampton, Ram Karmi, John Miller and Denise Scott Brown.

30   Hans Heyerdahl Hallen, letter to the author, 2 April 2015.

31   AA School Committee, 30 June 1955, AAA/SCM.

32   AA Council and Advisory Council, joint meeting, 21 June 1956, AAA/CM; Otto Koenigsberger, letter to Leo De Syllas, 30 Aug 1956, AAA/OK, 27.

33   AA School Committee, 20 June 1956, AAA/SCM; AA Council, 29 Oct 1956, AAA/CM.

34   Even the first course had attracted participants from non-British territories such as Peru, Laos, Nepal and the Philippines; later instalments featured government-sponsored students from Belgium, Germany and Portugal.

35   'Architecture in the Tropics', *Guardian*, 7 April 1958, p.7. For an in-depth discussion of the DTA and its successor, the Department of Tropical Studies, see Jiat-Hwee Chang, *A Genealogy of Tropical Architecture: Colonial Networks, Nature and Technoscience*, Abingdon/New York, 2016, pp 206–11, 217–27.

36   Chang, *A Genealogy of Tropical Architecture*, pp 217–18.

37   Chang, *A Genealogy of Tropical Architecture*, pp 225–6; see also, Mark Crinson, 'Imperial Modernism', in G. A. Bremner, *Architecture and Urbanism in the British Empire*, Oxford, 2016, pp 214–16.

38   Otto Koenigsberger, letter to H. J. W. Alexander, 30 Aug 1956, AAA/OK, 27.

39   Reyner Banham, *The New Brutalism*, London, 1966.

40   Kenneth Frampton, *Modern Architecture: A Critical History*, London, 1980, pp 262–8.

41   [Alison Smithson], 'House in Soho, London', *AD*, Dec 1953, p.342.

42   Peter Shepheard, for instance, referred to the 'new Brutalism' in his presidential address to the AA in October 1954. (Peter Shepheard, 'The Importance of Being Earnest', *AAJ*, Nov 1954, p.92.)

43   Robin Middleton, 'The New Brutalism or a Clean, Well-lighted Place', *AD*, Jan 1967, p.7. For instance, both Denys Lasdun and John Voelcker used the terms 'Brutalists' and 'Smithsons' interchangeably. ([Denys Lasdun, J. H. V. Davies], 'Thoughts in Progress: The New Brutalism', *AD*, April 1957, pp 111–12. John Voelcker, letter to the editor, *AD*, June 1957, p.184.) Ridiculing the preponderance of new stylistic movements, German critic Hermann Funke wrote: 'Brutalism has the smallest number of followers, namely two, Alison and Peter Smithson; but these two Brutalists are married to each other. So more may come.' (Hermann Funke, 'Wortmagie und vor allem viele Architekten', *Die Zeit*, 26 April 1963, p.18.)

44   Alison and Peter Smithson, 'The New Brutalism', *AD*, Jan 1955, p.1.

45   Reyner Banham, 'The New Brutalism', *AR*, Dec 1955, pp 354–61.

46   Quoted in 'Conversation on Brutalism', *Zodiac*, April 1959, p.74.

47   Banham, 'The New Brutalism', p.361.

48   A. and P. Smithson, 'The New Brutalism', p.1.

49   Reyner Banham, 'The History of the Immediate Future', *RIBAJ*, May 1961, p.253.

50   Quoted in James Gowan (ed.), *Projects: Architectural Association 1946–1971*, London, 1973, pp 30–31.

51   Colin Glennie, 'Architecture – A Personal Point of View', *AAJ*, April 1954, p.238.

52   Quoted in 'A Policy for the AA', *AAJ*, July/Aug 1954, p.52.

53   'Talk by Mr Lewis Mumford', *AAJ*, July/Aug 1953, p.49.

54   Quoted in Reyner Banham, 'Futurism and Modern Architecture', *RIBAJ*, Feb 1957, p.137.

55   John Outram, interviewed by Niamh Dillon, 27 November 2007, BLSA/NLSC:AL.

56   *AJ*, 1 Aug 1957, p.165.

57   Peter Cook, 'Responses', *Arena*, Dec 1966, p.139.

58   Peter Cook, 'Responses', *Arena*, Dec 1966, p.139.

59   *AJ*, 1 Aug 1957, p.164.

60   Quoted in 'Annual Prize Giving', *AAJ*, Sep/Oct 1957, p.62.

61   Malcolm Higgs, interview with the author, 19 Aug 2016. The bond between the three persisted beyond their diploma, but eventually they went their separate ways. Andrew Anderson moved to Norwich, where he set up a practice concerned with ecclesiastical conservation work. Malcolm Higgs pursued a career in academia, which he concluded as head of the Canterbury School of Architecture. Quinlan Terry became the partner of Raymond Erith and later inherited his practice. He developed into the leading neo-classical architect in the country and continues to run his practice as a family enterprise, supported by his son Francis, and his wife Christine, with whom he had studied at the AA. For a discussion of the Christian Weirdies, see Alan Powers, 'Flying Angels and Solid Walls', *AA Files*, no.64 (2012), pp 48–58.

62   Outram, interview.

63   Pattrick, quoted in John Summerson, 'The Case for a Theory of Modern Architecture', *RIBAJ*, June 1957, p.312.

64   'Curriculum Working Party Report', Feb 1958, AAA, 1991:31.

65   One year later, Gowan described the working party's curriculum in an article for the *Architectural Review*. Though it had by then been put into operation, his piece – oddly – lacks any reference to the AA. (James Gowan, 'Curriculum', *AR*, Dec 1959, pp 315–23.)

66   After one year, the progressive order of design tasks was limited to the middle years, i.e. the village in the second year, the town in the third, and the city in the fourth. The main reason for this was a basic flaw in the setup of the curriculum, which required students to tackle the largest and most complex architectural scale in their thesis year, when they were generally expected to work as individuals.

67   Ellis Woodman, *Modernity and Reinvention: The Architecture of James Gowan*, London, 2008, p.187.

68   Quoted in 'Annual Prize Giving', *AAJ*, Sep/Oct 1959, p.59.

69   Peter Smithson, 'Education for Town Building: An Outline of the Intention of the Architectural Association School Curriculum', *AAJ*, Jan 1961, p.191.

70   John Partridge, interview with the author, 23 April 2013.

71   James Gowan, *Style and Configuration*, London, 1994, p.12.

72   Robert Maxwell graduated from Liverpool in 1949 and worked for the LCC before becoming a partner in the practice of Douglas Stephen. He left the AA in 1962 to join the Bartlett, where he taught for 20 years. In 1982, he was appointed the dean of architecture at Princeton, and he later returned to the AA as a history lecturer. David Oakley graduated from the AA in 1952 and joined the team of George Atkinson, the colonial liaison officer of the BRS. Following his departure from the AA in 1963, he became a professor in New Delhi and a director of studies in Nairobi. In 1968, he returned to the United Kingdom to take charge of the Central Polytechnic of London.

73   In 1956, Pattrick introduced an informal 'fifth-year tutorial scheme', which allowed him, in addition to his studio tutors, to use the services of experienced practitioners who were otherwise too busy to teach at the AA. Two years later, the scheme superseded the previous tutorial arrangements in the fifth year, and 'assistant studio master' Korn became the only part-time member of the fifth-year staff who actually had a contract with the AA. Prior to that, the nomenclature did not clearly distinguish between formal 'tutors' and informal 'visiting tutors' (who, though remunerated, were not considered members of the teaching staff). This peculiarity might clear up a long-standing confusion among scholars over James Stirling's role at the AA. In March 1956, both Stirling and Gowan applied for a teaching post at the AA. Pattrick offered a position to Gowan but not to Stirling, who joined the Regent Street Polytechnic instead. Mark Crinson rightly states that Stirling 'was never appointed as a tutor'; it is, however, possible that Stirling acted as visiting tutor to a select group of students, as he himself claimed. (Mark Crinson, *Stirling and Gowan*, New Haven/London, 2012, p.311; James Stirling, 'An Architect's Approach to Architecture', *RIBAJ*, May 1965, p.233.)

74   Killick suffered from multiple sclerosis and died in 1971 at the age of 47.

7 In Search of a New Policy (1951–1961)

1   AA Council, 27 April 1953, AAA/CM.

2   AA Council, 4 Jan 1954, AAA/CM.

3   Casson, quoted in AA Council and Advisory Council, joint meeting, 27 April 1954, AAA/CM.

4   'Interview Memorandum – Architectural Association School of Architecture', 23 April 1954, TNA: ED 74/72. 'Direct grant establishments' were previously independent establishments whose catchment area was usually regional, or at least larger than the local authority in which they were situated, and the MOE's policy was not to make itself responsible for more than 50 per cent of their net running costs. In 1920, when the AA was first classified as a direct grant establishment, it was one of a handful of architectural schools in the country and the case for regional or even national relevance was strong – in 1954 it was politically untenable.

5   Quoted in AA Council and Advisory Council, joint meeting, 27 April 1954, AAA/CM.

6   Quoted in 'A Policy for the AA', July/Aug 1954, p.54.

7   *ABN*, 12 Aug 1954, p.175.

8   Mark Crinson and Jules Lubbock, *Architecture – Art or Profession? Three Hundred Years of Architectural Education in Britain*, Manchester, 1994, p.134.

9   'Report on Recent Events in the School, and Suggestions Toward a New Policy', June 1953.

10   Quoted in Council/Staff/Students' Committee, 30 Jan 1953, AAA/CSSCM.

11   Council/Staff/Students' Committee, 8 July 1953, AAA/CSSCM.

12   'President's Address to All Students', 15 July 1953, AAA, 1991:26.

13   Quoted in Council/Staff/Students' Committee, 18 June 1953, AAA/CSSCM.

14   RIBA Schools Committee, 3 Jan 1952, 5 June 1952, RIBA/ED 7.1.3.

15   *AJ*, 4 March 1954, p.267.

16   Over the three years in which they were run, about 140 assistants took advantage of these classes. Dozens of AA members, including former principals Robert Furneaux Jordan and Frederick Gibberd, volunteered to give free tuition.

17   Architectural Education Joint Committee, 16 March 1953, RIBA/ED 7.1.2; 'First Interim Report of the Architectural Education Joint Committee', May 1953, RIBA/ED 7.1.2, p.18.

18   Quoted in 'Annual Prize Giving', *AAJ*, Sep/Oct 1958, p.58.

19   RIBA Schools Committee, 15 Oct 1953, RIBA/ED 7.1.3; Architectural Education Joint Committee, 11 Feb 1954, RIBA/ED 7.1.2.

20   Architectural Education Joint Committee, 8 April 1954, RIBA/ED 7.1.2.

21   'Report of the Architectural Education Joint Committee on the Training and Qualification for Associate Membership of the Royal Institute of British Architects', *RIBAJ*, Feb 1955, pp 156–64.

22   *AJ*, 10 Feb 1955, p.183; 'Architectural Education', July 1955, *AD*, p.219.

23   RIBA Board of Architectural Education, 14 Feb 1955, RIBA/ED 7.1.1.

24   Leslie Martin, 'Conference on Architectural Education', *RIBAJ*, June 1958, pp 281–2.

25   'Principal's Report', att. to AA School Committee, 9 Oct 1958, AAA/SCM; see also, AA Council, 25 May 1959, AAA/CM.

26   Quoted in 'Annual Prize Giving', *AAJ*, Sep/Oct 1958, p.59.

27   Committee on the Oxford Architectural Education Conference, 4 July 1958, RIBA/ED 7.1.2.

28   AA Council, 19 March 1958, AAA/CM.

29   The classification of sandwich (or composite) courses shifted in the mid-1950s. The McMorran Committee had discussed them as a form of part-time training, whereas to the Oxford Conference they represented an experimental approach to full-time training, which was – and always had been – Pattrick's understanding.

30   AA School Committee, 9 Feb 1954, AAA/SCM.

31   AA President Bryan Westwood, quoted in 'Joint Education of Architects and Builders', memorandum, 25 May 1956, att. to AA Council, 28 May 1956, AAA/CM; see also, AA Council, 12 July 1954, AAA/CM.

32   AA School Committee, 8 Dec 1955, AAA/SCM.

33   AA Council and Advisory Council, joint meeting, 22 May 1957, AAA/CM.

34   Richard A. Butler, James Stuart and David Eccles, *Technical Education*, Feb 1956, TNA, CAB 129/79/40.

35   Antony Part, quoted in 'Note of an Informal Discussion between Officers of the Ministry and of the LCC [. . .]', 17 Dec 1957, LMA, LCC/EO/HFE/05/281.

36   Antony Part, quoted in Memorandum, 25 May 1956.

37   Antony Part, letter to J. R. Newman Booth (senior inspector, MOE), 1 June 1956, TNA: ED 74/72.

38   John Brandon-Jones, quoted in AA Council, 28 Oct 1957, AAA/CM.

39   'AA Council's Annual Report', *AAJ*, July/Aug 1958, p.47. Though a majority aligned itself with Brandon-Jones, the support was far from unanimous. Leo De Syllas, one of the main apologists of the scheme, disputed that Part 'intended to have what had been referred to as a "glorified polytechnic"' and pointed out that 'it would not be integrated education if it was solely run by architects'; and Anthony Cox 'could not but regret that the door had not been left open for further negotiations'. (AA Council, 14 May 1957, 28 Oct 1957, AAA/CM.)

40   Antony Part, letter to John Brandon-Jones, 4 Nov 1957, LMA, LCC/EO/HFE/05/281.

41   AA Council, 9 July 1958, AAA/CM.

42   Quoted in 'Annual Prize Giving', *AAJ*, Sep/Oct 1959, p.58.

43   AA Council, 10 April 1959, AAA/CM. Clarke Hall remembered the occasion with some bitterness: 'Although this course had been previously agreed, in my innocence I put it to a vote and lost it. [...] I had to go back to the Ministry telling them that the AA council didn't want to negotiate with them. From that moment on the AA never got any grants ever again. I was shattered about the whole thing.' (Denis Clarke Hall, interviewed by Louise Brodie, Oct 1997, BLSA/NLSC:AL).

44   'Report of the Proceedings at a Meeting of the Association', 25 May 1959, AAA, 2008:33.

45   AA Council, 8 June 1959, AAA/CM. Oddly, James Richards supported the motion to overturn the resolution which he himself had proposed.

46   'AA: Experiment or Expire', *AJ*, 14 May 1959, pp 717–18.

47   Quoted in 'A Policy for the AA', *AAJ*, July/Aug 1954, p.54.

48   Minute of Meeting, 13 Dec 1954, AAA, 2006:S57.

49   For comparison, at that time the annual tuition fees at the AA amounted to £180 for all students regardless of background. At most other schools, the fees for local students were in the region of £30; however, Birmingham, for instance, charged £208 to students from other counties and the London polytechnics up to £250.

50   Quoted in 'Annual Prize Giving', *AAJ*, July/Aug 1955, p.49.

51   The potential damage was not merely pecuniary as the AA, which absorbed five times more post-intermediate students than any of its competitors, had a long tradition of 'creaming off' top students from other schools. Some of the most distinguished architects who emerged from the AA had started their education at Cambridge, including Bill Howell, Edward Cullinan, Cedric Price, Roger Cunliffe and Philip Dowson.

52   AA Council, 25 May 1959, AAA/CM.

53   AA School Committee, 23 June 1959, AAA/SCM; AA Council, 23 May 1960, AAA/CM.

54   BAE, 25 May 1959, RIBA/ED 7.1.1.

55   AA Council, 28 March 1960, AAA/CM.

56   'The New RIBA Council', *AJ*, 20 April 1961, p.559.

57   AA Council, 9 Nov 1959, AAA/CM.

58   AA Council, 4 Jan 1960, AAA/CM.

59   AA Council, 25 Jan 1960, AAA/CM. Peter Chamberlin was a partner with Chamberlin, Powell and Bon, one of the leading architectural practices at the time; AA graduate Neville Conder had joined Hugh Casson in partnership following the Festival of Britain.

60   H. T. Cadbury-Brown, quoted in AA Council and Advisory Council, joint meeting, 30 May 1960, AAA/CM.

61   *AAJ*, July/Aug 1959, p.55.

62   Edward Playne, letter to John Eastwick-Field, 1 Dec 1965, AAA/OK, 43.

8   William Allen and the 'Art/Science Tension' (1961–1965)

1   'Director of the AA – Secretary of the AA – Principal of the AA', *AAJ*, March 1961, p.239.

2   Denys Lasdun, letter to George Wiltshire, 2 Sep 1960, AAA, 2003:37c.

3   James Cubitt, letter to H. J. W. Alexander, 6 Sep 1960, AAA, 2003:37c.

4   Mark Crinson and Jules Lubbock, *Architecture – Art or Profession? Three Hundred Years of Architectural Education in Britain*, Manchester, 1994, p.131.

5   'Brains in Bedford Square', *AJ*, 2 March 1961, p.307.

6   *AR*, April 1961, p.225.

7   Leo De Syllas, letter to H. J. W. Alexander, 30 Aug 1960, AAA, 2003:37c.

8   William Allen, letter to H. J. W. Alexander, 1 Jan 1961, MS, AAA, 2003:37c.

9   'Report of the Working Party on the Future of the Architectural Association', 23 May 1961, AAA, 2006:S34.

10   'Report of the Working Party on the Future of the Architectural Association', 23 May 1961, AAA, 2006:S34.

11   *Higher Education: Report of the Committee appointed by the Prime Minister under the Chairmanship of Lord Robbins*, London, 1963, p.70.

12   *Higher Education: Report of the Committee*, p.271.

13   AA Executive Committee, 19 April 1961, AAA/EC.

14   AA Council, 11 Dec 1961, AAA/CM; see also, Michael Austin-Smith, letter to Patrick Linstead, 20 June 1961, ICSTM, GB 0098 J AA/1. Michael Austin-Smith had graduated from the AA shortly after the war following a highly distinguished service with the Royal Horse Artillery. He was in a successful partnership with his wife Inette Austin-Smith, Peter Lord and Geoffrey Salmon, all of them fellow AA graduates.

15   Linstead, quoted in Edward Carter, 'The Architectural Association – Imperial College Project', 21 Nov 1966, AAA, 2006:S16b.

16   AA Executive Committee, 5 Nov 1962, AAA/ECM.

17   'The AA and the Imperial College of Science and Technology', 1964, AAA, 1991:7. The Grey Book was included as a loose insert in the March 1964 issue of the *AA Journal*.

18   Diana Lee-Smith, interview with the author, 5 May 2016. Lee-Smith's experiences at the AA inspired a life-long interest in the interplay of politics and educational institutions, which she pursued as a scholar and co-founder of the Mazingira Institute, an independent research and development institute in Nairobi.

19   Peter Cook, 'Responses', *Arena*, Dec 1966, p.143. Of the ten chairs and secretaries of the students' committee between 1962 and 1967 only one – David Usborne, chairman in 1964/65 – supported the merger, and only for lack of alternatives: 'My attitude [...] is one of qualified approval, Glickman's is one of unqualified disapproval.' (David Usborne, letter to the editor, *AAJ*, Jan 1965, p.186.)

20   AA Council, 16 March 1964, 27 July 1964, AAA/CM.

21   Michael Glickman, letter to the editor, *AAJ*, May 1964, p.328.

22   Edward Carter, letter to Graham Dawbarn, 5 Aug 1964, AAA, 2003:45c.

23   AA Council, 27 July 1964, AAA/CM.

24   Pressed on this point by a student, President Gabriel Epstein expressed the view that 'at least they had *not* got a mandate not to go on'. ('The AA & ICST Merger Plan: Any Questions?', *AAJ*, Nov 1964, p.118.)

25   William Allen, 'The Training and Education of Architects', inaugural lecture, *AAJ*, April 1962, pp 223–38.

26   Allen, 'The Training and Education of Architects', p.223.

27   Allen, 'The Training and Education of Architects', p.227.

28   William Allen, 'The Profession in Contemporary Society', *RIBAJ*, May 1960, p.253.

29   Allen, 'The Training and Education of Architects', p.224.

30   Quoted in 'School of Architecture: Annual Prize Giving', *AAJ*, Oct 1962, p.119; for comparison, see Richard Llewelyn Davies, 'The Education of an Architect', *RIBAJ*, Jan 1961, pp 118–20.

31   Allen, 'The Training and Education of Architects', p.238.

32   Allen, 'The Training and Education of Architects', pp 228, 230.

33   William Allen, 'The AA School Today', [May 1963], *AAJ*, Feb 1964, p.212; see also, AA Council, 23 Oct 1961, AAA/CM.

34   Jiat-Hwee Chang, *A Genealogy of Tropical Architecture: Colonial Networks, Nature and Technoscience*, Abingdon/New York, 2016, pp 222, 224–5.

35   For instance, in 1962, the DTS was invited to prepare a draft scheme for a new town in Bechuanaland (now Botswana); between 1963 and 1964, it carried out a reconnaissance survey for the government of Northern Rhodesia (now Zambia); and in 1965, it was commissioned to advise on the design of British High Commission buildings in Islamabad, Pakistan.

36   AA School Committee, 27 Sep 1962, AAA/SCM.

37   AA Council, 22 April 1963, AAA/CM; for a discussion, see Mark Crinson, *Modern Architecture and the End of Empire*, Aldershot/Burlington VT, 2003, pp 129–32; Hannah Le Roux, 'Modern Architecture in Post-Colonial Ghana and Nigeria', *Architectural History*, vol.47 (2004), pp 385–9.

38   The AA, which offered up to 80 first-year places, received 180 applications in 1962, over 200 in 1963, and 344 in 1964. For comparison, Liverpool, which had 35 available places (and demanded three A-levels), received 175 applications in 1961 and 250 in the following year. (Robert Gardner-Medwin, letter to Everard Haynes, RIBA Schools Committee, 9 Jan 1962, RIBA/ED 7.1.3.)

39   AA School Committee, 28 June 1962, AAA/SCM.

40   AA Council, 16 March 1964, AAA/CM. This was followed by another increase to £415 less than two years later.

41   AA Council, 27 May 1963, AAA/CM.

42   AA Council, 22 July 1963, AAA/CM. Korn had briefly run a similar scheme in 1946, when more than half of all AA students took an additional planning degree.

43   William Allen, 'Policies for Architectural Education', *Arena*, March 1966, p.223.

44   William Allen, 'Curriculum Review', memorandum to staff, 25 May 1965, ABA; William Allen, memorandum to council, 3 Nov 1965, private collection.

45   'Principal's Notes for Studio Staff and Lecturers', 1964, AAA, 1991:31.

46   For third-year students at the end of session 1963/64 the situation was such that their history course had halted after the first term of the second year, while the published third-year course had not been given at all. (AA Staff/Student Committee, 6 May 1964, ABA.)

47   Jack Morgan (chairman, students' committee), quoted in 'Annual Prize Giving', *AAJ*, Oct 1962, p.121; see also, AA School Committee, 22 March 1962, AAA/SCM.

48   'Report of the RIBA Visiting Board on the Architectural Association School of Architecture', March 1964; att. to AA Council, 26 Oct 1964, AAA/CM.

49   'Report of the RIBA Visiting Board', March 1964.

50   'Report of the RIBA Visiting Board', March 1964.

51   Anthony Cox, cited in AA Council and Advisory Council, joint meeting, 16 Nov 1963, AAA/CM.

52   James Cubitt, 'Critical State of the School and the Principal's Employment', memorandum to council, 9 July 1965, AAA, 2006:S34; see also, AA Council, 16 March 1964, 20 April 1964, AAA/CM.

53   AA Council, 30 Nov 1964, AAA/CM.

54   Michael Pearson, interview with the author, 14 May 2016; see also, e.g. Royston Landau, 'Towards a Structure for Architectural Ideas', *Arena*, June 1965, p.11.

55   Quoted in James Gowan (ed.), *Projects: Architectural Association 1946–1971*, London, 1973, p.63.

56   Leonard Manasseh, 'The Moment of Truth', presidential address, *AAJ*, Nov 1964, p.96.

57   Colin Rowe, letter to Alvin and Elizabeth Boyarsky, 24 May 1962, ABA.

58   Anthony Eardley, interview with the author, 4 April 2016.

59   Eardley, interview with the author, 4 April 2016; All Year Masters, memorandum to Allen, 20 Oct 1964, ABA.

60   William Allen, letter to Alvin Boyarsky, 11 June 1965, ABA.

61   Alvin Boyarsky, letter to William Allen, 1 July 1965, ABA.

62   Allen, 'Curriculum Review', memorandum to staff, 25 May 1965, ABA.

63   Allen, 'Curriculum Review', memorandum to staff, 25 May 1965, ABA.

64   Allen, 'Curriculum Review', memorandum to staff, 25 May 1965, ABA.

65   David Usborne, memorandum to James Cubitt, 5 July 1965, AAA, 2006:S34. This is the edited version of the original statement of 29 June, which Cubitt had rejected due to its being 'offensively worded'. (Cubitt, 'Critical State'.)

66   Unit Masters, memorandum to James Cubitt, 5 July 1965, AAA, 2006:S34.

67   Cubitt, 'Critical State'.

68   AA Council, 19 July 1965, AAA/CM.

69   AA Council, 19 July 1965, AAA/CM; William Allen, letter to Elizabeth Boyarsky, 16 July 1965, ABA. This course of events explodes a popular myth, whereby Boyarsky was sacked because of his opposition to the ICST merger. Many studio teachers rejected the merger, and some of them took a much more public stance against it – without any repercussions whatsoever. Those who were intimately involved in the ICST controversy remember Boyarsky's part in it barely (Michael Glickman, interview with the author, 28 May 2016) or not at all (Diana Lee-Smith, interview). While Boyarsky was no doubt opposed to the merger, it was his opposition to Allen which cost him his job. (The reasons for Balcombe's dismissal remain obscure, though it is clear that he, too, was critical of Allen's pedagogical approach.)

70   AA Council, 19 July 1965, AAA/CM.

71   See, e.g. John Voelcker, 'Technics of Architecture', *Arena*, May 1966, p.285.

72   AA Executive Committee, 18 Oct 1965, AAA/ECM.

73   William Allen, letter to Edward Carter, 1 Nov 1965, AAA, 2003:37c; see also, AA Council, 25 Oct 1965, AAA/CM.

74   Andrew Derbyshire, interviewed by Catherine Croft, 2003, BLSA/NLSC:AL.

75   Quoted in 'Annual General Meeting', *AAJ*, Dec 1962, p.198.

76   Michael Glickman, letter to the editor, *AAJ*, Dec 1964, pp 147–8.

9   Epilogue: Beyond the Sixties (1965–1990)

1   Otto Koenigsberger, 'The School's Work', *Arena*, Sep/Oct 1966, p.65.

2   AA Council, 31 Oct 1966, 27 Feb 1967, 9 Oct 1967, AAA/CM.

3   Simon Pepper, letter to the editor, *Arena*, Jan 1966, p.148; see also, AA Council, 13 Dec 1965, AAA/CM.

4   Otto Koenigsberger, letter to Robert Gardner-Medwin, 11 March 1966, AAA/OK, 43.

5   The so-called 'Colin Rowe-Lobby' (AAA/OK, 43) was a who's who of international architecture and included Peter Eisenman, Kenneth Frampton, John Hejduk, Richard Meier, Cedric Price, James Richards, Richard Rogers, Joseph Rykwert, Vincent Scully, O. M. Ungers, John Voelcker – and Aldo van Eyck.

6   Otto Koenigsberger, interview notes, [Jan 1966], AAA/OK, 43.

7   AA Council, 12 April 1966, AAA/CM.

8   Grahame Shane, email to the author, 26 April 2016.

9   *AJ*, 4 May 1966, p.1168.

10   John Lloyd, 'The Quality of Architectural Education', inaugural address, *Arena*, May 1967, p.278.

11   AA Council, 18 April 1966, AAA/CM.

12   For Lloyd's pedagogical approach, see Lloyd, 'The Quality of Architectural Education', pp 275–8; 'School Handbook', Sep 1967, AAA, 2007:50.

13   John Smith, 'Architecture in School', *ABN*, 14 Sep 1960, p.336.

14   Quoted in *Sunday Times*, 14 Nov 1965, p.9.

15   For a first-hand account, see Peter Cook, 'The Electric Decade: An Atmosphere at the AA School 1963–73', in James Gowan (ed.), *A Continuing Experiment*, London, 1975. Warren Chalk, Peter Cook and Michael Webb joined the AA in 1964, Ron Herron and Dennis Crompton in 1965, and David Greene in 1967.

16   Michael Pearson, interview with the author, 14 May 2016; Harry Hobin, email to the author, 13 May 2016.

17   Richard Hobin, letter to the editor, *AJ*, 24 Jan 1968, p.210; see also, Irene Sunwoo, 'Between the "Well-Laid Table" and the "Marketplace": Alvin Boyarsky's Experiments in Architectural Pedagogy', doctoral dissertation, Princeton University, Nov 2013, p.185.

18   Minutes of a meeting, [Nov 1969?], ABA. The minutes are undated but were most likely taken at a members' information meeting on 6 November 1969.

19   'The Architectural Association – Students' Union', 11 Dec 1969, ICSTM, GB 0098 J AA/10.

20   William Penney, letter to Jane Drew, unsent draft, 7 Jan 1970, ICSTM, GB 0098 J AA/11. Anthony Wade had read philosophy, politics and economics at Oxford before moving to Philadelphia to study under Louis Kahn. He joined the AA teaching staff in 1963 and took charge of the middle school under John Lloyd. He was dismissed in April 1970, when he publicly accused Lloyd of allowing Subud, the spiritual movement of which he was a member, to infiltrate the school. Wade subsequently became the head of the architectural school at Canterbury but died in 1976 at the age of 41.

21   William Penney, letter to John Dennys (acting president), 3 Feb 1970, AAA, 2006:S34; see also, Memorandum, 2 Feb 1970, ICSTM, GB 0098 J AA/11.

22   *AJ*, 11 Feb 1970, p.331.

23   *RIBAJ*, March 1970, p.93.

24   AA Council, 13 April 1970, 22 June 1970, AAA/CM.

25   AA Council, 21 Sep 1970, AAA/CM.

26   *AJ*, 23/30 Dec 1970, p.1472.

27   AA Council, 4 Jan 1971, AAA/CM.

28   AA Council, 8 March 1971, AAA/CM; see also, Charles Jencks, '125 Years of Quasi Democracy', in James Gowan (ed.), *A Continuing Experiment*, London, 1975, p.156.

29   AA Council, 16 Aug 1971, AAA/CM; see also, AA Council, 18 Dec 1978, AAA/CM.

30   AA Council, 19 July 1971, AAA/CM.

31   AA Council, 2 Aug 1971, AAA/CM; see also, Martin Pawley, 'Out on a Limb in Bedford Square', *Guardian*, 27 Aug 1984, p.9; for a discussion of the IID, see Irene Sunwoo, 'Pedagogy's Progress: Alvin Boyarsky's International Institute of Design', *Grey Room*, no.34 (Winter 2009), pp 28–57.

32   Alvin Boyarsky, candidate statement, June 1971, AAA, 2006:S34.

33   AA Council, 21 June 1971, AAA/CM.

34   AA Council, 26 June 1972, AAA/CM.

35   AA Council, 30 May 1977, AAA/CM; see also, SRC, '. . . there's a crisis on our hands!', [*c*.Oct 1976], AAA, 2007:55.

36   AA Council, 28 July 1971, 23 Aug 1971, AAA/CM.

37   AA Council and Advisory Council, joint meeting, 6 March 1972, AAA/CM.

38   Grahame Shane, 'Obituary: Alvin Boyarsky (1928–1990)', *Journal of Architectural Education*, vol.45, no.3 (May 1992), p.189; Irene Sunwoo, 'From the "Well-Laid Table" to the "Market Place": The Architectural Association Unit System', *Journal of Architectural Education*, March 2012, p.34.

39   Andrew Higgott, *Mediating Modernism*, London, 2007, pp 161–2.

40   Higgott, *Mediating Modernism*, pp 163–77; Sunwoo, dissertation, pp 210–46. Léon Krier, a former assistant of Stirling's, became a key figure behind the anti-modern revivalism in urban design in the 1980s; he is best known in Britain as the master planner of Poundbury. Bernard Tschumi turned into a leading thinker on deconstructivist architecture, which he promoted through his practice and a distinguished career in American academia. Brian Anson was a prominent member of the community architecture movement of the late 1960s and actively involved in its major battles, notably the one for Covent Garden.

41   Higgott, *Mediating Modernism*, p.162.

42   Sunwoo, dissertation, pp 168, 174.

43   AA Council, 26 May 1971, AAA/CM.

44   'Report of the RIBA Visiting Board', Aug 1976, AAA, 2013:91.

45   'Report of the RIBA Visiting Board', Aug 1976, AAA, 2013:91.

46   AA Council, 5 July 1976, AAA/CM.

47   Alvin Boyarsky, letter to Elizabeth Layton (RIBA), 29 Dec 1976, AAA, 2008:46; 'Report of the RIBA Visiting Board', Sep 1978, RIBA/ED, 7.1.6.

48   Higgott, *Mediating Modernism*, p.158; Sunwoo, dissertation, pp 111–13.

49   Higgott, *Mediating Modernism*, p.159.

50   AA Council, 19 June 1972, AAA/CM.

51   *HC Deb*, 25 July 1972, vol.841, cc.289–90W.

52   *Guardian*, 2 Aug 1972, p.4.

53   AA Council, 24 July 1972, AAA/CM.

54   Alvin Boyarsky, 'Tactics for Dealing with the Current LEA/DES Situation', 11 July 1972, att. to Forum, 12 July 1972, 2003:48a; AA Council, 24 July 1972, AAA/CM.

55   AA Council, 14 Aug 1972, 26 Feb 1973, AAA/CM.

56   AA Council, 9 Oct 1972, AAA/CM.

57   AA Council, 18 June 1973, AAA/CM.

58   AA Council, 28 April 1975, 12 Jan 1976, 8 Aug 1977, AAA/CM.

59   AA Council, 15 Nov 1971, 14 Feb 1972, AAA/CM.

60   See, e.g. AA Council, 26 April 1976, AAA/CM.

61   Higgott, *Mediating Modernism*, pp 177–8; Sunwoo, dissertation, pp 266–8; Igor Marjanović, 'Drawing Ambience', in Igor Marjanović and Jan Howard (eds), *Drawing Ambience: Alvin Boyarsky and the Architectural Association*, St Louis MO/Providence RI, 2014, pp 36–52.

62   Frank Duffy, quoted in AA Council, 22 July 1974, AAA/CM.

63   *AA Notes*, Aug–Oct 1973, p.1; *AA Prospectus*, London, 1983, AAL.

64   See, e.g. AA Council, 10 Oct 1977, 24 April 1978, AAA/CM.

65   AA Council, 29 May 1975, 23 June 1975, AAA/CM.

66   AA Council, 29 May 1975, 23 June 1975, AAA/CM.

67   AA Council, 26 April 1976, AAA/CM.

68   AA Council, 6 Sep 1976, AAA/CM; see also, SRC, '. . . there's a crisis on our hands!', Oct 1976.

69   *AA Notes*, July–Sep 1976, p.2; AA Council, 13 Dec 1976, AAA/CM; see also, AA Press Release, 5 June 1976, AAA, 2003:91.

70   AA Council, 5 July 1976, 5 Aug 1976, AAA/CM.

71   AA Council, 6 Sep 1976, AAA/CM.

72   AA Council, 11 Oct 1976, AAA/CM.

73   AA Council, 11 Oct 1976, AAA/CM.

74   AA Council, 14 Feb 1977, AAA/CM.

75   AA Council, 14 Feb 1977, AAA/CM; SRC, '. . . there's a crisis on our hands!', Oct 1976.

76   AA Council, 21 Feb 1977, AAA/CM.

77   AA Council, 21 Feb 1977, AAA/CM.

78   AA Council, 13 June 1977, 12 Sep 1977, AAA/CM.

79   See, e.g. AA Council, 10 Sep 1979, AAA/CM; 'Report of the RIBA Visiting Board', Dec 1982, AAA, 2012:15.

80   Robin Evans, '1975–1980 Projects: From Axes to Violins', *AA Files*, no.1 (Winter 1981–82), pp 115–20; Higgott, *Mediating Modernism*, p.173; see also, SRC, 'Just in the Nick of Time', election broadsheet, [May 1976], AAA, 2013:91.

81   Quoted in 'Report of Special Council Meeting on 30 October 1979', att. to AA Council, 8 Oct 1979, AAA/CM.

82   Higgott, *Mediating Modernism*, p.173.

83   Evans, '1975–1980 Projects', p.116; for an in-depth analysis of the role of the drawing in Boyarsky's AA, see Marjanović, 'Drawing Ambience'; see also, Sunwoo, dissertation, pp 313–15.

84   Charles Bremner, 'Exploding the World of Architecture', *Times*, 31 Aug 1988, p.8.

85   Higgott, *Mediating Modernism*, pp 175–6.

86   Andrew Higgott, 'The AA 1971–1990: A Narrative History', AAL, p.13.

87   AA Council, 16 Aug 1971, AAA/CM.

Conclusion

1   Quoted in 'Opening of the Centenary Exhibition', *AAJ*, Jan 1948, p.102.

2   Quoted in 'Annual Prize-Giving', *AAJ*, Sep/Oct 1952, p.47.

3   Alan Powers, *Britain*, London, 2007, pp 89, 93–94.

4   Edward Passmore, 'Exhibitions of Students' Work', *Builder*, 20 July 1951, p.91.

5   Michael Pattrick, 'AA Policy', *AAJ*, April 1956, p.244.

6   Geoffrey Salmon, 'Memoirs', AAA, March 2003, vol.4, p.91; Geoffrey Spyer, interview with the author, 24 July 2014.

7   Alan Powers, 'Flying Angels and Solid Walls', *AA Files*, no.64 (2012), p.48.

8   For a discussion, see Simon Sadler, *Archigram: Architecture Without Architecture*, Cambridge MA, 2005, pp 24–7.

9   Gerald Adler, *Robert Maguire and Keith Murray*, London, 2012, p.7, ff.

10   Reyner Banham, *The New Brutalism*, London, 1966, p.89.

11   For a discussion, see Mark Swenarton, *Cook's Camden*, London, 2017, p.20 *et pass*.

12   *AJ*, 4 May 1966, p.1168.

13   William Allen, 'The Training and Education of Architects', inaugural lecture, AAJ, April 1962, p.227.

14   Edward Carter, 'The Architectural Association – Imperial College Project', 21 Nov 1966, AAA, 2006:S16b.

15   Peter Cook, 'Cook's Grand Tour', *AR*, Oct 1983, p.36.

16   Quoted in 'Annual Prize Giving', *AAJ*, Sep/Oct 1960, p.76.

17   Quoted in 'Annual Prize Giving', *AAJ*, Sep/Oct 1960, p.76.

18   Mark Crinson and Jules Lubbock, *Architecture – Art or Profession? Three Hundred Years of Architectural Education in Britain*, Manchester, 1994, p.148.

19   Peter Cook, 'The Electric Decade: An Atmosphere at the AA School 1963–73', in James Gowan (ed.), *A Continuing Experiment*, London, 1975, p.138.

20   Edward Jones, quoted in James Gowan (ed.), *Projects: Architectural Association 1946–1971*, London, 1973, p.63.

21   Cook, 'Cook's Grand Tour', pp 35–6.

22   Alvin Boyarsky, interview with Bill Mount, 1980, ABA, cited in Irene Sunwoo, 'Between the "Well-Laid Table" and the Marketplace": Alvin Boyarsky's Experiments in Architectural Pedagogy', doctoral dissertation, Princeton University, Nov 2013, p.112.

Index

Note: page numbers in **bold** refer to pictured student work.

Illustration Credits

The reproduction of the illustrations listed below (by figure number) is courtesy of the following copyright holders: